THE JUDGE REPORT

Musings of a Conservative Republican Pro-Life
Catholic Red Sox Fanatic, currently hiding out in
Amsterdam, NY USA

By Robert N. Going

First Edition

DEDICATION
In the form of a blog entry

The Lunatic Who Saved Amsterdam
Mar. 18th, 2006 @ 02:23 pm

I have made it a point not to discuss passing controversies in the City of Amsterdam on this blog, but today I am making an exception. What follows is a proposed letter to the editor.

Dear Editor:

There is probably no person in the world who knows Michael Chiara better than I do, and I can assure you without equivocation that he is nuts.

That's right. Our City Assessor, Chairman of the Amsterdam Industrial Development Agency, the Master Plan Committee and the Mayor's Charter Commission and President of the Amsterdam Northern and Chuctanunda Railroad is totally and completely bonkers.

Not convinced? What man in his right mind would take the kind of abuse he takes day in and day out from politicians and demagogues and lately some people he had thought were his friends and still keep coming back for more?

It was Mike Chiara who fought, along with Joe Jacobs, to limit our City taxes to 1% of property value. It was Mike Chiara who led a taxpayer revolt to limit the annual increase in city taxes to three per cent. It was Mike Chiara who took an empty and theoretical industrial park out of bankruptcy and filled it with productive businesses with hundreds of employees.

Mike Chiara is one of the few people who recognizes that the principal reason our city has been decaying for seventy years is that our tax burden is one of the highest in the country. He knows we can't survive if we keep doing things the old way. He knows that developers would be churning away here if only our taxes didn't make new construction next to impossible.

So how to break the cycle? Mike looks at every possible way out, and he does this fifty times a day. He reminds me of New England Patriot quarterback Tom Brady who, if the team is down by twenty points with 38 seconds to play, is calculating what calls he will need to make to score enough times to win the game, instead of just playing out the clock as most of our elected leaders have been doing in my lifetime.

Now comes a proposal that could, if it proves to be legitimate, save the average taxpayer with a $60,000 assessment $500.00 or more a year for ten years. He thinks we should look at it, and make up our minds when all the facts are on the table.

And for that crime he gets attacked unmercifully.

Here's a guy with a good education, a fine intellect, an inquisitive mind, who has spent his entire adult life dedicated to making Amsterdam a better place to live, and now many of those very taxpayers he has fought for unselfishly have turned on him and pointed their fingers in his face and accused him of everything under the sun, simply because he has stated that a project which could result in cutting the city tax rate in half is maybe worth reviewing.

There are quite a few people, elected and unelected, who should be hanging their heads in shame for their treatment over the last few weeks of this good and decent man.

If the politicians in this town had followed Michael's advice over the years, there is no doubt in my mind that we would already be well on our way to recovery. If there were any justice in this life, instead of the lynch mobs preparing to burn him in effigy we would be erecting statues at each entrance to the city to Michael Chiara, the lunatic who saved Amsterdam.

Robert N. Going

INTRODUCTION

For several years now my wife has been casually wondering why I keep giving away my writing. With the exception of *Honor Roll*, which appeared in an anthology several years ago, I have never in my life received a dime for my writing, unless you count my salaries and legal fees for the court stuff.

In fact, just about everything in this book has previously appeared on the Internet, mostly at my blog, *The Judge Report*. You can find and read this stuff for free, but my family appreciates those of you who have purchased this book. It's still easier to curl up with a good book than it is to snuggle up to your Desktop PC.

I began the blog in 2005 when I found myself sufficiently riled up about the legal and moral issues surrounding the Terri Schiavo case. I was encouraged by Miss Dawn Eden, blogger *extraordinaire,* who liked an old piece I had written about Thomas More. When I began to slow down in my production, she publicly urged me to start up again, and I've been at it ever since.

I've always enjoyed writing, for as long as I can remember, and I have dabbled in all sorts of genres. My office is filled with the notes of 45 years worth of ideas, and some things I wrote about in high school (Bishop Scully, Class of 1969), resurrected themselves in my novel, *The Evil Has Landed*, about to be published at long last. I have a couple of dazzling movie scripts floating in my head, and the germ of an off-beat musical featuring the music of Richard Rodgers and a parody by me of the lyrics of Oscar Hammerstein II. That I did something like that once before in ninth grade, the yet-to-be-performed spy musical *North Atlantic*, will not hold me back.

The Judge Report (both versions) is rather eclectic. I've tried to arrange things topically here as much as possible, but some of this defies broad categorization. If I haven't captured your interest, keep reading. The next piece may be more to your liking. Although I have done some editing, the nature of a blog is such that there is an inevitable repetition of some details, particularly in the stories from the family history. Telling one generation's story simply requires some facts from another's.

Many of the pieces are light-hearted, sometimes satirical, sometimes sentimental.

I begin, though, rather grimly, with a series of articles I mostly wrote in the middle of the night while working as a Red Cross volunteer at Ground Zero in the fall of 2001. Time has tempered the emotions of those days. I'm glad I captured them while they were still raw.

Regular readers of my blog will doubtless note that I have left out most references to contemporary political events, both national and local. The former may emerge as a companion volume at some point; the latter, containing as it does the gruesome story of my foray into elective politics in the City of Amsterdam, NY, will likely be confined to the dustbin of history.

I have not included a formal biography. More than enough of my personal history will emerge as you peruse these pages.

Grampa Des Nichols used to entertain me with endless tales about different guys he beat up in his youth. Finally one day I said, "Hey, Grampa! Didn't you ever lose a fight?"

"Of course! I let the other guy tell those stories."

Just so.

Publishing this book has helped me fulfill one of my life-long fantasies. Next on the list is playing Harold Hill in *The Music Man*.

Robert N. Going
June 30, 2008
Amsterdam, NY USA

GROUND ZERO REMEMBRANCE

L ate one Sunday night in September of 2000 I worked feverishly to complete my first novel, a murder mystery. The words flowed off my fingertips and I rattled off thirty pages in that final session, lifting my fingers off the keyboard in a triumphal flourish as the words "The End" appeared on the screen in front of me. I looked at the system clock. After midnight.

Well, what do you know? My parents' wedding anniversary. A suitable day. Had they lived, it would have been 52 years.

The next morning I arrived at work (I was the Family Court Judge of Montgomery County, New York) in a euphoric mood, brandishing the last three chapters and epilogue, and pointing out "The End" to my staff. A wonderful day. A wonderful day indeed.

Things bounced along smoothly until early afternoon, when I was informed that an important fax was coming in for me. It was many pages long, and the machine ever-so-slow. I grabbed bunches of sheets and read feverishly. Finally, at the end, I learned that a referee appointed by the State Commission on Judicial Conduct had determined that I had violated the Code of Judicial Conduct. The groundwork had been laid for my removal from office.

Well, isn't this ironic. I guess this will go down as one of the most memorable days in my life. I'll never forget this one, that's for sure. For sure, I'll always remember the day Kennedy was shot, the day the Challenger exploded, and now the day I reached the bottom of my professional career.

Yes, sir. I'll remember September 11 as long as I live.

A year later, on the evening of September 10, 2001, I drove to Kennedy airport for the third time in three months, carrying with me my son James and his friend from Sardinia, our Rotary foreign exchange student Gianmario Crisponi. Jamie had flown out on July 10, the two 16-year-olds had flown in on August 10, and now it was time for Gianmario to go home.

The weather was a little wild. Storm clouds threatened as we crossed the Whitestone Bridge, and in the far distance Manhattan island was socked in fog, settled in so densely that the only recognizable landmarks were the top few floors of the Empire State Building and the Twin Towers of the World Trade Center.

I pulled over to the right lane so Gianmario could take his final photographs of his trip to America, a panoramic view of those three famous buildings.

He had actually seen them before, just after midnight on August 11 when I took them on the scenic route to Upstate, pausing to stroll without fear through Battery Park in Giuliani's New York for a view of Lady Liberty, then driving slowly up West Street for an in-your-face look at the World Trade Center, rising as it did then in awesome splendor far into the night sky.

As we pulled into the airport on September 10 the lightning and thunder had already started. Security was less tight at JFK than at Logan in Boston, so we were able to walk Gianmario to his gate. We said our good-byes.

"Shouldn't we wait until his plane leaves?" asked Jamie.

I thought about the long ride home, my empty stomach, the weather and the mounting tolls in the parking garage.

"He'll be alright," I said. "The worst thing that can happen is they delay the flight because of the weather. They'll take care of him. Nothing to worry about."

We went home.

The next morning I was home alone, approaching the end of the seventh month of an enforced sabbatical. I flipped on my computer, logged on to the Internet,and fired up my AOL Instant Messenger™, and casually glanced at the news bar scrolling across the top of the screen.

OH. MY. GOD.

The television took forever to warm up, but finally I saw the images of the smoke and one tower in flames, then realized the other one was gone, and before my eyes the North Tower crumbled into dust. Reruns of the second plane hitting, bodies flying or jumping from windows. No report yet on the two planes.

Gianmario.

Oh my God.

I never felt so helpless. Did his plane leave the ground? Did it get turned around across the Atlantic? Is he in that ball of flame dancing across my screen in slow motion?

Mary called from school where she was watching this with a class of four-year-olds. Had I heard from him?

I fumbled around the house and found his itinerary. Under the best of circumstances he would still be in the air, hopefully flying peacefully into Rome shortly.

Jamie called. No, I haven't heard from him. I'm sure he's ok. Yeah, maybe we should have stayed with him at the airport. Don't worry. He'll be alright. And yes, you may make an international call to his cell phone.

Anna IM'd me from Albany, from college. She is an EMT, and worked with the SUNY Albany Five Quad Ambulance Corps. They were already lined out the door donating blood at the school. They were talking about sending an ambulance down. So many people from school had family working there.

I love you, Daddy.

She was on her way over to her friend Beth's house to comfort her. Her father worked at the World Trade Center and no one had heard from him in the last four hours.

Later we learned that he had just gotten off his commuter train when the first plane hit. With hundreds of thousands of other people he walked out of Manhattan and across the Brooklyn Bridge. Cell phone service was disrupted (the local transmitters were on the North Tower) and regular service from the Verizon switching center had been blown apart by the falling rubble.

Jamie finally reached Gianmario, on the ground in Rome. His family was very happy to see him.

Anna came home later to pick up some American flags. The ambulances were indeed going to New York and she wanted them suitably attired. There were no more flags available in Albany (this was still September 11). She wasn't able to go herself, a last-minute injury.

There are few degrees of separation with an event of this magnitude. Bob, Jr. told us of a girl at his college whose cousin had been scheduled to be a flight attendant on one of the doomed planes. At the last minute, she traded off for another flight.

"Good news, huh?" he asks. Not really. "She talked her best friend into taking her place."

All day on 9/11 I was on line with my friend Lucianne Goldberg, political commentator and gadfly, who has her own talk show and was being constantly interrupted by other talk show hosts for her personal observations from New York. It happens that we both learned simultaneously of the death of Barbara Olson, who bravely phoned her husband, the United States Solicitor General Ted Olson, for guidance as her doomed plane plummeted toward the Pentagon. (Later he would find a note from her saying, "Wherever I am when you read this, know that I am thinking of you.")

Barbara Olson was a personal friend of Lucianne. Somehow, with everything else going on, Lucianne manage to find a quiet moment later that awful day and dug up this poem by Elizabeth Barrett Browning, which she placed the next morning on her web page at ***Lucianne.com*** as a tribute to Barbara and all the others:

IF God compel thee to this destiny,
To die alone, with none beside thy bed
To ruffle round with sobs thy last word said
And mark with tears the pulses ebb from thee,——
Pray then alone, 'O Christ, come tenderly!
By thy forsaken Sonship in the red
Drear wine-press,--by the wilderness out-spread,——
And the lone garden where thine agony
Fell bloody from thy brow,——by all of those
Permitted desolations, comfort mine!
No earthly friend being near me, interpose
No deathly angel 'twixt my face and thine,
But stoop Thyself to gather my life's rose,
And smile away my mortal to Divine!'

Within a couple of weeks, Anna had arranged the Red Cross classes for both of us. There were quite a few we had to take, but the agency was speeding things up because of the massive need for volunteers in New York City. We finished up over the first few weeks of October. I personally wouldn't be able to leave until after October 18, the day the Court of Appeals heard oral arguments in my case, the day they would begin to decide whether to terminate my 16 year judicial career. Another week went by, and I got the call.

GROUND ZERO DIARY
November 2, 2001

Nearly two months have passed and the fires are still burning. When the wind shifts, as it has for the last couple of days, the air becomes heavy, eye-stinging, lung irritating and carries with it the stark reality of what happened two blocks from where I now sit.

I am spending three weeks as a Red Cross Disaster Relief Mass Care volunteer, assigned to Respite Center One within the heavily restricted combat zone. Here we provide meals and comfort to the rescue workers, technicians, security personnel, etc. around the clock in the great tradition of the Red Cross. Folks are here from all over the country pitching in.

We never know from day to day who our co-workers will be. Yesterday it was five office workers from Orlando who were in town briefly on business for the Campus Crusade for Christ. They all came in to help for one day on the midnight to 8 a.m. shift. They figured they could sleep on the plane on the way home. They were here and wanted to help, and that was that.

We are surrounded by mail, posters, drawings from school kids all over the country. Hundreds, thousands, tens of thousands, and it all gets read and rotated on a regular basis. Sit down for dinner, and there's a stack of mail waiting for you. They've even separated the ones with return addresses so that the exhausted police and firefighters can sit down and write a quick thank-you. Most of it is incredibly moving. "Out of the mouths of babes." One youngster said he thought he knew what they must feel like, because he had a cousin who died. Another, with handwriting that I would guess was no more than fourth grade, simply enclosed a comforting verse from one of the Psalms.

Hopefully it will be the gravest event of their lifetimes, perhaps even more shocking and horror-filled to them than it is for us adults who have longer memories. Yet, they all seem to have understood it, grasped instinctively the terrible evil of it all, recognized the virtues of country and family and laying down one's life for others.

I arrived Monday night. It was a pleasant night, so I walked the 18 blocks up 8th Avenue to my hotel. Around 44th Street I was startled to come upon a full-size bronze statue of a fireman kneeling in sorrow over a fire helmet. The statue was on a tow-trailer and had already become a shrine.

It seems this statue had been commissioned for some place in Missouri. By odd coincidence it was delayed at Customs when it arrived in New York on September 9th.After the 11th, all agreed it would stay in New York. Lacking a permanent location, it is simply parked in the street.

A few blocks further up there is a firehouse, covered with messages of encouragement from people who now consider themselves New Yorkers even if they've never stepped foot here. And there were the portraits of the fifteen men from that company who were killed on 9/11. Now they were not just numbers, but flesh and blood: smiling, clowning, surrounded by friends and family.

"We are the dead," the poet said.

> *Short days ago we lived, felt dawn,*
> *Saw sunset glow.*
> *Loved and were loved. . .*

And now they lie beneath the rubble where their colleagues have carried on their desperate search all these weeks. Their friends wander over to our oasis, day after day, to catch a few hours sleep (each with a teddy bear donated from who-knows-where), watch some television, get a massage or a hot meal, play video games, anything to drive away the terrible reality they face on a daily basis. Some of the Red Cross volunteers do nothing more than sit around a table and chat. A friendly smile can cause amazing transformations.

It was a good week to be here. The three Yankee home games in the World Series gave them something to cheer about. Even I got into the act, dressing up as a Yankee fan for Halloween.

None of us know how any of this will turn out. But for now, it is enough to know that in some small way each of us can do something. As for me, I was here less than an hour before I was promoted to Third Shift Dessert Coordinator.

November 4, 2001

Yesterday while waiting with some fellow Red Cross Volunteers for the shuttle bus that would take us to our stations at Ground Zero I suddenly felt a hand on my back. I whipped around only to see a man walking briskly away from me down 42nd Street. I turned around and my companions were laughing.

"Get used to it," said one of the veterans who had been here a week longer. "That was a pat on the back. It happens a lot."

Perhaps because of my exceptional skill with a bagel-cutting knife (less than a week ago, I didn't even know there WAS such a thing), I have been invited to senior staff meetings. After about your second day you're considered one of the old pros around here. Virtually the entire staff turns over every three weeks, yet things seem to run very smoothly.

There was a lot of excitement here this week, first with the "gold strike" beneath the former North Tower of the World Trade Center. The Brinks trucks were running around all night for a couple of nights. Something over 200 million dollars worth was removed.

Then a couple of days ago the terrible confrontation between the firefighters and police, not far outside our door here at Respite Center One. Emotions had been running high, naturally. Faced with the awful dilemma of the sincere and worthy desire of recovering as many of the bodies as possible and the reality of the continuing danger of the site and the risk of more casualties, the Mayor has decided to cut back dramatically on the number of firefighters digging through the rubble for their lost comrades.

In the heat of the moment, things were said and done that has caused at least for now a dreadful schism. Several firefighters were arrested after punching out several of the cops. For us, it's worse than watching two of your children fighting, especially knowing all the while that the endless stress of this work has caused otherwise reasonable people to act in uncharacteristic ways.

We Red Cross workers don't have that problem. We took a stress management class the other night.

"Tell us about some things that are causing you stress and how you deal with them."

"Well," said one of the workers, "Yesterday the bus driver kept lurching the bus around, starting and stopping. He shook me up so much I could hardly think."

"And my husband," said another "he . . ."

"Wait a minute," I said. "Isn't anybody feeling any stress from that. . .that . . .," and I pointed to the window and realized I didn't have the words to describe what had happened across the street. That, what?

Tragedy? A tragedy is when you give your dog a bowl of water and it turns out to be antifreeze. Catastrophe? Not enough. Abomination? Too tame. How about:

Horror.

That horror that lurks and dwells in the back of our minds even when back home but especially here where we are facing it, surrounded by it, absorbed in it even while we go about our business pretending it's not there. ("The jury is instructed to pay no attention to that Mastodon in the courtroom.")

Yet there it is, just the same.

Last night we made a supply run that took us directly through Ground Zero. For now, two large sections of the North Tower still stand, leaning toward a neighboring building. The fires burn. One of the steel workers told us that some of the steel is still red hot, over 1200 degrees. One adjacent building still standing has a whole side blown off, and you can see offices and file cabinets and desks and computer terminals all neatly in place. The area where the firefighters used to gather is now largely empty. It is almost inconceivable that any more bodies will be recovered in any recognizable fashion.

Earlier in the day, passing through Grand Central Station, I passed one of the many memorial kiosks that have sprung up everywhere where families could post photos of their missing. I tried to read them all, trying to make these strangers come alive at least in my heart, but there were so, so many and it doesn't take long before your eyes just get too blurry to continue.

There was a single poster of the police officers who were killed, including one female, Moira Smith. Next to her picture was posted a long letter from a man who had met her on the way out of the World Trade Center, telling of her coolness and bravery and how she had personally saved him by looking him square in the eye and telling him firmly and authoritatively which way to go and to exit the building promptly. She saved hundreds, maybe thousands of lives by doing her job in a professional manner. It's likely she wouldn't have expected anyone's thanks.

All in a day's work.

I continue to read the mail from the school kids from across the continent. Today one had written, "Yea, though I walk through the valley of the shadow of death, I shall fear no evil."

I have now driven a Red Cross Emergency Response Vehicle through the valley of the shadow of death that was once the World Trade Center, and I have seen the face of evil.

November 5, 2001

Whenever I take the subway from midtown to my Red Cross assignment at Respite Center One, Ground Zero, I continue to be drawn to "New York's Wailing Wall" at Grand Central Station where families of the missing from the World Trade Center have posted heart-breaking requests for any information. Tonight I approached just as a young woman burst into tears.

"Oh my God! That's a girl I went to school with!"

And I quickly moved on.

My immediate supervisors, a husband and wife team from North Carolina, had Saturday night/Sunday morning off. Being acclimated to the third shift, they made a late, late night of it in the city that doesn't sleep.

Suzanne is a bouncy, friendly, delightful woman. When the night was petering out, a time "when the street belongs to the cop and the janitor with the mop," as Frank Loesser would say, a hollow man approached her.

"I know why I'm out this late," he said, "but why are you?"

So she explained what we are doing, and then he told his story.

He is a former cop who had taken a job as private security and driver for an executive at the Cantor Fitzgerald firm. He was in their World Trade Center office every day, except one. On September 11, they got a late start because they had to drive the executive's son to kindergarten. Virtually the entire company went down with the tower.

Suzanne stopped being bouncy when she told me the story. "I try to stay happy and forgot about all that, but you can't." They go home tomorrow. The Red Cross wisely sets time limits for their volunteers to prevent burn-out.

Today there was another memorial service for a firefighter at St. Patrick's. There is an altar in the church converted to a victim shrine. It gets a lot of attention.

On Sundays Catholic Mass is celebrated at Ground Zero, beneath an unusual icon. Discovered in the rubble, standing erect, rescue workers found a perfectly formed steel cross, and immediately rallied to it as a symbol of Hope. It stands at the front of the site in solemn defiance of all that is surrounding it. Many look upon it as a miracle.

I actually met the man who found it. He was introduced to me by the Fire Department Chaplain, Father Brian Jordan. Frank Silecchia is a huge, gentle man with hands three times the size of mine. Born in Brooklyn of a Jewish mother and a Roman Catholic father, he is a simple man with native eloquence and Faith to move mountains. We stood in the muck and mire midst the spirits of shattered dreams between the cross and the remains of the North Tower as he told me his tale.

Many of the buildings surrounding the World Trade Center had been crushed by the falling debris. In the hours and days following the massacre, rescue workers risked their own lives in the desperate hunt for survivors. This brought Frankie into one of those tottering shells, the Customs House, Building 6. Eventually he reached the basement, and there, in the center of the building, was a crater, and rising up out of the crater the steel cross, fully erect.

It was the morning of the third day. For twenty minutes he stood there, and wept.

It had been part of the North Tower, and as that structure came down, this cross had passed through the roof of the building, plummeted through floor after floor after floor, down, down, down until finally coming to rest where he found it.

"This is holy ground we are walking on," he told me. "All those people that died here, they're still here in a way. Don't you see?" and here he looked up to where the tower once stood. "Don't you see? Jesus was raised up on the cross, He died, and He descended to the dead. Then He gathered them up, and then," and now he turned to where his Cross stood witness, high over the widening pit, "then . . . Resurrection! And He rises and takes everyone with Him to the Father!"

Father Jordan, who was still with us, nodded, and it is hard to imagine a thousand volumes of theology and philosophy that could have explained things any better.

Still, to call this a miracle is ridiculous, of course. This can be no more an act of God than the '69 Mets. Both towers and the other destroyed structures had steel frames and doubtless thousands of such right-angle joints as might form what looks to us to be a cross. Right?

But symbols, which are all man-made, can nonetheless be powerful. What is the Liberty Bell other than an old decrepit piece of junk, or the tattered flag of Fort McHenry that we spend millions to preserve, or that Lady in the Harbor? But does not each in turn stir something in the soul?

For the Christian, the Cross is the ultimate symbol of triumph over Evil and Death. Secularly, when used by the Red Cross it becomes a symbol of Hope and Healing. Our long tradition of burying the dead under crosses goes beyond the principles of the Christian religion.

True, there have been times when the cross has been usurped for ignoble causes, but here at the Gates of Hell there can be no doubt of its purpose.

Understandably, some will object to such a prominent display of religion in a public place.

But if, on a crisp autumn day when the pipes play "Amazing Grace" and the drum sounds the Dead March, some widow or child or mom or dad glances up at that cross and thinks for but a moment, "I am the Resurrection and the Life," who among us should say them nay?

November 11, 2001

"Thanks," said the President of the United States as he shook my hand and looked me square in the eye after the international memorial service at Ground Zero on Sunday. Moments later Governor Pataki and Mayor Giuliani came by as well. Rudy signed my hard-hat.

It's nice to feel appreciated, finishing up my second week as a Red Cross Disaster Relief volunteer at Ground Zero in New York City. It was not the first thanks I had gotten that day. The first was a general thanks to the relief workers in a letter from a sixth grade girl in South Carolina. She had sent along a lucky penny to help us out, so I sent one back to her.

Then there was the thanks received from a police sergeant. A couple of us had sat with him at a dinner table in Respite Center One and listened.

"For the first couple of weeks, I just couldn't come down here," he said.

Stationed in the Bronx, on September 11 he was running an errand downtown. He saw the second plane hit, saw the flaming jet fuel incinerating everything in its path, saw bodies hurtling through the air, saw people jump, saw the whole thing come crumbling down.

"I hope you've worked through it," offered companion.

"Yeah, I'm ok with it now."

Right.

He is in charge of one of the security checkpoints. Says it's much better than duty at the Staten Island landfill, where the remains of the World Trade Center are sifted for body parts. Piece by piece, the rubble rides across a conveyor belt where workers using garden tools look for anything that might contain the DNA of a former human being, tossing same into buckets for later more detailed analysis.

So many stories. One of out regular volunteers is a 19 year old drama student with the singing voice of an angel, who comes down here to work the midnight to eight shift then runs cheerfully off to class. The school is in the upper west side of Manhattan. All phone service and public transportation were halted on September 11. A young man she knew was unable to contact his girlfriend, who was either in or near the World Trade Center. He borrowed a pair of roller blades and glided five miles to search for her (he found her safe and sound.)

Before the President arrived I attended Mass beneath the steel cross at Ground

Zero. We threw some scrap lumber down in the mud and laid some sheets of plywood over it and that was our sanctuary. The heavy machinery shut down out of respect. OSHA regulations notwithstanding, we uncovered our heads. At the remembrance section we were asked to call out the names of those who had died. There were many. So many Irish firemen it almost sounded like a reading of the Dublin white pages. The only hymn was "God Bless America", echoing unevenly off the burned out hulk of the World Trade Center.

It was Veterans' Day, and for that we gave thanks as well.

November 12

After working the midnight to eight shift, I had just settled into my pillow when the phone rang.

"Are you watching television?" asked my wife. "Another plane went down."

I tried to focus and tuned in on the early confused reports but the unmistakable rising smoke from Queens on an otherwise brilliantly clear day.

I was awake.

The phone lines to Red Cross headquarters in Brooklyn were all tied up. I decided to try to get there and see if I could help.

The Secret Service Agents guarding my floor were all pacing (they were protecting my floor neighbor, the president of the Congo). Outside on 42nd street an emergency traffic lane had been set up. Police were everywhere.

After determining the subways were still running, I dashed the three long blocks to Grand Central Station (not exactly ready for the Amsterdam High School Cross Country team, but I did pretty good), jumped on the train downtown and switched to the A-train to Brooklyn. Two young men stopped me to ask what I knew. They both lived in the Rockaway section of Queens, where the plane went down. I knew nothing.

At Headquarters they had me stand by. I wandered about the control room and was amazed at the efficiency of the operation. They already had a command center set up at JFK airport, two emergency response vehicles on the scene, accurate maps printed out of the crash site together with specific directions for getting there. Six more fully-manned vehicles were at the command center. One man on the telephone was clearly and professionally gathering information and repeating same.

When he hung up the phone he said very calmly, "Just so you are aware, they anticipate no survivors." And then, he swallowed hard and looked away.

A lot of arm-chair quarterbacks have been criticizing the Red Cross lately. Personally, I have been tremendously impressed by everything I've seen.

I was released and went back to my hotel.

November 19, 2001

Twenty-four hours a day a spot just outside the entrance to the Ground Zero work site is occupied by a changing but dedicated bunch whose sole function is to cheer and wave when rescue and relief workers enter or leave. Over at the morgue another group continuously recites Jewish prayers for the dead, and will do so until all the thousands of body parts recovered receive a proper burial. It seems everyone wants to do something.

We have quite a mix of folks volunteering here at Respite Center One at Ground Zero in New York City, where I am in my third and final week as a Red Cross volunteer. The core group on the midnight to 8 shift are three-weekers from around the country: North Carolina, Tennessee, Michigan, Indiana, Louisiana, California, Alaska, Washington State, even one from Canada.

Supplementing these are "local" volunteers, who are not necessarily from New York, who come in for a night or several or never leave. There are students and actors, lawyers, accountants, office workers, retired folks, etc. One night we had a lady cutting bagels who had been on *As the World Turns* for fourteen years. Many people stay all night and then leave to go to work. All are cheerful and wonderful.

This being a cosmopolitan city, there are occasional communication difficulties.

"Y'all know whut ah caint stan?" commented a spitfire from Nashville, "Et's these furren buhs drav-vers. Thy tok so funny, somtams ah caint unnerstan a WURD thy sigh, y'all know whut ah maine?"

Yes, I think I do.

Then there's Vikki.

Vikki is a "local" volunteer from Yorkshire, England, very near my wife's ancestral village. She is a policewoman there and was so taken by the events here that she dropped everything and flew to New York at her own expense and has been staying at the YWCA and coming in night after night to volunteer. If that isn't enough, before she left home she obtained an ankle tatoo of the Stars and Stripes intertwined with the Union Jack with the legend "God Bless America."

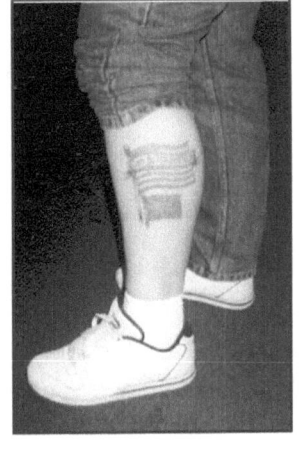

The other day she went shopping at a police uniform and paraphernalia store. Her speech betrayed her to an off-duty police officer. "You're Vikki, aren't you?" he asked. Upon ascertaining his honorable intentions, she permitted him to continue. "We've been looking for you. We heard all about you and want to do something to say thanks."

So the NYPD PBA set her up in a nice hotel room in midtown Manhattan for the duration of her stay.

Things are winding down here for our operation, and with each passing day more of our national folks are going home. As one of the principal Emergency Response Vehicle operators, it generally falls upon me to take them on a final tour of the Ground Zero area. One of the last stops is a pair of impromptu memorials. One we call the "Teddy Bear Site", where friends and relatives of the September 11 victims have left flowers, messages, and hundreds of stuffed animals. Across the walkway, ironically near a permanent memorial to police killed in action in New York, is a site dedicated to the various police agency and fire department personnel lost on that fateful day.

Among the many messages is a letter written to FDNY Captain Thomas Farino:

> *To Daddy*
> *I love you more than forever.*
> *I am glad for two reasons. One reason is that I am*
> *happy God is making you happy.*
> *Also my second reason is that you died in a very*
> *honorable way and the world thinks and is thankful*
> *that you saved people and you are a hero.*
> *Thank you Dad.*

In the last twenty-four hours the bodies of at least twelve firefighters have been removed from the rubble of the North Tower of the World Trade Center. This has coincided with the most spectacular Leonid meteor showers of our lifetime.

> *The heavens themselves blaze forth the death of princes.*

One cannot come to this place without being changed, and changed utterly.

November 24, 2001

"So you're a judge, are you?" inquired Vikki from Yorkshire after reading the article I had written about her activities as a Red Cross Volunteer in the *Amsterdam Recorder*. "That's funny. I had you pegged for a construction worker."

It is my last day after nearly four weeks at Respite Center One at Ground Zero in New York City. In some ways it is the most difficult.

"Just what exactly is the circulation of the *Recorder*," she asked.

"I'm not sure precisely," says I, "but I do know that the combined circulation of the *Recorder* and the *Reader's Digest* is something over 22 million." She was impressed.

Mary and the younger two children have spent most of the week with me and together we have witnessed this great city returning to some normalcy: the Macy's parade, the Radio City Music Hall Christmas show, lines around the block waiting to get into the brand new *Toys R Us,* the two hour wait to get into the Empire State Building Observation Deck. Of course, we couldn't help but notice that at any given moment about three quarters of the crowd were facing south, pointing in the direction of what once was. We went at twilight, and saw the effect of the gazillion watts of light being turned on at what had been the World Trade Center.

When Ronald Reagan was in the Army film office during the war, he came into possession of the footage of the U.S. Army liberating the Nazi death camps. He kept a copy for himself and showed this horror to his two sons on their respective twelfth birthdays. He wanted them to learn the possibilities of evil, of man's inhumanity to man, and to make sure they would never forget.

On Wednesday I took my family for a long walk around the periphery of Ground Zero so they could see for themselves, showed them the police and fire memorials, and the Teddy Bears. We took our time, reading as many of the tributes as were still legible, soaking in the wedding pictures, the printed church services, the decaying flowers, the birthday gifts come too late, the thousands of goodbyes.

On Friday my oldest child, Anna, came down with her college roommate. They worked with me here at the Respite Center on my last night. I took them to the same places, and drove them through the valley of the shadow of death. That will be my last memory of this place.

Calvin Coolidge said that each of us should strive to live our lives in such a way that we become the hero of our own life's story. I have seen plenty of people doing that down here. And it truly is a great feeling to get notes from your kids addressed, "My Dad, the Hero".

But I'm no hero, and I know that. I'm only here to make a small down payment on an old debt.

My father was in the Normandy campaign in the Second World War, and his father and uncle in World War I. My great-great grandfather was in the Army of Northern Virginia and survived Pickett's Charge at Gettysburg.

I'll never forget the day my older brother Jay came home from the Army and announced at the dining room table, jauntily, "Well, I nailed the plum assignment. I'm going to Vietnam." Our father's face beamed with pride, masking his fear; our mother's face full of fear, masking her pride. They were, of course, of a different and most remarkable generation.

But I fought the Battle of Albany State, supporting our troops without being one, waving the flag in the face of protestors, insisting on taking exams when others demanded the university be shut down.

Mine was the last year for automatic student deferments. The draft lottery was instituted and I pulled a high, safe number. The war in Vietnam ended half way through my senior year and the draft abolished for good about two weeks after I graduated.

By then there was nothing left to fight for. Morale in the military began a steady decline. Our people were booed when they came home. Our fortitude was put in mothballs.

By the time pride had been restored, I had a young family and a career. The opportunity to serve had passed, and as the years flew by I advanced and became settled in my ways until one day I realized that I had become one of those gentlemen Shakespeare's *Henry V* speaks of who "think themselves accursed" and "hold their manhoods cheap whiles any speak that fought. . ."

That is why I am here, now, because it is all I could think to do.

Some final thoughts. It will be hard to imagine any problem arising that would not pale next to the destruction I have seen here. I do not see myself wallowing in self-pity any time soon. Whatever I have to face is as nothing now. This is one terrific country and its people magnificent. More and more I have become convinced of the simple truths expressed so well by Mr. Greenwood:

> If tomorrow all the things were gone I'd worked for
> all my life,
> And I had to start again with just my children and my
> wife,
> I'd thank my lucky stars to be living here today,
> 'Cause the flag still stands for freedom and they
> can't take that away!

Epilogue

Prophecy is a funny business. The warning of the prophet only becomes obvious after the fact, they say. And so it was that less than twenty-four hours after writing those last lines, the Court of Appeals spoke. Suddenly, just after coming home, "all the things were gone I'd worked for all my life, and I had to start again with just my children and my wife."

But that's ok. After nearly four weeks at Ground Zero I realized that there are far worse fates than not being the Family Court Judge of Montgomery County.

We all had to undergo a mental health debriefing before being discharged. My worker said to me, quietly, "Tell me, how do you think you'll be able to go back and listen to the petty squabbles in Family Court after you've been here?"

I thought about it. "I'm not sure that I can."

Well. I'll never have to worry about that decision.

While riding the subway one day, I sat across from an extended family, consisting of a large black woman, her slightly retarded son in his early twenties, his sister, slightly older, and her boyfriend, a scrawny, swarthy fellow of uncertain ethnic extraction, perhaps native to anywhere from Morocco to Burma.

The son gave me a knowing look and tilted his head toward his sister's boyfriend.

"That's Osama bin Laden," he announced.

Pretty soon his mother and sister were whacking him affectionately.

"He's NOT Osama bin Laden!" the sister insisted.

"Don't pay any attention to him!" the mother warned me.

"Osama" was laughing. They were all laughing. I was laughing. Soon we were all chattering away.

New York has changed. We have all changed. A year earlier and everyone on that subway train would have been staring straight ahead. Now people talk, people laugh, people share. We are one.

Visiting firemen from Canada enter our car and people leap to offer their seats. A woman sees my Red Cross vest and follows me off the train to thank me and thank me again for being there.

I don't know how long it will last. I don't know what it all means. I leave it to the historians and the politicians and the experts to sort it all out.

But I do know this: something happened as a result of September 11.

And it is wonderful.

BEGINNINGS

John Paul the Great and How the Communists Were Destroyed
Apr. 1st, 2005 @ 08:02 pm

Before John Paul II there was another Polish savior of Europe, King John Sobieski, called upon by the countries of Old Europe to save Austria and the West from invasion by the Turks. Though the hour was desperate, Sobieski marched his troops two days out of the way, to the Shrine of Our Lady of Czestochowa, there to pray and copy her image onto their shields. He rallied the weary and wasted remnants of Christianity and gave them new life, and new hope. And victory.

From my birth in 1951 to our wedding in 1978 Mary and I had known only three popes. And then there were three in the first three months of our marriage. We come from a town with strong Polish roots. My wife and children have Polish blood. I grew up a couple of hills over where Polock jokes were all the rage in my youth.

It didn't take long. Approximately one day after the conclave I heard that the new pope had performed a miracle: he made a blind man deaf. And then came the one about explaining Easter, "when, three days after He suffered and died for our sins, He rose from the dead and stepped out of the tomb! Then He saw his shadow and there were six more weeks of winter."

And on and on. Some joke he turned out to be, just becoming one of the greatest men who ever lived. His story is oft-told now and will not be repeated. He will be known for all time as John Paul the Great. He is credited along with Reagan and Thatcher with bringing down the Soviet Union and destroying communism.

But there's a little more to the story that you may not have heard.

The picture that appears with my blog is of me with my daughter Anna, standing street-side at President George W. Bush's first inauguration, January 20, 2001. It wasn't our first trip to Washington with the kids, but their first presidential inauguration. Having been a Reagan delegate to the 1980 Convention, we were naturally invited to his inauguration. But then Anna came along on January 6, 1981 so we skipped that one. Four years later our third child greeted us on January 14, 1985 so we missed Reagan II as well. I went alone to Bush 41, parking myself on the same corner as this picture. Both Reagan and Bush waved to me, but then I was carrying a sign that said, "Thanks, Ron, for securing the blessings of liberty!" signed by Anna, Bobby and Jamie, and cleverly blocking the presidential view of the Keep Abortion Legal folks behind me.

Three months later, in April of 1989, we all went down to see the cherry trees and spent a couple of days touring and visiting old friends with their new foster-baby. Our last stop was the National Basilica of the Immaculate Conception. There are many, many side altars and chapels and we stopped in a few. We started to walk past one for Our Lady of Czestochowa. Eight year old Anna took my hand and said, "What is this one, Daddy?"

I told her, "This is where we pray for the people of Poland." Without another word from anyone, she walked to the altar rail, knelt down and said a prayer.

Two weeks later the world was stunned to hear that a coalition in the Polish parliament had thrown out the Communist government and lived to tell of it. The velvet revolution in Czechoslovakia and elsewhere swept across the east. The Baltic states declared their independence, their people holding hands in a line that connected the capitals of Estonia, Latvia and Lithuania, whispering to each other one word: Freedom. In November, the Berlin Wall came down.

All from the prayer of one little girl.

My Amusing Muse
May. 23rd, 2005 @ 08:50 pm

My muse this week, as several times before, is the irrepressible Dawn Eden, returned now from her junket to Beautiful Ohio, who answers emails indirectly by printing them. So, since she insists I kick-start this blog again, I begin at the beginning with my email to the *Petite Powerhouse*:

> I am a great fan of Ray Bradbury's *Martian Chronicles* which I have probably read a dozen times in the last 40 years. It was only a couple of years ago that I caught the full meaning of part of it when I stumbled on the lyrics to *"Beautiful Ohio"*. In the story about the third mission to Mars, the astronauts find an American mid-western town plopped right next to their rocket. The lads suddenly recognize their own relatives. They all run off to their boyhood homes. There's lemonade and ice cream, the sound of creaking porch rockers and through one of the windows a copy of the sheet music for *Beautiful Ohio* propped on a piano in the parlor. None of it is real, of course, just dreams of what used to be, prepared by the native Martians to lull them into complacency. (A dream that carries through to the All-American funeral with a band playing *"Columbia, The Gem of the Ocean"*).
>
> So Bradbury only gives us a glimpse of *Beautiful Ohio*, while winking at those who know the chorus:
>
> > *Drifting with the current down a moonlit stream*
> > *While above the Heavens in their glory gleam*
> > *And the stars on high*
> > *Twinkle in the sky*
> > *Seeming in a paradise of love divine*
> > *Dreaming of a pair of eyes that looked in mine*
> > *Beautiful Ohio, in dreams again I see*
> > *Visions of what used to be.*

Cool, eh?

Now, back to life issues. Life is baseball. Life is the Boston Red Sox.

Saturday I took the family, minus James still-away-at-college, to Cooperstown, to the Baseball Hall of Fame. Now a million stories have been written about what it's like to be a Red Sox fan. Stewart O'Nan has written one of the best, *Faithful* with Stephen King, and Stewart was in Cooperstown. Funny, poignant, wonderful. Made my day, I thought.

After the book signing we wandered through the hall, took some pictures with the World Series Trophy, on display for the weekend.

Bob Jr., 22, found me musing over something. "Dad, I think I just saw Bobby Doerr."

Bobby Doerr!! Hall of Fame Second Baseman for the Boston Red Sox! Ted Williams' best friend, from the minors, even. I spotted him, old guy in suspenders, approaching the exhibit of memorabilia from the Sox 2004 season. We greeted each other, he held out his hand. As I took it, I noticed the ring on the other hand.

A 2004 World Series ring.

Turns out the Sox had surprised him and Dom DiMaggio at a charity event a couple of weeks ago. Pesky already had his.

The Teammates.

Which reminded me that I was carrying a copy of *Teammates* in my bag. We got into a conspiratorial whisper about where we could meet the next day so he could sign it (my only missing autograph) as signing in the hall was strictly taboo.

Then we both looked at the exhibit. He pointed to Schilling's bloody sock. He choked a little. "That's really somethin', isn't it?" he said to me. I pointed to my son in the crowd and told Bobby about my Bobby. "He was 2 ½ years old when you were inducted into the Hall and I brought him down here and threw him on my shoulders so he could see everything." He seemed touched.

An old man wove through the gathering crowd. "Second base. Boston Red Sox." Bobby looked puzzled for a moment and I think we both thought this guy was saying that HE had played second base for the Red Sox, which certainly would have been some coincidence, but no, it was just a man who had once been a boy and who idolized this 87-year-old hero of his youth.

I slipped away. My day was complete.

****

That night my Muse appeared to me in a dream. Even though we have never met, when you're drifting with the current down a moonlit stream, strange things can happen. I dreamed that she had stopped by on her way back from Ohio (not otherwise inconceivable if she was driving, since I'm a short distance off the New York State Thruway and the beautiful Mohawk Valley provides a virtually flat route to Cleveland). Not much of a dream, but like I did with Bobby Doerr, I checked her left hand to see if she was sporting a ring yet. The only odd part is that my mother entered the room and I said, "This is my friend Dawn Eden," and my mother went up to my wife Mary and said, "Nice to meet you, Dawn." It's odd for several reasons. The first is my mother has never been blind or senile. Also she's been dead almost ten years.

Though it had never crossed my conscious mind at all the previous day, by the time this dream rolled around it was well past midnight, and was now Mom's 80th birthday.

My most wonderful, funny, twinkly-eyed all-perfect Mom was dropping in for a visit, happily assuring that

> *... in dreams again I see*
> *Visions of what used to be.*

Thanks, Mom. Thanks, Bobby. Thanks, Dawn.

A Visit to Canadia
May. 25th, 2005 @ 10:38 pm

Well, the Red Sox were playing in Toronto and Bob(22) has been spending a couple of weeks home after his graduation from Adelphi University (BFA)and Anna (24, BS-UA) is on a brief hiatus pending her AAS from FMCC on Friday which will make her an RN(P), so to celebrate all of the above the three of us hied our way to Canadia for the game, after dropping off Jamie at RIT.

The hieing across the border at Lewiston went less than smoothly. Seems the guards from Canada have gotten a little testy since our side announced we would be requiring passports and/or birth certificates in a couple of years, so they decided to pro-actively retaliate. And poor Anna had only seven forms of identification and neither passport nor birth certificate.

"This an INTERNATIONAL BORDER, SIR! WE REQUIRE PROOF OF CITIZENSHIP!"

"I have my driver's license," Anna meekly interjected.

"So did two of the 9/11 hijackers from YOUR STATE OF FLORIDA!"

So there we are, decked out in our team attire, driving in a Dodge mini-van with bumper slogans supporting Catholic Schools, the Wild Irish Dancers, Our Troops, the Boston Red Sox and George W. Bush, all atop a red-white-and-blue "God Bless America" and they'll take a photocopy of a fax of anybody's birth certificate as proof of citizenship, but they won't take the testimony of her mother's coach who actually witnessed her enter the USA as a citizen for the first time on January 6, 1981 at 7:46 am in Albany, NY and sang to her the *My Little Girl* sequence from the *Carousel Soliloquy* and who even knows that *in utero* she attended the

Republican National Convention in Detroit, Michigan where she much enjoyed the acceptance speech of Ronald Reagan! Most of this I did not say out loud.

And it was right about then that I just KNEW that a 1972 Renault with "ALLAHU AKBAR", "DEATH TO INFIDELS" and "KERRY/EDWARDS" bumper stickers had sped through there not five minutes earlier with two mid-eastern looking guys waving fake Saudi passports.

We were sternly warned. He let us in. We spent the rest of the trip strategizing how we would ever get Anna back to Amsterdam, NY, and what with the big graduation party scheduled for her house, this was no small matter. My idea was to take the Canadian Maid-of-the-Mist boat, have her "fall" overboard just as the American Maid-of-the-Mist was coming the other way, which would thereupon rescue the poor dear who tragically had lost all of her identification in the raging river. I thought this made more sense than covering her with a blanket behind the back seat of the van.

****

All of the early-arriving fans at thefacilityformerlyknownastheSkyDome seemed to be Sox fans. The vendors had more Sox material than Blue Jays'.

Incredibly, the official program for the evening of the Toronto Blue Jays featured Boston Superstar Johnny Damon on the cover. I asked one of the hawkers what gives and he leaned over and whispered, "It's the only way we could sell any."

I met and chatted with a fellow from Central Massachusetts who had flown up for the game. In 1940 when he was about twelve his dad had taken him to see a doubleheader at Fenway and in one of those games Ted Williams had made his only big league appearance as a pitcher (two innings, three hits, one run; coulda used him last night). In 1946 this fellow came home from the war in time for the World Series in Boston, but couldn't get tickets. I contemplated for a moment how much growing up he must have done in those six years. We talked about Williams and Bobby Doerr and all those players in all those heart-breaking series and I was really pleased to have met this man, because he was what 2004 was all about.

****

This is baseball? Oh,thefacilityformerlyknownastheSkyDome is comfortable enough.Heck, they have hotel rooms in center field. But it sure isn't the same experience you get in a dirty smelly cramped wonderful old park like Fenway. Seemed more like watching a River Rats hockey game at the Pepsi Arena in Albany. Same kind of crowd, mostly groups. We had $18 seats (American, I have no idea what they go for in euros or rubles or whatever it is they use up there) in what would be field boxes in most parks. But then it WAS a "Value Night". Value Night!!! They're playing a division rival and the DEFENDING WORLD SERIES CHAMPIONS and this is a Value Night!! What do they get for Tampa Bay games, I wondered only briefly, because the answer came up on the Jumbotron. For Tampa Bay, you not only get seats, but bring your sleeping bag and they'll give you a light supper and you can have a family sleep-over on the artificial turf. I'm not making this up.

You can see a game here for as little as two dollars (we paid twenty for standing room at Fenway the last time we went), yet it was probably the fifth inning before the crowd reached the announced 34,000 which is fewer than tiny Fenway has had at any time in the last two seasons. They give stuff away between innings. I was surprised that they haven't adopted the River Rats technique of using a giant sling shot to hurl tee-shirts and oil-change certificates into the upper decks.

A group of prepubescent school kids sat behind us. It appears that the teacher had organized them into two groups as a learning experience. The boys rooted for the Red Sox (borrowing our "Go Red Sox" banner left over from the big World Series parade in Boston) and the girls rooted for the home team, somewhat confusedly as they endlessly chanted, "Let's Go, Bluebirds".

Although they serve beer in the park (one thing they do well in Canadia), there was no sign of a townie testosterone section where loud-mouth know-it-alls (not unlike myself) should be analyzing every play. In fact, a feeble "Boston Sucks" effort seemed totally out of place and "BOOM-er" when Wells got in trouble in the 4th was just pathetic.

Poor Canadia. These people have no independent culture and no history of their own worth mentioning. (I recognize the sacrifices their boys made in WWII, but that was for THE KING, for gosh sake). That, and all those years of socialism have squeezed the life out of anything resembling individual initiative. It's not that they don't show enthusiasm. It's just that they have to be TOLD when to show it! They have an "In-game Host" who appears between innings and tries to bring up the noise level. We get to the bottom of the ninth with the score tied at 6 (we really saw some good baseball) and the fans have to be stirred up with this huge multi-media display that reminded me of the Great Leader sequences in Woody Allen's *Sleeper*. They all stood when they were supposed to stand, cheered and whistled when they were told to cheer and whistle and stamped their feet when it was time to stamp. It was positively Stepfordian. Animated drums drum up "Let's Go, Blue-Jays" with the words flashing (which I think confused the girls behind us) and an animated Jay, looking for all the world like an American Eagle, swoops down out of the lightning to destroy the opposition.

And as soon as the walk-off homer gives the Jays the victory, the place empties out as if nothing had happened. In Boston or New York the partying would have continued for half an hour and poured out into the streets. But there are no streets surrounding thefacilityformerlyknownastheSkyDome, just concrete and highways and the CN Tower.

Way too civilized. Give me old-fashioned American anarchy every time.

****

We crossed the Rainbow Bridge at Niagara Falls on a picture-perfect morning. We approached the American Border Guard.

Where were you born, how long have you been out of the country, where are you going.

"Have a safe trip home," the man said.

The free air never smelled so sweet.

Honor Roll
May. 28th, 2005 @ 07:44 am

My attic is a wonderful place: open, spacious, twenty feet from floor to peak, full-size windows on the ends and three dormers for light. It is everything an attic should be, filled with treasures of past generations, the accumulated junk of twenty-six years of marriage and remains of six or seven estates that wandered our way.

As I re-established my law practice a few years back, I spent a bit of time up there, searching out old files and forms and office supplies. One day, when my client base had doubled to two, I felt the immediate need for a notebook to keep track of things. There on a shelf was an old bound business journal, and I grabbed it. The first seventy pages were missing and the rest seemed blank. Perfect.

I figured it had belonged to my father when he practiced law forty years ago. I knew that I myself had never been so extravagant as to purchase anything in hardcover.

Flipping through it one day I realized that it was not as blank as I had thought. It was not my father's after all, but my grandmother's, dating back to when she led the American Legion Auxiliary in the late 1940's.

There were five pages of entries in the middle of the book, all in the neat handwriting of May Goodison Going Nichols, captioned *Deceased Amsterdam Boys of World War #2*. I suspect she never finished the project as the alphabetical listing ended abruptly with Corp. Donald Suchiel, September 22, 1944, France. There were, nonetheless, 136 entries.

The magnitude of my city's loss stunned me. In ten years of Vietnam there were, what? Less than a dozen deaths from this area?

Yet here were one hundred thirty six names from Private Leslie Ackerman to Corp. Suchiel. The vast majority were in the years 1944 and 1945.

Aldi, Alibozek, Anderson. These fellows probably had adjoining lockers in high school.

William Hassenfuss, December 7, 1941, Hawaii. I ice-skated on the field named after him when I was a kid.

Norman Briskie, Eugene Greco, Allen Pileckas, Lawrence Quackenbush, Thomas Quigley, Thomas Rutkowski. Didn't I know all these guys? Well, I was born in 1951, so I couldn't have, but I suppose it should not be unusual that lads of my generation would bear the names of the honored dead.

Theodore Canape, Anthony DeStefano, Thomas DiCaprio, Mullarkey, Munroe, Murawski, Natoli.

There's a note next to Sgt. Richard Morties. *"Returned from overseas after having been a prisoner of war. Killed while on leave in auto accident in Fort Johnson, October 6, 1945."*

Perkins, Petricca, Pettitti, Polikowski, Popielarz, Salvaleauskas, San Fillipo.

Sgt. Nicholas Foti, June 6, 1944, France; Private Harold Premo, June 6, 1944, Normandy; Pvt. John Schilling, June 6, 1944, France.

In another corner of the attic were letters my father had written to his mother during the war, including this one dated June 19, 1944 as he was about to sail for France and the fortnight-old Normandy campaign:

> *Dear Mom,*
> *I'm sorry that I haven't written you sooner but I honestly haven't been able to. This is the first letter I've been allowed to write and will probably be the only one for a time so please be patient and don't worry. I'm safe and well so there is no cause for worry. We received our first mail in some time yesterday and yours of June 6 was among them. I also received the first copy of the newspaper but no packages. . . .Have been attending Mass and receiving Communion daily as we have the Catholic Chaplain with us. I thank God for that opportunity. It's a great help at a time like this. My love to all and regards to Dez. Please continue to write and be patient until you hear from me.*

All my love

Bud

Don't worry.

Pvt. Theodore Demanski, June 13, 1944, France; Pvt. Thomas Cronin, June 25, 1944, Normandy; Sgt. George Brown, July 6, 1944, Normandy; Pvt. William Hutchinson, July 27, 1944, France.

Lt. Lewis Di Leillo, October 4, 1944, France. Missing, presumed dead, after leading a rear guard action to protect retreating troops. The presumption proved to be correct. Remarkably, I attended his funeral.

What a strange thing indeed to be about forty years old and participating in the last farewells of someone who had died in his early twenties nearly seven years before you were born. What a miracle that they had found his body, at last, and brought him across the sea to Amsterdam, to St. Mary's, where crusty old veterans lined up in solemn salute to their fallen forever-young comrade.

The reading at his funeral Mass was from Deuteronomy 30:4:

> **"Though you may have been driven to the farthest corner of the world, even from there will the Lord, your God, gather you; even from there will He bring you back."**

The Man With the Briefcase
Jun. 4th, 2005 @ 06:58 pm

It's early June and yet another anniversary of the Tiananmen Square Massacre passes with barely a notice.

How blithely we forget those tens of thousands of brave Chinese people who in peaceful defiance of their autocratic state met in the Spring of 1989 to celebrate the concept of Freedom, raised a statue to the *Goddess of Democracy* (an homage to our own "Liberty Enlightening the World") and were rewarded with tanks, and guns and death.

China has always fascinated me, but more so since meeting my brother's father-in-law, Charlie Chow.

Charlie was a teenager when the Communist Revolution swept over China.

One dark night men came for his father, a judge.

The family never heard from him again.

Charlie alone managed to make his way to Taiwan. Because of the Revolution he never graduated from high school, but managed to attend college in Taiwan, Republic of China (I use the title "Republic of China" not only to be historically accurate, but because I know it will annoy the despots in Beijing when they read this).

He married, had the first of five children, and was off to graduate school in the United States before he could attend his college graduation. He never attended graduation ceremonies for his Masters degree in Missouri either, since by then General Electric had hired him and the family moved to the Schenectady area. It was not until he received his Doctorate that he finally stood on a platform to receive his just accolades.

His mother and siblings remained behind in China, completely locked out of contact with their son and brother until the 1971 Nixon trip. Then, slowly, things loosened and Charlie was among the very first expatriates to be allowed to visit, with his wife.

It was an emotional time for them. China was a very closed society, just a few years removed from the "Cultural Revolution" that had ripped the nation apart. A government "translator" was assigned to the fluent Chows and accompanied them everywhere. The "Mao" clothes were still required and poverty ran deep.

To carry his papers, Charlie had brought along a briefcase, the kind used by millions of businessmen daily in this country. His relatives were enraptured by it. It was the finest thing they had ever seen. The Chows came back with hundreds of slides, and it seems that nearly half of them contained a shot of one relative or another beaming broadly, holding that briefcase.

Charlie offered to leave it behind. "Oh, no, you mustn't," he was told. "Not even the highest members of the Party in our district have anything as fine as this. We would be open to criticism and suspicion."

So they took the briefcase and little else, walking out of China with only the clothes on their backs and bedroom slippers on their feet.

****

In early June of 1989 I was glued to the television, watching joyfully as the people took to the streets and stopped the army with flowers and peaceful assembly. But when June 4 came and all hope dashed, I returned to more mundane matters.

On June 5, 1989 the Montgomery County Republican Committee planned to meet in the Courthouse in Fonda to endorse candidates for the coming election.

I was seeking re-election as City Court Judge of Amsterdam, and would be expected to say a few words. I really didn't have any prepared, and knew it wouldn't make a whole lot of difference what I said.

I caught the first part of the network news before leaving for Fonda, and saw the most startling thing: in the middle of Tiananmen Square where thousands had only the day before been killed, arrested or dispersed, here stood ONE MAN, standing alone before a line of tanks, refusing to let them pass. Whichever way the lead tank zigged, he zagged.

He had no idea that he was being filmed as all cameras had been barred and the international press excluded from the area. Yet there he stood, nonetheless. In a nation of a billion people he stood up for his God-given right to be one.

The footage, taken from a distant window with a telephoto lens, was fuzzy, yet I could see that he was carrying something in his hand.

To me it looked like Charlie Chow's briefcase.

****

"We meet here once a year and do the same thing over and over," I told my fellow Republicans. "It's so trivial, what with everything else going on in the world."

And I told them of the man with the briefcase stopping the tanks, and I reminded them of our little militia peacefully assembled on Lexington Green in 1775, standing with their weapons down as the Red Coats approached, because they were confidant that the British soldiers would never fire on their own people. And then I remembered that this was the eve of the 45th anniversary of D-Day, and mentioned the courage of men like Judge Malcolm Tomlinson who went ashore ahead of the troops to help guide the naval bombardment, and the courage of people of all time who were willing to risk even death for a noble idea that was bigger than all of us.

"So the fact that we meet here every year and decide for ourselves who we want to hold public office is quite trivial.

"And so magnificent.

"And it is well that we pause and reflect every once in a while about what a truly wonderful thing we are doing here."

And I sat down.

****

They took the man with the briefcase away.

They say he's dead now.

And we never learned his name.

Rudy the Great
Sep. 1st, 2005 @ 01:22 pm

MAYBE it's not fair to compare, but what the heck. On the one hand you have this current slap-dash, disjointed, whadowedonext FUBAR incompetence down in New Orleans and environs where both nature and humanity have spun out of control.

And then there's Rudy. All hell broke loose. They had emergency plans and equipment, but those got wiped out, too. What did it take, one maybe two seconds for him to improvise? By giving orders, he created order out of chaos.

One just can't imagine the NYPD driving past thousands of dehydrating people and giving them no help, no information, no instructions, no water.

How hard would it be for SOMEONE to tell the dispatchers to put out an APB saying "Five hundred buses will be arriving in twelve hours to bring you to safety at such and such an intersection." It doesn't even have to be a great plan or a good plan for that matter. ANY plan would do to restore order and give hope.

How long should it take to say, "We need the National Guard and we need them NOW!" I know the Governor of Louisiana's heart is bleeding over all the suffering, but how about shutting down the tears and DOING SOMETHING.

In New York it seemed like every piece of construction equipment in the northeast was mobilized and in place in the first 24 hours. In New Orleans days have gone by and they still have not made any concerted effort to stop the leak. It seems that even though they had a plan to drop 3,000 pound sand bags into the hole, the straps they needed to carry the bags were still in Baton Rouge.

What happened to all the city buses? Like the Bus Named Desire which replaced the old street car? Couldn't they have been lined up outside the Superdome? Shouldn't there have been a thousand ambulances and paramedics?

On the fringes, things seem to be under control. The Red Cross has huge contingency plans and a nation-wide network of experienced people who can set up shelters everywhere on a moment's notice. Ditto the Salvation Army and the Southern Baptists whose portable kitchens for thousands pop up wherever needed. The manner in which the City of Houston has opened its doors is heartwarming.

But the governments of Louisiana and the City of New Orleans? Pathetic.

But I guess your Rudy Giulianis don't come around that often. Now we know it's not just a case of greatness being thrust upon him.

****

Back in 1977 I proposed to my wife during a concert in our home town featuring the Preservation Hall Jazz Band of New Orleans. Many of the nonagenarian musicians had played with Louis Armstrong, back when they were inventing music. (Their music was featured in Woody Allen's *Sleeper*).

We finally got to New Orleans in the summer of 2001, there for the big party at the D-Day Museum for my uncle the Admiral's retirement and the Change of Command Ceremony. It was everything New Orleans is supposed to be: blasted hot, stifling humidity and pure fun. We ate at *Emeril's DelMonico Restaurant* one night, took a carriage ride through the French Quarter, ferried across the Mississippi to the antebellum mansion that served as the Admiral's Quarters, saw a genuine New Orleans Jazz Funeral and Parade, and, of course, heard music everywhere.

Preservation Hall looks (or is made to look) exactly as it would have in the 1920's, and as though not a dime had been spent on decor since the 1870's. Most people stood, though there were a couple of benches and cushions on the floor directly in front of the band, which is where we perched. The ancient trombonist was so close to Mary that the slide passed over her head on a regular basis.

It was pure heaven. Five bucks admission for three hours of solid entertainment. Even when they repeated songs, they weren't even close to the same arrangements. (Actually there is nothing "arranged" about any of it.) Every once in a while they would break into "When the Saints Go Marching

In" when someone would slip them a twenty, and then you'd see people gathering on the street outside the dirty windows hollerin' and stompin' and just having a grand old time. It was, I think, the most enjoyable evening of my life.

And now, it may never happen again.

Is the city dead?

Yesterday the screen was filled with refugees slogging through the flooded, sewage-filled streets, carrying their meager possessions and not having a clue as to where they were going or what would happen to them.

And yet, on one street corner a man took out his trumpet and played and played and played. One man tooting, "He's Got the Whole World in His Hands."

NATIONAL REVIEW at 50
Oct. 6th, 2005 @ 05:57 pm

Politically, I guess I was something of a prodigy. I remember watching the 1956 Democratic National Convention on television. I was 5. By 1960 I had forced my way into a picture with Richard Nixon. I tagged along with my Dad as he helped lay the foundation for the Conservative Party in New York in 1962. A year later when he ran for the Republican nomination for Alderman of the Second Ward of the City of Amsterdam that little escapade probably cost him the election which he only lost by seven votes. It's hard to believe now, but there was actually a whispering campaign going on. Did you know that Frank Going is a CONSERVATIVE?

That was around the time he first subscribed to *National Review*. He had already been hooked on Bill Buckley for a while from his books and columns. Bill had made his imprint on society at a very young age. I'm quoting here from distant memory, but it seems to me that there is a scene in *The Manchurian Candidate* (the book) where a bunch of the usual right-wing crackpots are gathered, and also "that fascinating young man who wrote about God and Man at Yale."

Before Talk Radio was capitalized and went national, it existed in a few of the big cities. For us in upstate New York sundown meant we could start picking up WNBC in New York, with Long John Nebel from 8-9, Brad Crandall from 9-midnight, then Long John again in an all-night marathon to 5 a.m. It was on one of these shows that we first heard the voice of William F. Buckley, Jr.

We were astounded at his rich baritone (my father and I). He could talk and debate without end. He was a Conservative Prophet, almost single-handedly bringing the message to the masses. There I am, in junior high school, soaking it all in. Then came the Goldwater Campaign, and Buckley's quixotic run for Mayor in 1965 that firmly established the Conservative Party in New York.

When I was in college in 1971, I received one of those funny letters from *National Review* urging me to subscribe. I wrote Buckley, telling him I couldn't afford the magazine, but to keep me on the mailing list because I so much enjoyed receiving his missives. A couple of days later I received a note from his personal secretary, Frances Bronson, that Mr. Buckley had arranged for me to receive a free subscription for one year.

In 1995, when my Mom died, the magazines were still coming. At that point I decided it was time to pay and took over the responsibility.

I met Buckley on a few occasions, particularly when he hosted a series of discussions on "Four Reforms" at Russell Sage College in Troy. Russell Kirk tagged along for one. Bill told me to look him up when I came to New York and he'd take me to lunch. Unfortunately our schedules never meshed and it didn't happen.

Dad couldn't make it to Troy. He was too sick by then.

He had told me once how much he would love to spend an evening with Bill Buckley.

"What would you say to him?" I asked.

"I'd say, 'Bill, talk. . . . Just talk.'"

Consider the Lilies of the Field
Oct. 9th, 2005 @ 11:17 pm

The Little Sisters of the Poor paid our parish a visit this weekend and the good Sister post-homilist told us some wonderful "God will provide" stories. They just have their faith and let God take care of their needs. And He does, on a regular basis. It helps, no doubt, that the things they "need" are really for aiding somebody else.

Mother Teresa was once approached by the American Knights of Columbus who offered to set up a foundation to meet the every need of her Missionary Sisters of the Poor so that she wouldn't have to worry about finances. She turned them down flat. God takes care of us, and it is better for our faith that we not know how He will do it.

Mom once initiated a little miracle like that, asking my brother to pick up some carrots if they had any at the shop where he was buying his Sunday paper. No carrots. (It was likely a bookie joint). So he set off for home cutting across a field.

There in the middle of his path in the middle of nowhere lay a fresh bag of carrots.

****

A news item a couple of weeks ago mentioned that FEMA had begun reimbursing "faith based" organizations for their services in the Katrina hurricane. Another item noted that a society of funeral directors which had mobilized its members to provide free assistance in New Orleans was told by FEMA that their help was not needed. Instead FEMA laid a lucrative contract on a single mortuary firm.

We have already learned how the Red Cross and Salvation Army were turned away from New Orleans by the state government of Louisiana.

What was it Reagan said? "Government is not the solution to our problem; government is the problem."

Why are we discouraging private charity and/or cheapening its worth by subsidizing it? The truly remarkable stories coming out of the hurricanes are the ones about people opening up their homes to strangers, and offering them jobs, and caring for and comforting them.

I'm serious. Get the government out of it. Love thy neighbor still works in this country, thank God.

[UPDATE 10/11/05]

As further proof that their beloved grandmother still watches over them, I spoke with Jamie on the phone last night. Recently a neighbor to his apartment tossed out a player-piano (and no, Dale, her name wasn't Ethel Tothelmeyer). So Jamie and one of his roommates push the thing from the dumpster to their apartment. It was monstrously heavy and the two of them could not negotiate the two stairs to the front door.

"How are we going to do this?" Jamie lamented.

At that very moment a big panel truck rolled down the street and stopped. Across the side of the truck was painted, "We Move Pianos." Three big guys jumped out, laughed, picked up the piano and brought it inside.

My Dinner With Anna
Oct. 22nd, 2005 @ 12:36 am

Parenthood really has its delightful moments. On Friday we spent our first "formal" evening at Anna and Pete's new house. Now they've been married for a year and a couple of months and in the house for a couple of months and we certainly spent plenty of time down there stripping wallpaper and painting and varnishing and slapping down pizza and wings and that sort of thing (and Mrs. Judge making and hanging drapes), but this was really the first time that we enjoyed the "finished" house with a real meal in the dining room and a leisurely evening of games to follow.

Anna was born mature, but she just keeps blossoming. The meal was outstanding in every way, from the maple-crusted salmon to the rigatoni in pesto sauce, to the garlic and maple red potatoes to the apple and raisin bread pudding. Wow. And I forgot the rosemary and something bread dipped in olive oil appetizer.

Poor Peter is sick with his fifth bout of tonsillitis this year, so it was just Anna, Mrs. Judge, me, Louisa (our 15-yr-old baby) and Louisa's friend whose great-great grandmother was the sister of my great-grandmother (who died in 1899). We settled in for a game of *Balderdash*, the object of which is to make up answers to extremely obscure trivia questions. ou get points if someone else guesses your answer for the real one, or if you guess the real one.

Mrs. Judge volunteered to read the answers and, as always happens when Anna is around, we laughed and laughed and laughed for hours. Sometimes Mary was just choking and convulsing so hard she couldn't get the answers out.

Mostly they were short responses, but in the category of movies you get the title of a genuine but virtually unknown film and you have to make up the plot. *Toxic Zombies* was something of a challenge because essentially all the plots came out the same. If you've seen one toxic zombie movie, you've seen them all. But *Little Cigars* brought a whole wave of imagination (the real answer had something to do with midgets; I forget whether they were Cuban).

My response was "The story of a poor orphan girl who is forced to work at an exploding cigar factory and falls in love with a band wrapper." Well, for some reason that just grabbed Mrs. Judge's funny bone and there she is a-shakin' and a-hoppin' and the tears running down her face and that got the rest of us going and I hate to think what poor Peter was thinking in his sick bed overhead.

Much as I'd like to take credit for the plot, it really belongs to Mr. Timothy Blanchfield, a gentleman featured in *Who's Who Among American Teachers* and former Educator of the Year of the Germantown (NY) School District. This, of course, is not the Tim Blanchfield I know.

I know Tim, among other things, as the ninth grade student in Mrs. Going's (yes, Mom's) English class who had never read a book. This small fact did not cause him the slightest hesitation when called upon to give a three minute oral book report. He simply created a title and author and extemporized a much longer version of the afore-mentioned plot. For fifteen minutes.

Now Mom enjoyed the presentation as well as anybody, but duty required her to take *some* deduction for the fact that the book report was missing an essential element - a book - and therefore Tim did not receive full credit. A "C" I think.

Mom was no pushover. She could pretty much tell when somebody was faking it, even a pro like Tim. Once she received a written book report on *To Kill a Mockingbird*:

> "This is a book about a Southern lawyer, Atticus Finch (Gregory Peck) . . ."

Being we were in a Catholic school, when Mom approached the young lady with the question, "Did you really read this book?" she was conscience-bound to confess that she might possibly have seen the movie at the Tryon Theater one night.

Mom would have really enjoyed our dinner with Anna. She would have laughed harder than any of us. And she would have been so very, very proud of her grandchildren, as am I.

COURT STORIES

Keeping the Loco in loco parentis
Nov. 4th, 2005 @ 09:23 am

The Federal 9th Circuit Court of Appeals came down with an interesting case yesterday, which I have not read in its entirety, which raises some fascinating legal and constitutional questions. It involves parental rights, among other things, but the issues are clouded in the somewhat strange fact pattern. So let's just discuss this for now from a cultural perspective.

The parents of young elementary school children were asked to allow their children to participate in a study about attitudes. Each parent executed a consent form. Whether it was informed consent remains an issue. As I understand it, there was no mention of sexual content. These are some of the questions the 7-10 year olds were asked to rate as to how often they thought about these things:

> a. "Touching my private parts too much."
> b. "Thinking about having sex"
> c. "Thinking about touching other people's private parts."
> d. "Thinking about sex when I don't want to."
> e. "Washing myself because I feel dirty on the inside."
> f. "Not trusting people because they might want sex."
> g. "Getting scared or upset when I think about sex."
> h. "Having sex feelings in my body."
> i. "Can't stop thinking about sex."
> j. "Getting upset when people talk about sex."

****

While you are pondering the appropriateness of the above for such an age group and returning your jaws to their natural position, let me interrupt the flow of my narrative (it's ok; Melville did it all the time) and tell a little story about definition of terms. I do this to point out the general uselessness of such a survey without a clear understanding of what the words mean to the surveyees.

I began practicing in Family Court just after the HLA paternity test was introduced (later augmented by DNA testing). Before that nearly every paternity case went to trial, because the older blood tests only served to exclude a person who was not the father in about 10% of the cases. (Now it is in the 99% range inclusive). Therefore the proof rested on actual testimony of times, dates and circumstances of sexual relations.

About a year earlier, young attorney Rick Partyka was assigned to represent a paternity defendant. The Department of Social Services Attorney, John Kosinski, brought the case to seek child support to reimburse the county for welfare costs. The other names are fictional.

DSS Attorney Kosinski puts Miss Doe on the stand and quickly elicits the important facts: date of her last period, opportunity and access on May 3, May 5, May 6, May 8, etc. He sits down.

Well-prepared Mr. Partyka cross-examines.

"Isn't it true that when you had sex with my client on May 3rd that he had a prophylactic on that occasion?"

"Yes, that's true."

"And isn't it also true that he had a prophylactic on May 5th?"

"Yes."

"And he also had a prophylactic on May 6 and May 8, didn't he?"

"Yes."

"And isn't it true, Miss Doe, that on each and every occasion that you had sexual relations with my client, he had a prophylactic?"

"That's right. Yes."

Partyka sits down triumphant.

"Re-direct, Mr. Kosinski?"

"Just a couple of questions, your honor. Miss Doe, when you were answering Mr. Partyka's questions, he used a big word: 'prophylactic'. Let me ask you this, do you know what 'prophylactic' means?"

"I think so, yes."

"Well, tell us in your own words what it means?"

She blushed. "It means he came."

****

S ays the Court:

> ...there is no fundamental right of parents to be the exclusive provider of information regarding sexual matters to their children, either independent of their right to direct the upbringing and education of their children or encompassed by it. We also hold that parents have no due process or privacy right to override the determinations of public schools as to the information to which their children will be exposed while enrolled as students. Finally, we hold that the defendants' actions were rationally related to a legitimate state purpose....
> ...In summary, we hold that there is no free-standing fundamental right of parents "to control the upbringing of their children by introducing them to matters of and relating to sex in accordance with their personal and religious values and beliefs" and that the asserted right is not encompassed by any other fundamental right. In doing so, we do not quarrel with the parents' right to inform and advise their children about the subject of sex as they see fit. We conclude only that the parents are possessed of no constitutional right to prevent the public schools from providing information on that subject to their students in any forum or manner they select.

And how about this little comforting thought found in a footnote:

"I understand answering questions may make my child feel uncomfortable. If this occurs, then, Kristi Seymour, the research study coordinator, will assist us in locating a therapist for further psychological help if necessary."

****

Here is my thought for the day: if there are certain fundamental rights reserved to the people, and the right to raise and educate your children as you see fit isn't one of them, then what is?

I realize that this is probably long-settled law ("super-precedent"), but what right does the government have to enforce compulsory education anyway? Every single state requires it.

There was no such animal at the time the constitution was adopted. Public education was the brainchild of Horace Mann in the 19th century. (The site of his birth is across the street from the first Brunelli's Supermarket in Franklin, MA. That's an inside-family thing.) We all accept it as the right of government now. Children can be pulled from their homes and placed in custody for not attending school and their parents charged with child neglect. Why?

[Personal to members of the Senate Judiciary Committee: I'm just attempting to provoke discussion and thought here. Nothing should be construed as reflecting any opinion I might have or be used as the basis for conjecture as to how I might rule on a particular issue which might come before me.]

****

John Kosinski had a Christmas party later that year. As Rick Partyka and his wife were leaving, John shook his hand and said, "Glad you could prophylactic, Mr. Partyka. I hope you can prophylactic again next year."

In the Least-Worse Interests of the Children
Nov. 30th, 2005 @ 11:22 pm

While browsing through my hard drive I came across this custody decision I wrote in Family Court several years ago. I think it needs a broader audience. -RNG

STATE OF NEW YORK
FAMILY COURT   COUNTY OF MONTGOMERY

D V,
        Petitioner

                        DECISION AND ORDER
-against-
                        File # xxx
                        Docket # V-xxx-2000
C V,
        Respondent

ROBERT N. GOING, JFC:

The Petitioner seeks an Order of Custody for the subject children of his marriage to Respondent, namely DI V, d/o/b xx/xx/95, and DA. V, d/o/b xx/xx/97. The parties separated in February of 2000 and since that time the children have been residing primarily with their mother in a new location pursuant to a temporary order of this court while the petitioner has been sharing substantial custodial time with the children at the marital residence.

Ordinarily, in a Decision such as this, THE COURT would be reciting in the third person all the appropriate facts and circumstances which would lead IT to a wise, just and appropriate solution which would provide ever-so-obviously for the best interests of the children. I am breaking with this tradition because I think these parties need to hear the truth, and that is that there is nothing I can do that can possibly set right what these parties have set aside, nor can I make anyone whole, nor can I remotely provide for the best interests of these children.

When parents break up, they inevitably attempt to convince themselves that the children will be better off, and I suppose that is occasionally true, particularly when one party or the other has been abusive toward the children or toward the spouse. But in most cases the parents are just trying to justify their own actions and their own human frailties. In a case as this one, where we have two parties who are clearly decent, considerate people and loving and effective parents, any solution short of a reestablishment of the family unit will bring nothing but heartache, disappointment, confusion, anger, guilt and frustration for the children, no matter what their ages and it is foolish and even perhaps a trifle cruel to think otherwise.

I have not been told what led to the marital breakup. I do know that I saw in the courtroom two people who are hurting, and hurting badly. I know from the testimony that both are heavily invested in the children and their welfare, that both have been actively connected to the children on a daily basis, that from all outward signs they were what most people would consider an ideal family.

It is nearly axiomatic that the introduction of children into a household can put stress on the husband/wife relationship. Economic tensions, time inevitably shared with the children lost to the parents, the old freedom of movement gone, seemingly forever. And yet, every family from the beginning of time has faced these same stresses, and most have survived. It takes effort, it takes time, it takes compromise, it takes careful listening, it takes a few tears. But it can work. If two people have loved each other enough to bring children into the world, they ought to be able to reach back into that reservoir created by the marriage vow to find the strength that they need to continue, to endure and to triumph. The two most powerful sentences in a marriage are "I'm sorry" and "I forgive you." It doesn't matter awfully much who says which.

But, as these parties have chosen another path, I must render a decision, not, unfortunately, in the best interests of the children, but in the least worse.

As far as parenting goes, I find these parties equally prepared for the responsibilities of parenthood. As they share similar philosophies and goals and are able to communicate exceptionally well regarding the children, Joint Custody is appropriate and will continue. Among the other factors considered by the Court (there is that cold and impersonal third-person "Court" again) are the work schedules of the parties, the alternative arrangements when a parent is not available, the fact that the Respondent has another child by a previous relationship who is close to his siblings, along with all the other usual factors provided by statute and case law.

On the basis of all those considerations, the Court finds that it would be in the least-worse interests of the children to have primary physical custody with the respondent/mother, that the petitioner/father should have open and liberal custodial time with the children, including continuing the schedule set forth in the Temporary Order of February 29, 2000, namely alternate weekends from Friday at 4:00 P.M. until Sunday at 6:00 P.M. and each Wednesday from 4:30 P.M. to 8:00 P.M. and such other and further times as the parties may agree, as the Court is confident they will. Further, as it appears these children are spending substantial time with babysitters and other care providers, each parent shall have the right of first refusal of time with the children when the children require the services of an outside care-provider, and it is

SO ORDERED.

Finally, in the best interests of the children, I request that the parties search and review long and hard those commitments which they once made to each other for life.

Dated: May 18, 2000

_____
Robert N. Going, JFC

Memories
Mar. 3rd, 2006 @ 09:27 pm

The object of the wake was a genuine American original who made it to 87 and who had been one of my big supporters when I ran for mayor in my head-strong youth. I probably hadn't seen him in fifteen years or more, though I would bump into one or another of his kids from time to time. The funeral home rocked with his children and grandchildren and great-grandchildren.

One of the daughters approached me with delight. I had seen this reaction before. When you are a Family Court Judge, there is only one function that gives you and others any kind of happiness: the adoption of children. Many, many times people have stopped me in stores or on the street or coming out of church to re-introduce me to the fast-growing youngsters I had made permanent parts of their families. Nearly always the child will politely shake my hand while the parent beams. So it was here. With a wave she pointed out her nearly-twelve twins: a pretty young lady with a sweet smile, and her handsome brother, a lad in a stroller of sorts, still physically and mentally disabled as he had been when I first saw him when he was no bigger than a melon. Mom bragged about how he had defied all expectations and could now say a few words. She couldn't have been happier. Dad sat with him, chatting and paying attention to his every noise.

I went over and said hello to Dad, and sat with the boy, introduced myself, and told him how I remembered when he was the size of the little baby across the room.

What I wanted to tell him was how much joy he had brought into the world, but I think he understood that in his own way.

There isn't much of Family Court that I recall happily, but those adoption highlights are gifts that keep on giving, and it doesn't take much of that kind of reward to make a fellow shove the rest into a nearly-forgotten compartment of the brain.

Fond memories.

God bless them all.

****

"Your honor, I object to this petition. The Department of Social Services has ridiculously over-stated their case. They've painted a picture of my client as if he's some kind of monster. That just isn't fair."

I stood up. I could barely keep my composure. "Judge," I said, "if 10% of what we've learned in this investigation is true, this man is one of the worst monsters who has ever lived."

The third grader shifted continuously at her desk. The teacher became increasingly annoyed, finally telling her to sit back in her chair.

"I can't. It hurts."

A trip to the school nurse revealed the black and blue marks on her back, still showing the clear outline of the two by four that had been used to convince her it was time to go to sleep.

Later we learned of the near-ritual sexual molestation of the girl and her three younger siblings by their father, a convicted child molester who had done time in state prison for that crime. All had been beaten mercilessly and the mother seemed completely indifferent. The family had moved from county to county ahead of the Social Services investigators.

We convinced the judge, my predecessor, to remove the children. Permanently. The older girl became one of those difficult to place kids. When she hit puberty the repressed rage kicked in. I don't know what happened to her after that. She'd be in her twenties now.

But in the deepness of the night, when memories have nothing to hold them back, I see her still.

She won't let me forget.

****

The mother was pregnant when the case started. When she gave birth, the

Department, mercifully, took immediate emergency custody.

Twins.

A girl and a tiny little disabled boy.

His Birthday
Apr. 19th, 2006 @ 11:13 pm

The witness, a relatively young man, early thirties maybe, sat erect in his brown shirt. He had just the faintest fuzz of a moustache.

It had been a fairly routine custody battle up to that point, but custody trials are rarely boring for long.

"Sir, is it true you keep a photograph of Adolph Hitler in your wallet?"

He denied it, but I don't know if that qualified as a "Big Lie" or just routine neo-Nazi deception.

Law Guardian for the children showed him some notes in his own handwriting, which he acknowledged. "PS: how do you like the stationery?" he had asked his then beloved, speaking of the Southwest Native American design commonly known to the world today as the swastika.

A brief interruption as the court reporter sneezed. From around the room came:

"God bless you!"

"God bless you!"

"God bless you!"

"God bless you!"

"Gesundheit!"

At that point I needed to call a brief recess, which is just as well for him. Gave him a chance to clean out his wallet.

****

When play resumed, his wallet was briefly produced and the spot where Ann-Margaret may have once been was now empty, remarkably.

The testimony turned to more mundane matters, such as who picked up whom at what date and time, etc. etc. Witness was able to corroborate most of his testimony with the aid of a handy pocket calendar, which he produced in evidence. I glanced over it while the questioning continued.

When no one else had anything to ask, I thought I'd try my hand at clarifying a few points.

"Sir, could you perhaps explain to me why you have circled the date April 20th with the notation 'his birthday' next to it?"

Witness couldn't recall.

"Is it just a coincidence that April 20 is the birthday of ADOLPH HITLER?!?"

And now a kind of creepy silence fell over the courtroom and I could see the gears buzzing in the heads of all three lawyers. How the heck does THE JUDGE know that? [I'm pretty sure they weren't thinking of me in capital letters, but hey, it's my blog.]

****

Ah, there's no mystery to it. I know from my history learning that Douglas MacArthur gave his farewell address to the Congress on April 19, 1951. The next day they had that big tickertape parade for him in New York. Mike Riccio, my predecessor as Police Court Judge, was at that parade as a young man and he told me about it, also mentioning that it had been his birthday, a date he shared with *Der Fuehrer.*

So, if you happen to run into Mike Riccio on Thursday, give him a real big smile and try to be especially nice.

It's his birthday.

What Can We Do?
Apr. 21st, 2006 @ 12:55 am

One evening some years ago when I could have been home watching *Seinfeld*, I found myself on a panel at the middle school discussing the problems of teenage hoodlums in the community before a large group of very angry parents.

At the time I was both a City Court Judge and the attorney for the Department of Social Services where, among other things, I dealt with child abuse cases and placement of juvenile delinquents. I was somewhat amused to see one of our graduates in the audience with her mother, both of them applauding wildly at every mention of cracking down on the wayward youths of our fair city.

I didn't have any kids in the middle school being harassed on their way home. Mine were safely in St. Mary's where they were receiving a fine education in a quiet atmosphere.

"Judge Going, what can we do? How do we stop this?"

Part of me gets a chuckle when I'm looked on as the Answer Man. I got the City Court job because no one else wanted it. I did no campaigning and didn't even attend the meeting where I was nominated. I ran without opposition. (Actually, that's not true. I had plenty of opposition, just no opponent). But by simply donning a robe and taking an oath of office, suddenly I was looked upon as though I possessed the Wisdom of the Ages. I admit, it can go to your head. Especially when they stand up when you walk into a room.

"You want to know what you can do. Well, that's not easy, but you can all do something. Let me tell you a story."

And so I told them about the Alternatives to Incarceration program we had established wherein minor offenders performed community service projects as part or all of their sentence. I sat on the advisory board. The director had forms for every participant, quite detailed. He also did home visits.

After a couple of years he compiled statistics. The age group was primarily 16 to 25.

Number of adult criminals married and residing with spouse: zero.

Number of teens residing at home where father and mother are married and living together as a family unit: zero.

"People ask me, what percentage of the kids who appear in my court and Family Court come from broken homes. The honest answer is: all of them.

"You want to know what you can do. Well, you can't solve all the problems of the world by yourself, but you can at least make an effort to take care of your own little corner of the universe. You want to do something for your kids? Start at home."

****

I wandered into the parking lot after the meeting and opened my car door.

Some punk kid had rifled my glove compartment and swiped all my spare change.

Mystic Dwarves
Aug. 20th, 2006 @ 09:05 am

It took three years, but a Filipino judge has been removed from the bench for consulting with three invisible dwarves.

> In a letter to the court he said: "From obscurity, my name and the three mystic dwarves became immortal."

> However, the Supreme Court said dalliance with dwarves would gradually erode the public's acceptance of the judiciary as the guardian of the law, if not make it an object of ridicule.

Now this just goes to show the cultural differences between some countries.

Several years ago I had a litigant in a custody case appear before me in Family Court. The evidence from a prior proceeding had indicated, among other things, that he regularly conversed with three spirits: one named Barney, one named Aunt Bea, and a third one, who resembled a smelly old woman, who refused to give her name (to him, that is; none of them testified in court). He was able to fill us in on a lot of the secret details of the life of the mother of his children because he could send the spirits down to her trailer to spy on her. It seems she didn't have the gift, so she couldn't see them, so it was a perfect setup for him.

In the previous proceeding another judge had ruled that he could not have unsupervised visitation until he had undergone a psychological evaluation, so I ruled from the bench to dismiss his current petition because he still had not done so.

The litigant interrupted me and started screaming, saying, among other things, "WHY?? I DON'T UNDERSTAND THIS!! WHY SHOULD I HAVE TO GET A PSYCHOLOGICAL EVALUATION???"

Whereupon your usually genial host and kind-hearted judge replied, "Because it appears to me that you are more than a little nuts."

I was, of course, duly and publicly admonished by the New York State Commission on Judicial Conduct for that remark.

I've often wondered whether they had three extra commissioners sitting that day.

The Longest Day
Aug. 27th, 2006 @ 08:55 pm

The out of town lawyer couldn't help it. She didn't know the territory, so when her client told her that the child's grandfather couldn't have been the one abusing him, the lawyer naturally bought into the tale of the other older guy with the same first name who maybe the kid thought of as a surrogate grandfather. Yeah, he must be the one.

I'll spare you the details. The third party "grandfather" had nothing whatever to do with it, but that didn't keep out of town lawyer from subpoenaing him and dragging him into Family Court and asking him all sorts of embarrassing questions and treating him as a hostile witness. All for nothing.

When the lawyers had all finished their questions, he was about to step down, but I stopped him.

"Wait a second. The Court has a few questions of its own."

We judges like to refer to ourselves as "The Court". Always be wary of anybody who thinks their first name is "The".

"Sir, if you can recall, can you tell The Court where you were at approximately 6:00 a.m. on June 6, 1944?"

****

He was 18 years old, just one of thousands of scared young privates on board a landing craft, being tossed around on rough seas on the English Channel heading straight for a piece of Hell called Omaha Beach. Like a lot of men that day he got cut down early on and fell bleeding behind some rocks where he passed out.

They found him on the second day.

Months and months in the hospital, rehabilitation, and finally he came home and rebuilt his life and raised a family in his home town and minded his own business.

-63-

Every once in a while, like when *The Longest Day* premiered at the Mohawk Theater in 1962, he would make a public appearance and maybe tell his story to whatever new young reporter they had working that week.

I saw that movie in the theater in 1962, when I was 11, and again when they re-released it in 1964 for the twentieth anniversary of D-Day, and numerous times on television, and again this afternoon. There's just something about the film and the event that gets me in the gut.

Maybe because Dad was one of those guys in England waiting to be shipped across to help out, as he was a couple of weeks later. Maybe because it's just one of those moments in history when great forces and great ideals converge to form a few hours that will be remembered forever.

Maybe it's because of that dream I had once about wandering to the edge of a cliff and finding a monument there and looking down over the cliff to the beaches and sea. In my dream I somehow knew it had something to do with D-Day, but I didn't know what.

I recognized the spot when Reagan spoke there on June 6, 1984. It is called Pointe du Hoc.

****

Out of town lawyer squirmed uncomfortably at her table as "grandfather" told his story.

No one else had any further questions, so I let the hero step down and leave the courtroom.

Law Guardian felt sorry for out of town attorney, so she made a motion to strike all the testimony about 1944 on the grounds that it was irrelevant to the current proceeding.

"Your motion is carefully considered and, respectfully, denied," The Court said.

The Good Doctor
Feb. 15th, 2008 @ 10:33 am

Some years ago in Family Court I presided over a *Munchausen's By Proxy* case. The allegations were that the mother of the child was deliberately trying to make the child sick to draw attention to herself. She went from doctor to doctor demanding painful diagnostic tests that none of them thought were necessary. Evidence was produced that she had been grinding up some pills into the child's food, something which she initially denied.

Enter the Good Doctor. The defense produced a "Doctor of Nutrition" who had been using "alternative medicine" to treat the child, unbeknownst to the family physician. Using various doctoral techniques such as pulling on the thumb, gazing into her irises and balancing pills on her chest to determine the proper dosage, the doctor was able to diagnose and treat her for a variety of serious organ dysfunctions.

Upon cross-examination it appeared that the doctorate was obtained in a crash course from the nutritional supplement manufacturer who supplied all the doctor's patent medicine cures.

The less than respectful Social Services Attorney insisted on addressing him as "Mister".

****

A couple of nights ago I lay awake for several hours suffering from severe back and hip problems and the CSPAN re-run of the Waxman Committee hearings starring Roger Clemens and Brian McNamee, or should I say "Doctor" Brian McNamee who in his advertising claimed to have a Ph.D. in Behavioral Sciences with a Specialty in Nutrition.

Turns out his doctorate came from an internet degree mill. He told the panel he was shocked to learn that the University he attended on line had no campus or credentials. But he still likes to call himself Doctor.

Now Roger Clemens is not the most sympathetic witness in the world, being not a particularly nice guy to begin with, but for all the smears against him, I thought he held up pretty well, whereas McNamee was exposed in lie after lie after lie. His time frame for when and where he injected Clemens proved to be impossible, his personal ethics were shown to be non-existent, and his supposed physical "proof" non-convincing and easily explainable.

Yet the most vile and loathsome man ever to sit in the United States Congress, Henry Waxman, heaped praise on this scum for his courage and forthrightness and essentially told Clemens that even if there wasn't any proof he was still a liar.

I don't particularly like Roger Clemens and if he's lying he deserves everything he has coming to him, but on the testimony and evidence produced thus far, I am not impressed, the good doctor's credentials notwithstanding.

SUPREME COURT

Harriet Miers
Oct. 3rd, 2005 @ 12:56 pm

THE JUDGE . . .

. . . is not impressed.

Harriet Miers II
Oct. 7th, 2005 @ 07:23 am

I have been wearing my brain out trying to figure out what the heck Bush was thinking. What is it about presidents hitting their second terms? Do they burn out all their political instincts running for reelection? For a guy who acted pretty courageously and decisively on a number of matters in term one (when he was a minority president), it is astounding to me how he's suddenly turned to mush. Consistent mush.

There is no justification for this appointment. None.

George Will has had his say. And now Krauthammer even more direct. (He calls for the withdrawal of the nomination. I concur.)

Harriet Miers III -The Smoking Gun?
Oct. 9th, 2005 @ 07:35 am

Michael Isikoff investigates the reactions of the informal conservative think tank which rallied support for Roberts. It appears they are not, as a group, overwhelmed by the nomination. Isikoff got ahold of some of the exchanged emails, and they certainly look legitimate (i.e. those great legal and political minds had a reaction very similar to my own). Here is the sentence that ought to send chills up and down the spines of those who have been working feverishly for a generation to build a conservative "bench", both in baseball and judicial terms:

Michael A. Carvin, the lawyer who argued the president's case in *Bush v. Gore* before the Florida Supreme Court, was riled by a newspaper article about Miers. The story reported that Miers had once been quoted saying she wouldn't belong to the Federalist Society, an influential conservative legal group, because she viewed it as "'activist' and 'partisan'." In an e-mail to the group, Carvin—who did not respond to repeated calls for comment—wrote, "This is becoming more embarrassing as every day passes."

Any person holding such a view of the Federalist Society has no business being nominated for the Supreme Court of the United States by a Republican president.

Harriet Miers VI - Once More Into the Breach
Oct. 12th, 2005 @ 09:40 am

Enter the President

ROVE

O that we now had here
But one ten thousand of those conservatives
That do no work for Miers!

THE PRESIDENT

What's he that wishes so?
My crony Rove? No, my dear crony:
If we are mark'd to lose, it is enough
That we can blame elites; and if to win,
The fewer men, the fewer favours owed.

THE FIRST LADY

You said "the fewer men." I trust you mean
To also speak of those of whom it's said
A ceiling made of glass must yet be pierced.

THE PRESIDENT

Quite so! I pray thee, wish not one man more,
Or even of that other sex as well.
By Jove, I am not covetous for gold,
Nor care I of the ratings of the polls;
It yearns me not if commentators scorn;
Such outward things dwell not in my desires:
But if it be a sin to clone O'Connor,
I am the most offending soul alive.
No, Fate, dear Rove, has brought me to this place:
The only status that I yearn is quo,
And only I discern the woman's heart.

ROVE

The bloggers claim you've not the promise kept.

THE PRESIDENT

Too bad. Too bad. They say I'm like my dad.
Well read my hips, I need you not at all,
You pundits and you weird neanderthals!
Rather proclaim it, Rove, through talking points,
That he which hath no stomach to this fight,
Let him depart; his White House pass be gone,
No bridges for his state and bases closed.
We would not lie in that man's company
That fears his fellowship to lie with us.

THE FIRST LADY

The women, Bushie! We have status too.

THE PRESIDENT

Status quota. Ha! I made a joke! [all laugh]

This day we'll call the feast of Harriet:
And if she should the Senators survive,
We'll stand a tip-toe when the day is named,
And shout "Hear! Hear!" for dear old Harriet.

Old men forget, and women too, my dear,
And trust me (Ha! I made another joke!):
The Right to other matters will be turned,
And naught will come of this, o be assured.

But we shall not forget but once *their* names:
Kristol and Will, Krauthammer, K-Lo, Rush.
And mark you Goldberg too, the kid, not mom
(Who did many a kitten drown to win this fight).
Be them, their flowing crap, freshly remember'd.

And Harriet's day shall ne'er go by,
From this day to the ending of the world,
But we in it shall be remember'd;
We few, we happy few, we broth of blanders.

Harriet Miers VII -This Does It for Me
Oct. 26th, 2005 @ 12:45 pm

In case it wasn't already clear, I am opposed to the nomination of Harriet Miers for the Supreme Court.

The latest, and for me final straw is this story in today's Washington Post:

> Supreme Court nominee Harriet Miers said in a speech more than a decade ago that "self-determination" should guide decisions about abortion and school prayer and that in cases where scientific facts are disputed and religious beliefs vary, "government should not act."

> In an undated speech given in the spring of 1993 to the Executive Women of Dallas, Miers appeared to offer a libertarian view of several topics in which the law and religious beliefs were colliding in court.

> "The ongoing debate continues surrounding the attempt to once again criminalize abortions or to once and for all guarantee the freedom of the individual women's [sic] right to decide for herself whether she will have an abortion," Miers said.

> Those seeking to resolve such disputes would do well to remember that "we gave up" a long time ago on "legislating religion or morality," she said. And "when science cannot determine the facts and decisions vary based upon religious belief, then government should not act."

> "My basic message here is that when you hear the courts blamed for activism or intrusion where they do not belong, stop and examine what the elected leadership has done to solve the problem at issue," she said.

These are not the words of an "originalist", these are not the words of someone who thinks judges should not legislate from the bench, these are not the words of a conservative. This is not what the president should be seeing when he looks into the heart of a potential nominee.

I am convinced that she is not only woefully unqualified for the position, but that she would be horribly bad as a justice from every perspective that matters to me as a lawyer, former judge, and Conservative Republican Pro-Life Catholic Red Sox fanatic. (While I'm not sure what her position on baseball would be, I feel confident in asserting that she would screw that up as well.)

STOP, Mr. President. STOP! Please!

[UPDATE] Wow! That didn't take long! Now, Mr. President, about my application . . . I got a B- in Constitutional Law. That's good, right?

Dear Mr. President: Constitutional Law and My Application
Oct. 27th, 2005 @ 05:05 pm

Dear Mr. President:

In the UPDATE to my last post I said that I received a "B-" in Constitutional Law. That was rash of me, but be assured the error was unintentional. I've had my people do some vetting for me and discovered that I actually received that grade for a course on the First and Fourteenth Amendments, but those are still important ones, right? And "B-" is not a bad grade for law school, really.

Now, in order for my application to be complete and accurate, I must let you know that my actual grade in Constitutional Law was a "C-". WAIT! WAIT! Don't stop reading. There are a few things you need to know about that.

FIRST, my professor was a card-carrying member of the ACLU! (Ask your Dad about that one!)

SECOND, that same professor joined the National Lawyers' Guild BECAUSE the Attorney General (not Gonzales, another one) had declared the Guild a Communist Front organization!

Mr. President, this guy was NOT a Strict-constructionist, he was NOT an

Originalist and he was NOT a Nixonian! I mention the latter because the night before the Final Exam, President Nixon was on television with Sir David Frost talking about, of all things, CONSTITUTIONAL LAW. Well, this was serendipity if ever there was any, so I listened very carefully when President Nixon explained to THE WHOLE WORLD, that if THE PRESIDENT orders something to happen, it CANNOT be UNCONSTITUTIONAL, because by the very nature of the office ANYTHING the President does IS CONSTITUTIONAL! I learned more in that one hour than I did in a year from that LIBERAL professor!

SOOOOO, the next day on the final exam I managed to work in President Nixon's wisdom on Constitutional Law (he went to Duke Law school, did you know that?) and explained to my COMMIE-LOVER Professor how CONSTITUTIONALLY the President can do whatever he damn well pleases!

And THAT, Mr. President, is how I got a "C-" in Constitutional Law.

-Robert N. Going

PS Please don't share this letter with Sen. Schumer. I think some of this stuff we need to keep below the radar, if you know what I mean.

Dear Mr. President: Balancing the Court and My Application
Oct. 28th, 2005 @ 12:25 pm

Dear Mr. President:

I see you haven't made a decision about my application yet, and I've still got my fingers crossed! Here's something else you might want to consider.

Now, I have been puzzling over something that makes no sense to me. During your first term, the New England Patriots won TWO Super Bowls, and the Boston Red Sox won the World Series. You'd think that would make SOME people real happy about the job you were doing, but NOOOOOO. You got CLOBBERED in New England. What's up with that?

I think the answer is that you have never appointed an avowed Red Sox fan to high office. People remember stuff like that. It's not fair, I know, but this is a democracy and sometimes you have to look beyond people's skills and potential and, dare I say it, PANDER to certain interest groups, just so they don't feel left out.

Remember you are President of the UNITED STATES, not just Texas, and there are like a whole big lot of people who watched your mom and dad jumping up and down and rooting for the HOUSTON Astros, and that just goes to remind them that, well, it's been a long time since the Red Sox had a seat on the Supreme Court.

This is just something I think you ought to consider when making your next appointment.

-Robert N. Going,
Conservative Republican Pro-Life Catholic Red Sox Fanatic

PS Do you think Schumer and Mrs. Clinton would dare oppose someone from Upstate New York? I don't!

Alito
Oct. 31st, 2005 @ 08:44 am

Dear Judge Going:

Thank you for expressing your interest in the position of *Associate Justice of the Supreme Court of the United States.*

It is always difficult to choose when there are so many well-qualified candidates, such as yourself, available to fill a single position.

We are sorry to inform you that President Bush has chosen to go in a different direction and the vacancy has been filled.

Please be assured that we will keep your application on file for six months should there be any further openings in this or similar positions.

Very truly yours,

Marjorie Mennerhoff
Administrative Assistant to the Assistant Administrator in Charge of Administration
Office of Presidential Appointments

P.S. On a personal note, the candy and flowers were greatly appreciated. A record of your donation is on permanent file in the Bureau of Government Ethics.

The Way We Were
Jan. 10th, 2006 @ 09:00 am

> "But this was back in the late 1960s and early 1970s. It was a
> time of turmoil at colleges and universities. And I saw some
> very smart people and very privileged people behaving
> irresponsibly."
> -Samuel Alito 1/9/2006

You youngsters can have no idea what it was like to be a conservative
Republican on a college campus in that era. I entered the university in the fall
of 1969, when the radical left was still hepped up from the thrill of the 1968
Chicago convention riots and enthralled by the example of Mao's Cultural
Revolution.

Now, I was not on a major Ivy League type campus, just a state university. But
the Reds were well-organized if not overly-competent. There were a couple of
feeble attempts that were more farcical than practical, like breaking down a
snow fence around a small plot that was being planted with trees and benches
and hijacking it as "People's Park" for no obvious purpose since that was the
intended use of the space anyway. Then there was the poor guy standing on the
small fountain during the October, 1969 Student Moratorium (we were
supposed to cut classes and denounce all the usual suspects) who tried to
deliver a stem-winder with all the passion of George Goebel talking about
Spooky Old Alice. "Am I calling for revolution?" (Glances at his note card.)
"Maybe."

But, as the year went on, things got more tense. By Spring we had the Kent
State shootings and the radicals used that as an opportunity to firebomb one of
the dormitories. (Actually the imperialist "Flag Room" where the flags of all
nations hung multiculturally). It wasn't a game anymore. Several times we
exited the dorms in the middle of the night. Students took turns on 24-hour fire
watch.

As in China, the leaders were demanding that the colleges be closed. Anyone
who refused to cooperate was denounced and terrorized. Final exams were
forbidden.

A group of us risked their ire by showing up for our Roman History final. About twenty minutes into it, we heard loud noises in the hall and a group of thugs burst in and filled the back and side of the classroom (accompanied by a newspaper photographer). The leader got several of them to start thumping their fists in unison against the blackboard. He began talking about how this was the sound of the jack-booted Nazis who were running the university and compelling us against our will to take exams.

Professor Hans Pohlsander rose from his desk and pointed a finger at him. "DON'T TELL ME ABOUT THE NAZIS! I was in school in Germany when they were in power and I know what they were like. You know what they were like? THEY WERE EXACTLY LIKE YOU! YOU ARE THE NAZIS!"

The girl sitting across from me turned around and said, "Will you people get out of here? We're taking this exam because we want to take it!"

I wish I could report on something brave or heroic that I said or did. I hope I at least made a face, but I frankly don't remember doing even that.

The Nazis left. After a short while, Professor Pohlsander thanked everyone for remaining and told us to take the exams with us, consider it an open book test, and return them to his office by Thursday.

The gutless university closed and we never did take the rest of our finals.

If Sam Alito has memories like that, I'll be mighty happy to see him on the Supreme Court.

The Scalia Gesture
Mar. 29th, 2006 @ 08:24 am

Gosh, it seems the reporting world is all agog over Supreme Court Justice
Antonin Scalia and his alleged chin flip to an obnoxious reporter after Mass the
other day, described as "an obscene gesture". Well, I'm half-Italian and the
gesture in question is not unknown in my family, and although we come from
northern Tuscany and speak a more pure form of Italian than the dialect of the
Scalia family, I have taken a course in Italian hand language and feel I have at
least as much expertise as the reporter involved, and less emotion.

It is indeed possible that the gesture could be interpreted as obscene, but it is
a very nuanced move and it really all depends on the intensity of the torque of
the wrist action. It could mean anything from, "Whadya some kinda moron?"
to "Gedouddahere before I break your head" to . . . well, it's a continuum. We
weren't there, so the good justice should get the benefit of the doubt.

Back when I was in law school the local (Italian-American) municipal court
judge invited me to court one day as an observer. Featured was a case involving
a very agitated deaf-mute (forgive me, I'm not up on the politically correct term
this week). A conscientious sign language interpreter was giving a dead-pan
simultaneous translation for the court. The litigant got more and more
frustrated, pacing in the well of the courtroom, and at the end of a long, silent
speech, turns to the judge and gives him a good, solid chin flip.

While, without missing a beat, the interpreter translates, "I am very upset with
these proceedings, Your Honor."

There. That's all Tony was trying to say. So let's fuhgeddaboudit.

Plessy v. Ferguson
May. 18th, 2006 @ 08:51 am

On May 18, 1896, the Supreme Court handed down the infamous "separate but
equal" decision which put the national imprimatur on "Jim Crow" laws enacted
in the post-war South.

Read the decision carefully, for there is much in it. Pay special attention to Harlan's stirring dissent. An example:

> The law regards man as man, and takes no account of his surroundings or of his color when his civil rights as guarantied by the supreme law of the land are involved. It is therefore to be regretted that this high tribunal, the final expositor of the fundamental law of the land, has reached the conclusion that it is competent for a state to regulate the enjoyment by citizens of their civil rights solely upon the basis of race.
>
> In my opinion, the judgment this day rendered will, in time, prove to be quite as pernicious as the decision made by this tribunal in the *Dred Scott* Case.

Sometimes the Supreme Court makes rulings for which they, and we, should be ashamed. This is a classic example. And it acted as "super-precedent" for a long time after.

My Week at NRO
Jun. 16th, 2006 @ 05:18 pm

I've been running a pretty good streak lately getting my comments posted (however uncredited) at my favorite Blog, *The Corner at National Review Online*. Here's a couple from this week:

Starts with John Derbyshire's post on Thursday:

> **Whose Gulf?** [John Derbyshire]
> Iran has banned The Economist for printing a map in which the blue blob between Iran and Saudi Arabia is called "The Gulf" rather than "The Persian Gulf." The latter, according to Iran, is the only permissible name.
>
> Here's my question. Since only about half the population of Iran is Persian ("Persian 51%, Azeri 24%, Gilaki and Mazandarani 8%, Kurd 7%, Arab 3%, Lur 2%, Baloch 2%, Turkmen 2%, other 1%"), shouldn't they prefer "Iranian

Gulf"?

Which prompted this, courtesy of me:

Meme Meme Tekel Upharsim [John Derbyshire]
A reader, responding to my post about Iran: "You know what
they say, Derb: One man's Mede is another man's Persian."

[And no, Derb, if weighed in the balance you would surely not be found
wanting. Wait. Maybe he was talking about me.]

Then today Jonah Goldberg opened up a discussion on the Supreme Court
"No-Knock" ruling of yesterday:

Knock, Knock [Jonah Goldberg]
Do any of our legal eagles have a problem with yesterday's
Scotus decision? Personally, I think knocking is nice and
should be done where appropriate. But if the police have a
warrant, why should people have a constitutional right to
hearing a knock? Listening to NPR this morning Nina
Totenberg made it sound like the jackbooted
sensible-shoe-wearing thugs of the police state were on the
verge of having the right to break into your house and charge
whatever they wanted on your pay-per-view without asking.
Are the conservatives on the court really poised to throw out
the exclusionary rule and warrants entirely? I find that hard
to believe.
Posted at 10:54 AM

AHA! Something I actually know something about! First, I had to clarify some
misconceptions about the case. (It helps if you read it first.)

To Knock Or Not To Knock [Jonah Goldberg]
From a reader:

I believe there is some confusion over what the court
actually said. They did NOT say it was ok to enter without
knocking. In fact, the parties conceded as a given that the entry

-80-

in this case was improper.

The discussion and the decision were entirely about whether the EXCLUSIONARY RULE applies in this case, and a majority decided that it did not. In other words, valuable and otherwise valid evidence of guilt could still be presented to the jury. The plurality decision pondered whether the exclusionary rule, adopted in the early 60's, was still necessary at all, pointing out that there are other remedies available to both serve as deterrents to police misuse of authority and remedy existing violations, such as federal 1983 civil rights actions and civilian oversight of police.

Excluding evidence of guilt is, after all, a pretty draconian solution when you think about it. The Warren Court felt that it was the only way to control the police. This court is starting to think that maybe it isn't.

On the facts of this case, I think that the existence of an actual warrant for the items seized is what brought Kennedy over. The others (*i.e.* The Good Guys) look plenty ready to declare the Mapp Rule an idea whose time has passed.

So, about that next vacancy on the Supreme Court, Mr. President: I believe you still have my application? 'Cause if not, I could always send you another one.

Catherine Cortez Masto
Nov. 17th, 2006 @ 09:11 am

Now just why do you suppose The Judge Report would be featuring a picture of a Democrat, the newly elected Attorney General of Nevada Catherine Cortez Masto?

Because her husband Paul, former White House Secret Service Agent, is a native of Amsterdam, and her father-in-law Paul is on our Golf Commission, and her mother-in-law is my dear friend Tilda Masto, who is my accompanist whenever I appear with the Galway Players and am permitted to sing.

So congratulations to the Masto family and best wishes to Catherine as she undertakes her new responsibilities.

And, oh, by the way, I may be persuaded to relocate if the price is right and you need someone with vast experience in criminal law, not to mention judicial wisdom.

****

CONFIDENTIAL TO GWB: This does not mean that I have lost interest in that Supreme Court nomination I had mentioned previously. It's important that we, like, try to appear a little bipartisan under the circumstances, you know what I mean? Ask Karl. I'm sure he'll agree.

Attorney General
Aug. 27th, 2007 @ 10:16 am

Dear Mr. President,

I see from the New York Times that you will soon have a vacancy in the office of Attorney General of the United States.

Now, I happen to think I'm well-qualified for this job. First of all, I am an attorney. Second, I am one of the very few people in this country who knows that the Attorney General is one of four original cabinet positions appointed by

President GEORGE WASHINGTON! (We call him George W. around here).

Third, people keep saying that being Attorney General is a good thing to have in your background when you get nominated for the Supreme Court, at least that's what the word was when you put Mr. Gonzales there (guess that's not working out too well, huh?). Anyway, since I'm already qualified to be a Supreme Court Justice (except in New York, but that's another story), well, why not just put me in the AG suite till the next slot opens up? Stevens doesn't look all that hot lately, BTW.

Of course, some of those liberals up there on the Hill probably would be shocked and dismayed instead of awed if you suddenly threw out the name of a conservative Republican pro-life Catholic Red Sox fanatic, so maybe we could slip this through as one of those recess appointments. Then we do that again next year and before you know it, we're both ready to retire. Unless Fred or Rudy or somebody wants to appoint one of us to the Supreme Court.

There I go again.

You know we had one ex-president on the Supreme Court. His name was Taft, not the one that just wrecked the Republican Party in Ohio, one of his remote ancestors, I think. And there's nothing in the Constitution that says an MBA can't be on the court (Notice my brilliance in Constitutional Law, Mr. Prez?), so heck, with nine chairs there'll be room enough for both of us!

Oh, and I have a blog.

Very truly yours,

Robert N. Going
Conservative Republican pro-life Catholic Red Sox fanatic currently hiding out in Amsterdam, NY but willing to relocate

PS Uh, if you should be looking through the blog archives you can probably skip over some of that stuff about Harriet Miers.

You know how stale topical humor can get.

Attorney General II
Aug. 28th, 2007 @ 08:32 am

Dear Mr. President,

Wow! You sure can move fast when the mood strikes you!

I gather from the headlines that you plan on asking Clement to be Acting Attorney General and then maybe if he works out giving him the starting position.

Now, Matt Clement is an interesting choice. You're thinking baseball and more importantly Red Sox, so I see you're taking some of my advice to heart. That's good. And Clement hasn't been doing much except working out for the last year and a half, whatever that means, so he's available, and what with the way the Red Sox starters have been doing, not to mention the bull pen, there's frankly mot much room on the roster for him, even when they go to 40 next week. So, short-term it makes some sense.

BUT.

You know how the jokesters are. Think about it. Do you really need to have Leno and Letterman and Chris Matthews holding up that film of Clement taking the line drive to the head in 2005 and making it the symbol of the last days of your administration? Not good.

And really, Clement wasn't with the team long enough to have inspired loyal fans. We saw him in early 2005 at Fenway and he pitched a hell of a game, even if it was against Tampa Bay. But a great half-season that ended up going nowhere isn't the stuff of which legends are made.

I'm thinking maybe Gabe Kappler. Sure he was just a back-up outfielder, but he was on the 2004 World Champs, so everybody loves him. It used to be neat to see him and Johnny Demon (that's what we call him now) stand in the outfield between innings with their shirt numbers saying "19 18" for us guys in the bleacher seats (get it? Of course after this season they'll have to put Dick Cheney and Sean Connery in the outfield to make a similar joke- "2 007". Like the Rangers have a chance. Hah!).

And Kappler's like Jewish, and whether it's true or not, most people think he'd probably make a smart lawyer, and perception's the key to everything in politics.

But then, he's got a nice job managing one of the minor league clubs, so he probably wouldn't be interested.

But I am.

And I still might be your best choice, even if my cutter's a little wobbly.

Robert N. Going
Conservative Republican pro-life Catholic Red Sox fanatic currently hiding out in Amsterdam, NY but willing to relocate

[**UPDATE:** Turns out it's PAUL Clement, not Matt after all. Sheesh. Matt I could understand, but what the heck has Paul got that I haven't got?]

Job Opening
May. 14th, 2008 @ 08:57 pm

Dear Mr. President:

I see where the Solicitor General of the United States Paul Clement is stepping down, and he's the guy in your justice department who handles the cases before the Supreme Court. I think it was pretty mean of him to quit just when you and Laura were all excited about the big wedding. (BTW, may their first child be a masculine child!).

I know what you're thinking: who the heck am I gonna get to fill this job what with the administration coming to an end and all. Like, who's gonna drop everything just so he can tell his grandkids, "Hey, guess what? I was Solicitor General for six whole months" (or whatever).

Well, it just so happens Mr. President that through a peculiar combination of circumstances I am available and willing. Oh, sure, I realize that I've been holding out for one of those Supreme Court vacancies, or even AG, but you know, I've been thinking it over and figure that Solicitor General would be ok for now if my country really needs me, and God knows they do. (See, in one small way I'm like that Obama guy: I'm ready to do God's work when called, and btw my number's in the book; which reminds me, did you know God's direct line is et cum spiri-2-2-0? That's an old altar boy joke you can ask Benedict about next time you see him and I'm sure he'll chuckle, especially if you follow it up with the "Dominick go frisk 'em" one which always gets a belly laugh at the communion breakfasts, at least it did before 1965).

So how about it? I'm sure I wouldn't embarrass you, like *that* would make a difference at this point, and the arguments in the Supreme Court are pretty much all done now until October, and I'm sure we could ask the CJ to postpone any appearance of mine until after the November election and after that, if I screw up, who's gonna give a crap anyway?

Not that it matters, because I'm doing this to serve my country, but does this job come with health insurance and/or a limo?

Yours in strict-construction-originalist mode,
Robert N. Going

PS I have Scotusblog on my LiveJournal Friends Page, so I'm up to date with the current cases and I'm perfectly willing to take either your side or Cheney's on the DC gun issue should it come up again, whichever way you guys decide.

MOVING RIGHT ALONG

A Night at the Opera
Nov. 13th, 2005 @ 11:44 am

Mary decided it was time for a quiet evening at home with a movie, curling in front of the electric heater (the new boiler hasn't arrived yet). I had a fleeting moment of hope when I saw the title was *Phantom of the Opera*, but I quickly realized she would not have chosen the Lon Chaney classic or the quite good color version from the 40's.

No, I was subjected to a night with Andrew Lloyd Webber, one of those major compromises you make to keep a marriage fresh if you ever hope to see Clint Eastwood again.

To the critics who hailed this production as a masterpiece, what the hell were you smoking? From beginning to end it ranges from the merely awful to the god-awful.

Now, I am actually a fan of the underlying story, and, as I say, it's been done well heretofore, which I think adds a special unhappy dimension to this production. It's not as if it were an adaptation of *Tammy and the Bachelor*. This is the wholesale destruction of a work of depth and nuance.

The cinematography wasn't all that bad. The acting was pretty much non-existent, however, and the characters so one-dimensional they might have been sucked into a black hole in The Simpsons. There are some of us who in the past could have readily identified with The Phantom, even rooted for him, like we do for Judd Frey in *Oklahoma!*. Not this time. The girl who played the girl exhibited a range of emotions from A to A, and the guy on the white horse was just another guy on a white horse who gets to kiss the girl with all the passion of a department store mannequin.

Even the makeup sucked. Your average car accident produces scarier looking deformities than the ones shown here. Were the producers afraid of offending the facially-challenged?

Mark Twain wrote of experiencing the German Opera:

I find that there is nothing the Germans like so much as opera. They like it wholeheartedly, as a result of habit and education. Our nation will like it too, by and by, no doubt. One in fifty of those who attend our operas likes it already, perhaps, but I think a good many of the other forty-nine go there with the idea of learning to like it.

Which brings me to my final and most important point. Andrew Lloyd Webber composes excruciatingly terrible music.

Why hasn't anyone ever noticed this? Instead, every first-year drama student is taught to proclaim him a genius, when all he really is is loud. There's nothing like the pounding of a few kettle drums every third or fourth bar to let the audience know it's time to think this is wonderful and soaring and emotional and original, when actually it's just a reprise of the last song and the song before that and the twelve songs from his previous show. This is the heir to Rodgers and Kern and Porter and Berlin and Bernstein?

I shudder.

And not because the Phantom scared me. He didn't.

Television: The Good, the Bad and the Ugly
Dec. 8th, 2005 @ 09:14 am

I managed to arrange my schedule over the last week to watch three adults and I forget how many kids play John Paul II on the dueling docudramas from ABC and CBS.

The two hour ABC version aired last Thursday was necessarily rushed, devoting only one hour to the 26 ½ year papacy. The parts about his young years were quite excellent and moving, and the rest had its moments, but there were at least three occasions when they took broad literary license to imagine conversations between the pope and variously his assassin, Gen. Jaruszelski and Archbishop Romero, which also supposed the unlikely circumstance that John Paul II would be confessing his sin of having opposed liberation theology. Also, the Pope segments were too low-key, capturing the words but failing to capture the dynamism of the young pope and his tumultuous first return to Poland.

Not so with the CBS version airing Sunday and Wednesday, which clearly relied on much of the Pope's own memoirs and had far superior production values. While the childhood years were glossed over (I may paste on that part from the other version), the Nazi years and his priesthood and bishopric were well touched upon, and Jon Voight's performance in part 2 was quite outstanding.

Having read Weigel's biography, I can see how it would really take a year-long miniseries to truly capture all the drama and importance of this great man's life and teachings, but for the time allotted I must give CBS applause for an outstanding and faithful effort.

****

Unfortunately, due to the football-delayed Sunday schedule I was forced to endure what is truly one of the most grueling hours on tv today, that incredibly bad *Cold Case* show, where, on the night when they were presenting the champion of the Culture of Life, they produce an episode in which a high school couple conceives a child, but the wicked and obviously crazed school nurse shows fetal pictures to and otherwise talks the guy out of financing an abortion. The cops naturally greet this story with horror and disgust. I flipped it off and read a book when the nurse became the chief suspect in the lad's murder.

****

Then on Tuesday, *Law and Order, SVU*, lately the best written of the three regular series, turned itself over entirely to the gay/lesbian/wacko lobby with a plot and dialogue so preposterous that I hesitate to even attempt to summarize it. There were many kickers, but probably the worst was when the grandparents of the girl with two mommies find naked photographs of the little girl with the lesbian partner stroking her thighs. With the help of their lawyer, they commence a custody battle, after which they are, naturally, charged with felony hate crimes.

But, not to worry. They cut a deal and testify against their lawyer, who is also charged, since he was the one who fed them phony statistics about kids growing up in gay homes, when ALL of the studies show how wonderful it really is.

Not since *Mission to Moscow* have I seen such an unadulterated propaganda piece.

I think, however, that this was such an act of desperation that it must mean that we are actually winning the culture wars.

Who Dropped the Tali-bomb?
Jan. 18th, 2006 @ 09:46 pm

News item:

> ISLAMABAD (Reuters) - Pakistani intelligence sources on Thursday identified three of four al Qaeda members believed to have been killed by a U.S. airstrike last week, though they have yet to recover the bodies.
>
> One of the dead was said to be Abdul Rehman Al-Misri al Maghribi, a son-in-law of al Qaeda second-in-command Ayman al-Zawahri.
>
> Another was Midhat Murfi al Sayid Omer, an expert in explosives and poisons who carried a $5 million U.S. reward on his head.
>
> The third man named was Abu Obaidah al Misri, al Qaeda's chief of operations in Afghanistan's eastern Kunar province.

****

"Who dropped the Tali-bomb in Midhat Murfi's chowder?"
Zawahri was pissed, so he hollered all the louder.
"Why it seems they got all three,
"The al-Misri's company,
"And Midhat Murfi's innards are all out-er!"

[Editor's Note: I thought this punny parody was hilarious when I wrote it and eagerly awaited the comments. Not one! Not even a groan! I thought it was perfectly obvious that it's sung to the tune of *Who Threw the Overalls in Mrs. Murphy's Chowder*. Maybe the kids don't know that one.]

High Noon for All Seasons
Jan. 30th, 2006 @ 10:28 pm

Dawn Eden, having discovered *A Man for All Seasons*, the movie, and also having discovered that it was directed by Fred Zinnemann who also directed that other great film about one man standing alone and risking everything, *High Noon*, took it upon herself to challenge me to write a theme song for *A Man for All Seasons* using the melody from *The Ballad of High Noon*.

So, here it is.

> ### *High Noon for All Seasons*
>
> **Do not forsake me good King Henry**
> **For this divorcing "Nay".**
> **Do not forsake me good King Henry-**
> **Wait! Hold that blade!**
>
> **I am your good and faithful servant,**
> **So full of wit and not a bore,**
> **I don't know why it's so unnervin'**
> **To call your wedding**
> **No more than bedding**
> **And say your Anne Boleyn's a whore.**

-91-

What is this thing called Church of England?
Protestant/Catholic doctrine minglin'
Look at those people lining up,
Signing that oath.
I made a vow to Higher Power,
Now I am waiting in the Tower.
Look at that axe man standing tall-
What if my top part should leave me?

Do not forsake me good King Henry,
Just 'cause I take my cues from Rome.
In school I wish I'd had more mem'ry
And learned ebonics
Instead of phonics
To say that I beheading home.

Let it swing, let it swing.
Let it swing, let it swing!

Gilboa
Feb. 10th, 2006 @ 09:11 am

Say, I hope my New York City readers enjoyed their coffee and convenient flushes this morning. A lot of that water comes from about seventy miles south of me, the Gilboa Reservoir. That multi-billion gallon man-made lake is formed by the damming of the upper reaches of the Schoharie Creek.

Most of you have probably never heard of the Schoharie Creek, because it flows north, away from you, through the broad farm lands of the Schoharie Valley, then down through a long chute before plunging into the Mohawk River near the Shrine of the North American Martyrs in Auriesville, NY. The combined waters then sweep east past Amsterdam and Schenectady and eventually cascade over the Cohoes falls where they join the Hudson River and head south. I assume you know about the Hudson.

The dam holding back the Gilboa Reservoir is falling apart. You probably haven't heard about that, though your city Department of Environmental Protection declared its repair a top priority back in 1997.

There has been some discussion about it up this way, however. For several months we have been working on contingency plans and pouring over old studies and examining worst-case scenarios. If the dam goes, you people might have to open up your valves a little wider on some of your other water sources. The villages of Middleburgh and Schoharie (which once had an entire David Letterman show devoted to it) and numerous other hamlets and crossroads would be wiped out. Seventy miles downstream, we're luckier. We'll get four or five hours advance warning (well, they originally said eleven, but who knows?). By that time we should see some houses and churches and schools and farm stands floating by.

When the wall of water crashes into the Mohawk, there will be no room for the regular river, so that will back up twelve miles or so, which ought to take care of Randall and Yosts and Fultonville and Fonda. And the main line of the old New York Central (I forget what they call it these days) and the New York State Thruway. (Back in the 90's a non-dam-related flood destroyed five bridges over the Schoharie, including the Thruway bridge. Ten cars plunged over the edge before an alert stroller stopped traffic). Taking the big turn at Fort Hunter might slow things down some, and then our mini-tsunami will start rinsing West Main Street and Carmichael and Division Streets and Guy Park Avenue. Sir William Johnson's family homes which have been around since before the Revolution should get damp. The original plan suggested the first floor of St. Mary's Hospital might be under water, but hey, a lot of this is speculation.

Our plans call for evacuating 3,500 people or so to high ground. Our bus garage will require scuba gear, so we're moving the buses. No hope for the sewage treatment plant. The river bridge will probably survive, though it won't lead anywhere. We'll be sending some fire trucks and police cars to the south side for the duration. There won't be any power or hardly any form of communication for a while. The top of the flood wall protecting the south side will be six feet under. Several thousand homes and businesses and such will be destroyed.

Then the waters will recede here and move on to Schenectady where they might do some real damage.

Have a nice day.

Dreamtown, USA
Feb. 16th, 2006 @ 09:27 pm

Back in the summer of 1973, shortly after I graduated from college, I plopped down a hundred and fifty bucks and grabbed myself a Greyhound *Ameripass*, good for thirty days of unlimited travel across the United States and Canada. I figured that this might end up being the last care-free summer of my life. I called it early retirement. Like, why wait until you're too old to enjoy it? I've never regretted the decision for a minute, even though I missed a couple of job interviews and would not have full-time gainful employment until I finished law school six years later.

There was no particular rhyme or reason to my itinerary. Sometimes I just took the next bus out and headed wherever it was headed. I had a hundred adventures, even traveling with people I met on the way for several days at a time. I had a big suitcase and very early regretted not having a big backpack instead, like the night I was looking for a flat place to sleep on the side of Mt. Rushmore beneath the highway (there wasn't one), and more particularly the next morning when I dragged that thing back up to the road, emerging with a great view of Washington's profile and several gallons of sweat.

From there it was hitch-hike time (no buses in that part of SD), passing by herds of buffalo, touring the Wind Cave National Park ("Now many of you may be familiar with the terms stalagMITES and stalacTITES. We don't have any of those. If you suffer from claustrophobia, perhaps the Wind Cave is not for you") and ending up in Hot Springs, South Dakota.

Now, this has got to be just about one of the goofiest excuses for a community in all of America.

I loved every minute of it.

Hot Springs is the cultural capital of the Black Hills

That's what they advertise, and who can argue? "There are over 4,250 friendly people." I didn't meet all of them, but the ones I came across certainly met the description. They had a local museum, which seemed worth a look. Thing was,

I recognized most everything in it as having a twin in Des Nichols' house on McCleary Avenue, even down to the same kitchen table.

The really big attraction was (and is) "The Plunge" as the locals call it. Or, more formally, the Evans Plunge. Here we are in this drive all day to get there or get out of no-place and holy crap they've got this giant indoor swimming pool with a gravel bottom feeding off 87 degree mineral water. They had Tarzan ropes (can't be too many plaintiffs' lawyers out there) so you could act just like you would have at the old swimmin' hole when your parents weren't watching. And the slide! That must be why they call it The Plunge, 'cause you climb way, way up on this ladder and (this was about the only rule in the place) you lie on your stomach with your arms outstretched like Superman and drop head first, picking up speed as you go along and then FLY across the top of the water for about a mile or so before settling into that warm, buoyant, wonderful spring.

Heaven.

The bus out of town didn't leave until 2 in the morning, so after The Plunge closed for the evening we had to wait at the taxi office , which I think was actually this guy's living room. I remember sitting on his couch watching *Seven Brides for Seven Brothers* until about 11:30, which is when a different bus pulls into a nearby town and the only cab in the region has to go over there and pick up the folks coming on to Hot Springs. So the cab guy apologizes, but we have to fend for ourselves for an hour or so till he gets back. The routine is to send the bus people over to the police station to kill time, since they're open 24/7 whereas everyone else in Hot Springs is peacefully resting up for the morrow.

The policeman at the desk buzzed us right in. I think the only other cop on duty was the one who showed up a few minutes later with the town drunk who, appropriately, was placed in the drunk tank which they had to hose down every time he threw up. They weren't treating him badly, though. More like George Bailey bringing Uncle Billy home one more time. The desk guy shook his head with a baffled look. "What would make somebody drink that much?"

And I thought, "This would be a nice place to live."

I went back to the cab stand and boarded the next bus out.

I've never set eyes on Hot Springs, South Dakota from that day in July of 1973 to this.

But in my dreams . . . .

Quis Custodiet Custodes?
Apr. 2nd, 2006 @ 09:47 pm

Not too many of you know who Thomas Spargo is. A few days ago he was in the news briefly when the New York State Commission on Judicial Conduct announced that they were removing him from office as a Justice of the New York State Supreme Court. That really came as no surprise, since they had already decided to do that several years ago, even before he entered his present office, for reasons that will be evident if you continue.

Tom Spargo at one time was counsel to the New York State Republican Party. In the process he learned a whole lot about election law, and became probably the foremost expert on the subject in the State of New York. He became very much in demand around petition gathering and election time, and had clients across the political spectrum.

For whatever reason, he ran for the post of part-time Town Justice in the Town of Berne, a sparsely populated area mostly in the Helderberg Mountains south of Albany.

He was allowed under the rules to maintain a private practice, with a few non-relevant limitations. Which is how he happened to be in the State of Florida in November and December of 1980 when the whole world was watching. Tom Spargo was one of those people who was there when the three election inspectors, all Democrats, decided unilaterally to move their review of the hanging chads behind closed doors.

You may remember the scene of the neatly-attired Republicans storming the office in outrage, and ultimately preventing the stealing of the presidential election in the backroom. Spargo was seen in one of the shots, and his long personal nightmare began.

When a judge is removed from the bench, it is little-noted that the charges which initiated the investigation are unfounded. Such was the case here. Nothing about *Bush v. Gore* survives as an offense. But Spargo had the audacity to challenge the authority of the Commission in Federal Court, and initially he won. This only served to enrage the Commission Staff and the Commission itself.

Meanwhile, Spargo got himself elected to State Supreme Court (which in New York is a lower-level court). Every iota of his judicial career now became open to scrutiny on a long-term fishing expedition, because the sad fact is that once you challenge the authority of the Commission on Judicial Conduct, or deny the allegations against you and force them to prove their case with actual evidence, you are doomed. Every day of your judicial career will then be spent defending yourself. In Spargo's case he quickly ran up legal bills of $140,000 to keep a job that pays $136,000 a year.

Every year plenty of good judges throw in the towel and resign rather than fight. Because you can't fight. Because you can't win.

Judges running for election always give hand-outs to the voters. Pens are popular and can be expensive. I gave out emery boards ("And you can use them on your spark plugs, sir!") which ran a couple of cents each. Spargo, they say, gave out five dollar gift certificates outside a convenience store to four or five people and (horrors!) bought a few rounds of drinks at local watering holes. I'll bet that shocked the heck out of the Commission.

I guess as proof of malfeasance, they point out that though the Town of Berne is heavily Democrat, he won by 85 votes out of 1,200 cast. And now I think you can see what this whole thing is really about.

Some friends of his put together a legal expense fund to, I assume, not only defend Spargo, but also to pay for some much-needed court action to curb the abuses of the commission. This became the mortal sin of mortal sins, and on the flimsiest evidence and raw conjecture (which is even obvious from the decision they themselves wrote, which ignores any evidence to the contrary and focuses on the bare minimum needed to convict) they decided that he was pressuring lawyers to contribute. It is so much baloney, and that's the best they could do.

Judges, as a rule, bend over backwards to protect the rights of the accused, a tradition ingrained on the collective psyche by the Bill of Rights via *Magna Carta*. In New York, judges themselves have no such protections.

The Commission, an appointed body, serves as investigator, complainant, prosecutor, judge, jury and executioner. Appeal is only to the State Court of Appeals, another non-elective body. The People who elected the judge have no say whatsoever in his fate.

The Commission alone has the power to decide what constitutes a violation of judicial ethics. A large minority of the Commission, and the Commission Staff, have held to the position that a judge may not accept the endorsement of the Right to Life Party. I have been told by former Deputy Chief Administrative Judge Joseph Traficanti that, at least pre-Lewinsky, some members of the commission held to the belief that ANY relationship between a judge and an employee, no matter how consensual, constituted sexual harassment because of the power differential. Others have felt that consensual is ok. Who decides? The majority of the Commission. They adapt the facts to the nearest possible violation of the canon of judicial ethics.

This is not meant to be a direct comparison, but Professor Daniel Moriarty of Albany Law School has pointed out that three cultures in the twentieth century adopted similar rules for their criminal code. Those three were Stalinist Russia, Nazi Germany, and the puppet government of the free city of Danzig. Not exactly worthy precedent.

Most troubling of all in a case like this is that nearly every issue comes down to WHO IS TELLING THE TRUTH.

So how many members of the Commission have had the opportunity to examine the credibility and demeanor of Tom Spargo and his accusers? Exactly none. How many of them actually read the several days worth of transcript? It is unlikely that ANY have done so.

And the standard of proof for judges? Not proof beyond a reasonable doubt, not clear and convincing evidence, but rather the bare minimum "preponderance of the evidence" which means that one arbitrary peppercorn more weight on one side or the other is enough to decide the whole case, to decide whether a person elected by the people shall be removed from office.

In the course of the investigation, the rankest form of hearsay is accepted, and they who have become jurors in the case had already been exposed to every rumor from every source, thus risking bias, and had been forced to prejudge every aspect of the case before a single word of sworn testimony was received.

The Commission answers to no one, so it should come as no surprise that they frequently violate their own rules and governing law. Contrary to the rules, members of the commission routinely are given *ex parte* briefings on the cases before them by the members of their staff who are serving as prosecutors. There is nothing resembling a level playing field.

"Quis custodiet custodes?" said the Roman Juvenal.

"Who will guard the guards?"

****

And so, Tom Spargo becomes the latest victim of this tyranny, and hopefully the final victim of *Bush v. Gore*, but I doubt it.

Aside from a letter of support to him, which went unanswered, I have had no contact whatsoever with Tom Spargo since the summer of 1980 when, though a bare acquaintance, he arranged to get a balcony pass for my pregnant wife at the Republican National Convention in Detroit, Michigan. It was an act of kindness and graciousness which seemed to come so easily to him that I determined it must be habitual. Such virtues will carry him well in his forced retirement.

Hang in there, Judge.

LIFE

And Now We Wait
Mar. 18th, 2005 @ 11:24 pm

The Supreme Court's *Dred Scott* decision in March of 1857 purported to settle the slavery issue once and for all. Then, on December 2, 1859 the Abolitionist John Brown was executed for his part in the raid on Harper's Ferry. Although generally viewed as a crackpot, the cause for which he died stirred such emotion that all over the northern states people stood in silence and church bells tolled at the hour of his death. A cultural chasm opened; the moral and spiritual revulsion arising from this national focus on the slavery question galvanized public opinion. The election of Lincoln followed soon after, and civil war. In the end, the moldering body of John Brown and the Truth of his cause led to a new birth of freedom.

Tonight, a woman lies dying in Florida. By her husband's orders she is slowly being starved to death. He will not even allow ice chips in her mouth to ease her suffering. The courts and therefore THE LAW have sanctioned this barbarism, just as once they did back-flips to justify and institutionalize slavery.

But a strange thing is happening again. The death watch for Terri Schiavo is bringing together people from all over the country, even all over the world, to stand in solemn witness to her right to life. As each hour ticks by and the end draws nearer more and more consciences will be examined, more and more conversions made, more mystic chords touched. Her passing will stir this nation, and her moldering remains will give life to the Truth.

The end is inevitable. The Culture of Death is on trial and no earthly court can save it now.

Ye shall be as gods
Mar. 26th, 2005 @ 10:23 am

Whittaker Chambers called it the world's second oldest religion: "Ye shall be as gods." That temptation in the Garden has manifested itself in many forms over the centuries. Currently it's hanging out in a courtroom in Florida and similar places.

I've been on the bench. I know what it's like to be all-powerful. Every decision I rendered was with the sure knowledge that there was very little likelihood of being overturned on appeal, or even of an appeal being taken. Part of my training as a Family Court Judge came from Judge Judy. Several of us spent an afternoon with her in New York County Family Court and learned the importance of including certain phrases in our decisions: "This Court has had the unique opportunity to examine the credibility and demeanor of the witnesses in this case." That was a good one. What Appellate Court could overturn you on factual issues with language like that? The prevailing party has always "met the statutory standard of proof." From other judges I learned to dismiss strong opposing arguments by writing, "The mere fact that . . .", etc.

And so it is that Judge Greer can make life and death decisions based on conflicting testimony, and never be overturned. He, after all, had the unique opportunity to examine the credibility and demeanor of the witnesses. The mere fact that Michael Schiavo never mentioned his wife's wishes for seven years, and that no one else ever remembered them until after her court-appointed law guardian suggested Michael might not be credible, has no bearing on the decision. All a judge need do is reject the credibility of people he doesn't want to believe and accept the testimony of people he does, and then fill his decision with language from statutes and case law which support his result, and that is that! It's very easy. And it actually is "due process of law."

Once in a while a case like this comes along when very reasonable people can ask, "What judge in his right mind could find clear and convincing evidence of Terri's physical state or her intention to die based on this conflicting testimony?" But absent wrong-doing, the trier of fact will receive great deference from the courts above and the courts beside.

That's the way the system works. I HOPE everyone understands that now.

And yet, one need not have years of legal training and judicial experience to suspect that something is really wrong with a system that not only allows but even DEMANDS that an innocent disabled woman be starved to death.

She's Dead, Of Course
Mar. 31st, 2005 @ 07:44 pm

> *Matthew 13:15 -- For this people's heart has become calloused; they hardly hear with their ears, and they have closed their eyes. Otherwise they might see with their eyes, hear with their ears, understand with their hearts and turn, and I would heal them.*

I'm not quite as optimistic as I was on March 18 (see "And Now We Wait", above). While it is doubtless true that the vast majority of folks have no understanding of the details of the Schiavo case, the callous indifference that so many have shown is disheartening. Yes, the true believers are fired up. Yes, it is encouraging to see Jesse Jackson part-way back to where he belongs (it has been so terribly sad to see him transformed over the years from a committed, articulate pro-lifer to a sleazy vote-hustling politician. There is still time, brother). And yes, there have been some conversions in all this, and mystic chords touched.

But oh, the ordinary people who were rooting for her death, the nickle-and-dimers who worried about how much it was costing to keep her alive, the eyes-closed-ers who just couldn't stand to hear about it any more!

I took a stress test the other day. My cardiologist likes to get people talking while on the treadmill. She asked me what I thought about the case with what seemed like an all-powerful-doctor tone in her voice. I reached my maximum pulse rate much quicker than expected, though I may have read too much into it.

We talked a lot about Terri Schiavo on my radio show Wednesday, and I concluded by remarking how ridiculous and revolting it was that we even needed to bring this up. And yet, here we are. A woman is dead, and the reasonable people are ok with it. It's just us fanatics that need our heads examined.

On the other hand, even the major media realized that there was something about this that deserved attention. Why? I think that just maybe, in their heart of hearts, they're starting to feel a little bit uncomfortable. Good. Let them think about it some more.

Perhaps you haven't noticed, mademoiselle, but in Casablanca human life is cheap.

I hope you opened some eyes, Terri. May yours be ever bright.

Wrongful Life
Jul. 16th, 2005 @ 06:38 pm

A number of years ago a married woman of our acquaintance underwent prenatal testing. She and her husband received the sad news that their daughter would be born blind and deaf. She was strongly urged by medical professionals to abort the child (my word). Her faith would not allow it, and her stubbornness gave her the strength to stand up to the new gods.

But how many women have that strength, and how many men support them? In a previous post, in a footnote comment, I linked to a chilling article by George Neumayr, executive editor of The American Spectator titled The abortion debate that wasn't in the Seattle *Post Intelligencer*. The statistics are horrifying.

Most of us know at least one person with Down Syndrome. Most lead fairly normal lives. I seem to recall one teenager starring in a television drama several years ago.

Some experts believe that since 1989, 70% of all conceived Down Syndrome children (my word) have been aborted.

Read the article for the rest. It will make you sick, I hope.

As a lawyer and former judge, I am particularly concerned with the part played in all this by the courts. Under our system of Common Law, causes of action are developed over time not by the legislatures, but by the courts. Trial lawyers push the limits all the time, which is how, without any action taken by elected bodies, suits for Wrongful Birth and Wrongful Life have cowered the already ethically challenged medical profession into not only acquiescing in, but actually promoting the New Eugenics.

A doctor fails to perform prenatal testing, or fails to discover a potential birth defect, or fails to adequately inform the mother (my word) of her "options", including the RightThatDaresNotSpeakItsName, and the doctor or his insurance company can be on the hook for all the trauma caused the parents, and the support of the child forever. Is it any wonder that doctors use their professional status to urge, even demand, abortion when there is the slightest chance of an "imperfect" child?

The Culture of Life says that every life is a gift from God. The greatest triumph of our humanity has been our care for the weak and the helpless and the hopeless among us. In the Church we call such things works of mercy. Their essence is contained in the Beatitudes.

Will the Culture of Life prevail, or will the attitude of Senator Clinton, who argued that the partial birth abortion law should be defeated because it did not contain an exception for the mother (my word) to abort a disabled child (my word)?

Even if medical science can show us with absolute certainty the physical future of our progeny, by what right does anyone destroy that life?

Our friend gave birth to a baby girl who is, by the way, a perfectly normal high school kid today.

A Person's A Person
Aug. 14th, 2005 @ 01:41 pm

Mom got a special present the Christmas, I think, when she had the first four grandchildren around: *Horton Hears a Who!* by Dr. Seuss, of course. It was the perfect gift, from my sister, who knew how much Mom would enjoy reading to the kids.

Many years have passed and the rascals have grown. I imagine the book ended up in Mary's pre-K collection at St. Mary's. I had forgotten about it until we took our 15 ½ year old baby to see *Seussical the Musical* the other night, which blends the two Horton plots with various other Seuss characters and situations in a delightful romp.

Horton is an elephant whose big ears hear what no one else can. He alone knows that on a speck of dust resting on a clover is a tiny world of tiny people just like us. They talk to him, and he promises to save them, no easy task in a world where society only appreciates the life it can witness with its senses.

"A person's a person, no matter how small," proclaims Horton.

In the climax, the society is about to destroy the life Horton knows exists. The Who people are begged to make enough noise so that the big world will recognize them as worthy of protection. Eventually a small boy's voice is heard, and all ends well (giving the Who people an opportunity to return in the *Grinch* sequel).

Take another look at this fable. In a week when we are outraged at the repugnant cartoon put out by Planned Parenthood Golden Gate which calls for the drowning, decapitating and blowing-up of pro-life supporters, among other things, here is a gentle reminder of the value of life, even a life we can't (or won't) see.

When you hear the Who people crying out from their cone of silence, remember for a moment Terri Schiavo's family desperately trying to get her to say, "I want to live."

When you see Horton standing up for what he believes in the face of ridicule, think of all those folks on the front lines trying to save one life at a time.

When you hear the NARAL monsters rage, try to realize that it is your duty, even if you are the only one, to remind the world that

A person's a person, no matter how small.

That's Character, Gentlemen
Aug. 15th, 2005 @ 11:05 pm

When I was a freshman at our parochial high school (lo those many years ago) one of the seniors suffered a head injury in the last football game of the season. They rushed him to the hospital and lucky for him it was just a minor concussion. Unlucky for him, as it happens, his blood alcohol count was higher than .00.

Before the game even ended, the administration discovered the booze on the team bus.

Ah, those were the days. A school-wide assembly was called. We stood in the crowded auditorium and listened intently as four perpetrators were identified by name. Each received a suspension from school, each banned from all athletic activities for the remainder of the school year. For the seniors, that meant no chance at all to play on the championship basketball and baseball teams. It was the ultimate disgrace, akin to Chuck Conners having the buttons ripped off his shirt before being kicked out of the fort in the old *Branded* television show.

And then an amazing thing happened. When the assembly ended, a student emerged from the crowd and approached the principal.

"Father, when they were passing the bottle around, I took a swig, too."

He took the same punishment, and to this day I still look at him with awe.

Three years later and now we were seniors at the new high school. A bunch of us were hanging around the guidance office one day with Father Gustas, and somebody wondered out loud about how a Catholic school managed to grab this obviously brilliant and over-qualified biology and human physiology teacher.

"I'll tell you how," said Father Gustas. "He was doing biological research at one of the top pharmaceutical companies in the country, making three or four times what we're paying him. Then one day they assigned him to work on a team developing a 'morning after' birth control pill. They were only working on animals, not humans, but he knew where it was going. He quit. And came here."

He paused and looked us over.

"That's character, gentlemen."

I thought of that today, reading an article on the Web from the Lincoln, Nebraska *Journal-Star* about the death of Judge Joseph W. Moylan who served over twenty years as Douglas County Judge.

Back in 1993 Nebraska had a parental notification provision for minors seeking an abortion. Under certain circumstances that notification could be waived by a judge. Such a case came before Judge Moylan. He reviewed the case carefully and determined that under the law he was required to grant the relief requested.

And so he resigned.

He resigned!

At the height of his fame, in the prime of life.

> Said Moylan at the time: "My personal belief is that someday we'll all meet at the final judgment and give an accounting of our lives. I've got a lot of things I wish I didn't have to account for, and I don't care to add something like this to the list."

-108-

I've always been in favor of parental notification, but when I became a Family Court Judge and there was some talk about a similar law in New York, it dawned on me that I might find myself in the same situation. I wrote about the struggle judges sometimes face, afterwards, when talk is cheap.

Judge Moylan made his decision when his career, his reputation, and his family's future were on the line.

That's character, gentlemen.

What Is Man?
Aug. 24th, 2005 @ 05:54 pm

I was a boy, once, lying in the back yard, gazing up at the stars and contemplating the immensity of the universe, not unlike the shepherds of past millennia. When I grew older and learned the actual distances of the stars my awe only grew.

I was 18 and just out of high school when Apollo 11 landed on the moon. Neil Armstrong mouthed the famous first words, but it was Buzz Aldrin who got the last word on the way home, quoting from Psalm 8:

> When I consider Thy heavens, the work of Thy fingers,
>   the moon and the stars, which Thou hast ordained;
> What is man, that Thou art mindful of him?

Which leads me, naturally, to sex.

Any two dogs in the street can copulate and reproduce, not likely even connecting the two. We share much in common with the other animals, including DNA. And yet, Man alone, of all the creatures, has the ability to inspire others, through art and poetry, through courage and character, through self-sacrificing love.

Animals reproduce. Man procreates. We believers profess that at the beginning of each new life is the creation of an immortal soul, created not by us, but by God.

Just think about that for a minute. If we believe that there is eternal life, a life for us beyond this one, then we must accept that that life begins with a unique soul to go along with our unique DNA.

Therefore, at the moment of conception there exists not just a sperm and an egg, but the all-loving touch of the Creator of the heavens, the moon and the stars. The loving act of procreation joins with the ultimate Love, the Maker of us all, who bothers to become involved directly at each of our beginnings.

What is man, that Thou art mindful of him?

Didn't You Ever Wonder
Aug. 27th, 2005 @ 09:18 pm

"Before we got married my husband was married to someone else. They were separated."

I could see that this casual conversation with a co-worker had taken a sudden turn. I don't know how it happens. It's not like I'm particularly attentive, I don't think. Certainly no one in the family has ever accused me of that. Yet for some reason bare acquaintances suddenly start pouring out their life stories to me. Must be the "Uncle Judge" mystique.

"I got pregnant." (Taking the corner at 95 now).

"We couldn't get married. He wasn't divorced yet."

Makes sense.

"I was young. I still lived at home with my parents. I was sure they wouldn't understand. I didn't want to shame them."

You know, I really don't know you all that well. Are you sure you want to . . .

"I had a choice."

There was a tinge of bitter irony as she voiced that oft-employed euphemism.

"Eventually we got married, obviously."

Obviously.

"Later my unmarried sister got pregnant and I was surprised. My parents welcomed my sister and the baby with open arms."

The tinge got bitterer.

"It was my choice, I guess. I had a choice."

She looked up at me.

"Didn't you ever wonder why I seem so sad all the time?"

A Person's a Person II
Oct. 18th, 2005 @ 08:16 am

STOP THE ACLU is running a story about how the ACLU is defending a woman who gave birth to a drug-addicted baby, on the grounds that a fetus is not a person under Maryland law and thus not subject to protection from the abuse of the mother.

Back when I was a real judge we were prohibited from commenting on stuff like this, but I was granted such a rare opportunity when judging a Moot Court competition featuring law students from around the country. The case being argued contained the same facts as this one (except that the state law was not in issue; the argument was strictly on the Federal Constitution).

What fun I had. The woman arguing in favor of the child abuse cited *Roe v. Wade* and I interrupted her to ask how she could cite a case which specifically gave states the right to regulate fetal destruction in the third trimester? She fumbled a bit, and then dove into the developing case law post-*Roe* which hinged on the idea that a fetus is not a person, and thus not entitled to protection.

I glanced down from the bench at her African-American co-counsel.

"Then I take it you are in full agreement with the majority decision of the Supreme Court in the case of *Dred Scott v. Sandford*?"

She confessed that she was not familiar with that case (!).

"Well, the *Dred Scott* case holds essentially that if a certain class is not defined as having personhood, then they are not considered persons under the United States Constitution."

Poor student lawyer started to nod in agreement.

"Such as Negroes."

She mostly sputtered incoherently after that.

Well, I guess I wasn't being fair. But then, I don't think it's awfully fair to abuse your children, either. Born or unborn.

Death By Justice
Mar. 19th, 2006 @ 09:02 pm

When I was twenty some friends and I were walking on a deserted section of beach in Key Biscayne when we came across the body of an elderly gentleman washed up on shore. It was, I think, my first experience with death outside a funeral home. About a year later I was waiting for a bus at the top of the circle at the State University of New York at Albany when I glanced up just as a young woman exited the 22nd floor of the State Quad tower and plummeted to her death. I didn't see that part, as the low rise dorms were in the way, but the ambulance sounds not long after confirmed that this was not a hoax.

Over the years I've known quite a few people who died in fires and car accidents, one of the latter being my son's godfather, a sheriff's deputy on duty.

My profession has brought me into contact with half a dozen people who died from drug overdoses before they hit 35. I've known teenage suicides. I've known murderers and murder victims (at least one of whom, I am confident, was both).

Yet none of these terrible violent deaths can compare to the horror of the judicial murder of Terri Schiavo, who began dying one year ago. They told us starvation was a peaceful and non-suffering way to die, but they gave her morphine. They told us that her brain was essentially dead, and that she was not conscious of the world around her and that she could not possibly be feeling pain or fear.

They did an autopsy afterward and confirmed that much of her brain was indeed non-functioning.

But not the part that controlled consciousness.

She knew what was happening.

She knew what they were doing.

She couldn't tell them to stop.

Unborn Child
Apr. 19th, 2007 @ 08:35 am

Pardon me if I'm not dancing in the streets over yesterday's Supreme Court ruling in *Gonzales v. Carhart*.

Not that I disagree with the decision. It's ok as far as it goes, which is not too far. All it says is that this particular statute, which seeks to ban a medical procedure by which a fully-developed viable unborn child is yanked feet-first through the birth canal until its head is locked in the cervix, whereupon its skull

-113-

is pierced and brains vacuumed out until, presumably, death occurs, is not UNCONSTITUTIONAL on its face.

It still might be unconstitutional in some cases, of course, and there are other, unbanned, methods available which would allow for the same result, so what's the big deal suggests the majority, while the shrill voices of the dissenters (and ALL the candidates for president in the party of Jefferson) are left kicking and screaming like, well, a new-born baby.

Roe v. Wade was fairly new when I was in law school and even the most radical left-wing card-carrying-member-of-the-ACLU law professor wasn't convinced it was good law, nor good policy. I remember him explaining the "viability" issue left open by the court. (You may recall that *Roe* divided a baby into three trimesters and declared that no regulation could take place for the first trimester, some for the second, and then marked the beginning of the third trimester as when "viability" happens and thus a stronger governmental interest is created).

The Professor pointed out that advances in science and medicine were already moving back the viability time clock and that we could expect future courts to narrow the *Roe* decision without having to overturn it.

Which shows that prophecy is a difficult business when dealing with a body like the Supreme Court which has the power to make its own rules and public policy as it goes along.

So why not just say what is obvious to nearly everyone: that a fully-developed fetus which unquestionably could survive and thrive outside the womb has every bit as much right to life as nine ladies and gentlemen wearing black robes?

I said fetus there deliberately.

The thing that sent dissenter Justice Ginsburg into apoplexy yesterday? Justice Kennedy continuously referred to the victim of this grim and ghastly barbarism as an "unborn child".

And therein appears the very first crack in 34 years in this wall of madness.

This and That

You Throw Tomatoes
May. 19th, 2006 @ 04:12 pm

(A musical review of the DaVinci Code [the movie] with sincere apologies to the ghosts of George and Ira and *Let's Call the Whole Thing Off*)

> *If you say "awful" and I say "offal",*
> *We'd both say, "That offal's awful!"*
> *Opie, Hanksy, they deserve our thanksy:*
> *They made the whole thing worse.*
>
> *You say "Dull-Vinci", I'll say, "Duh-Vinci"*
> *That means DaVinci is no Oscar cinchy.*
> *Opus Dei need not worry, maybe*
> *They cast da "Vinci curse."*
>
> *And oh, when the music swells, why then the critics frown.*
> *And oh, if the movie smells, why we'll just blame Dan Brown.*
>
> *So don't be moan-y, just save your money.*
> *Magdy wasn't the Saviour's honey,*
> *And we know He didn't have pro-geny,*
> *Or inspire an albino monk---*
> *Let's say the whole thing stunk.*

YAAAHHHHHH!!!!
Jun. 7th, 2006 @ 09:56 pm

Mary and I popped up to Glens Falls this evening to exchange cars and have dinner with Bob at his favorite gourmet sandwich shop. He's working as Master Electrician at the Adirondack Theater Festival again this summer.

While savoring the corn chowder we were rather overcome by the sound of a political meeting breaking out across the small room. A group of about twenty or so were listening enthusiastically to a talk by a woman school-teacher-union type from "Democracy for America", a "grassroots" organization left over from the Howard Dean campaign, and clearly they were Dean-worshipers all, applauding every mention of his name, sporting Dean buttons and otherwise salivating over the prospect of another run for the roses.

Glens Falls is a lovely little town. ("Why," a friend asks, "do the liberals get all the nice places?"). It's nestled between Saratoga Springs and Lake George and when the wind blows from the east you can almost smell Vermont, that strange mixture of incense pots and aging McGovernism that occasionally finds its way into the water and atmosphere of upstate New York.

I guess I should have expected something like this. After all, our grilled cheese sandwiches were made with pesto. But still, to see so many of them gathered in one place, these antique revolutionaries (*i.e.* they were mostly around my age), frankly startled me. I hadn't seen anything like it since my college days. They weren't making any more sense tonight than they did in 1970, but, Lordy! they were still so . . . earnest.

Wife and son hustled me out of there for some reason, just as that old twitch started to come back. I never even got to raise my hand.

Oh, well. Guess I'll have to save my energy for the next debate on Hawaiian independence over at my local breakfast joint where the eggs still come with homefries and my choice of sausage or bacon and either coffee or . . . no coffee.

I wonder what would have happened if I'd just yelled, "ANN COULTER!" on my way out the door?

Where Are They Now?
Jun. 11th, 2006 @ 09:02 am

A column by Nick Coleman in the Star-Tribune of Minneapolis-St. Paul conjures up memories of the battles in the late forties for control of American Liberalism between the communists and their various fronts and the pro-Americans. In the middle of it all was Hubert Horatio Humphrey.

I've been re-evaluating Humphrey for a long time now. He was on the periphery of my first political memories, the 1960 presidential campaign. Later, when he was vice-president, I heard him speak at the National CYO Convention (where he had been dispatched overnight by President Johnson to thank us for our resolution supporting the troops in Vietnam).

Boy could he talk.

He had the energy of a three-year-old and just bubbled with enthusiasm and delight to be with us. They finally had to practically give him the hook so they could get on with the scheduled program.

He was his party's nominee for President of the United States in 1968, losing in a very close race to Richard Nixon in a year when the Democrats were ripped apart over Vietnam and George Wallace was carrying a few of the southern states as an independent.

He tried again in 1972, but his time had passed. By then his eloquence had devolved to classic double-talk, being "absolutely 100%" against the involuntary bussing of little school children, "except as a tool."

I always dismissed Humphrey as just a typical liberal democrat who probably didn't really believe in anything.

But fade back to 1948, the first presidential election post-Roosevelt. The former Vice President of the United States, Henry Wallace, led the "Progressive" wing of the democrats (i.e Socialists, Communists, Fellow-Travelers, Dupes). Minneapolis Mayor Hubert Humphrey fought them, and fought them hard. He rescued the Democrat-Farm-Labor Party of Minnesota from their clutches and battled them nationally, helping found the anti-communist Americans for Democratic Action which became the ultimate Liberal organization of the fifties and sixties. The Wallaceites walked out of the 1948 convention and ran independent.

You'd think that would be enough for one year. But the old Roosevelt coalition also included the "Solid South". No Democrat had ever been elected president without the support of southern Democrats. That is why the Democrats were also the party of Jim Crow, encouraged in that tradition by that virulent racist Woodrow Wilson during his two terms as president.

Hubert Humphrey believed in Civil Rights for all. He came from a white toast state, so had no particular personal stake in the matter. He just thought that it was the right thing to do and that no great national party should be the party of segregation and repression.

So he led another battle, on the floor of the convention, for a party plank supporting Civil Rights for blacks.

He won.

Strom Thurmond and the Dixiecrats walked out, and the old white South would never again be a force in Democratic politics.

****

When he was dying, Humphrey shared a hospital with the super-depressed socially-exiled Richard Nixon. Knowing he had only weeks to live, he bounced around the hospital cheering up the other patients. He spent a lot of time with his old political nemesis. He probably saved his life.

Nixon's first return to Washington after August, 1974 was to Hubert Humphrey's state funeral in January of 1978. Hubert had personally arranged for the invitation. Devoid of the old pomp and power, Nixon stood almost anonymously with the other guests in the Capitol Rotunda. Muriel Humphrey spotted him and dashed over to give him a big hug. "Dick!" she exclaimed, long before any Republican had even bothered to say hello.

****

I'm wondering. Just exactly where do we find the likes of Hubert Humphrey today?

Quatre Avec Sprite
Jun. 21st, 2006 @ 09:10 am

Well, I see the controversy continues down at *Geno's* in Philadelphia, home of the world's greatest cheese steak. Seems the little sign they put up suggesting that customers speak English seein' as they're in America has got the human rights crowd up in arms. It didn't take long for the phrase "Jim Crow" to be devalued by that crew, and I'm relatively sure that casual comparisons to Hitler are only moments away.

Sen. Rick Santorum, knowing a wedge issue when he sees one, has stepped in bravely and forcefully on the *Geno's* side. It'll be interesting to see where Casey comes down on this critical matter.

I don't think this rebellion is gonna catch on, though. It's hard enough finding a food joint where the staff understands when you speak English, so what's the point?

This is by no means a solely American issue. A few years ago I took the family up to Montreal for a couple of days and lemme tell ya those folks up there insist on French and French only. If you're driving, you'd better learn your *droit* from your *gauche* pretty quickly or you will get real lost.

Armed with two years of high school French (I can find the library in any town in the francophone world), I marched boldly into a local Wendy's, reviewed the options, and announced to the attendant, "QUATRE AVEC SPRITE!"

As I say, some problems are universal. She leans into her microphone and addresses the foreign workers in the kitchen.

 "Gimme a number four with Sprite."

-119-

The Wrong War
Jun. 21st, 2006 @ 10:24 pm

With apologies to Harry Turtledove, consider if you will this alternate history scenario:

Franklin D. Roosevelt, out of great consideration for his wife's uncle Teddy and never being one to avoid political expediency when the opportunity presents itself, joins the Republican Party and is elected President of the United States in 1936, soundly whupping one term wonder Alfred E. Smith who is widely perceived to have brought on the Great Depression by his misguided policies of international neutrality, hard liquor and First Saturday novenas.

With the return of Prohibition, the nation's productivity soars and the Depression is soon over. FDR sweeps to re-election victory in 1940. His opponent, Sen. Joseph P. Kennedy of Massachusetts, having carried no states, concedes defeat in a rather nasty farewell press conference at which his second wife Gloria bursts into tears just as the newsreel cameras zoom in for a closeup.

Then, on December 7, 1941, a date that will live in infamy, the United States of America is suddenly and deliberately attacked by naval and air forces of the Empire of Japan.

The war then proceeds as you have seen it on the History Channel.

In 1944 FDR narrowly defeats Sen. Harry S. Truman and is sworn in the following January for an unprecedented third term. A routine Senate resolution congratulating the President sparks a mini-filibuster, much to the chagrin of Vice President Robert A. Taft.

> SENATOR KENNEDY:
>
> Lies, lies, lies! That's all we have gotten from this administration! It's been over three years, three long, bloody years since we suffered a surprise attack on our naval forces in Hawaii, and believe me I support the troops, and what has President Roosevelt done about it?

Hirohito is still at large!

His armed forces wander the Pacific with impunity! He grows stronger every day! We are no closer to catching him than we were on December 6, 1941!

So what does this president do?

Does he make any effort to go after our sworn enemy?

NOOOO!

Instead he decides to invade FRANCE! Our oldest ALLY, Mr. President! A country that has NEVER done us any harm! A country against whom we have no complaint, and yet here we are, slaughtering innocent women and children and civilians. For what? Where is the honor? Where is the glory?

No, this president is just engaged in some sick, sick, sick super-macho effort to make up for what happened in 1917-18.

It appears to me that the Roosevelt family is engaging is some sort of personal feud, trying to even up the score with our long-dead glorious president, that great Democrat Woodrow Wilson who led our nation to victory after the country soundly rejected Mr. Bull Moose Roosevelt, a man who though a little wacky at least wore the uniform of his country on a battlefield.

Does this chicken-hawk President, who spent the last war in a cushy, privileged government job, think leaving thousands of bodies on Omaha Beach makes him some kind of San Juan Hill hero?

SICK, Mr. President. SICK! SICK! SICK!

I ask you, Mr. President, did we find Hirohito under a rock in Normandy? Was he hiding in a church in Ste. Mere Eglise? Was he in Paris? Was he at The Bulge?

OOPS! We can't talk about The Bulge, can we Mr. President? Your Secretary of War certainly bungled that one, didn't he? And by the way, why hasn't he been removed?

Why can't this administration ever, ever admit its mistakes?

How many lives, Mr. President? How many of our boys are going to be killed fighting the wrong war in the wrong place at the wrong time?

Sure, we all admit this Hitler character may not be the nicest guy in the world, but what did he ever do to us?

Why are we fighting this war? I say, let the people of Europe sort out their own differences. If they prefer dictatorship to democracy, and it's pretty clear that they do, what business is that of ours?

And, oh! Where are these so-called super-weapons that General Marshall warned us about? I haven't seen any. NOR HAS ANYBODY ELSE!

They never existed, did they?

No jet planes, no jumbo-bombs.

Was this just another LIE to drag us into an endless war in Europe, a bottomless quagmire, while across the Pacific the Emperor is laughing in his japants?

Mr. President, I DEMAND that we pull our troops out of Europe NOW!

A River Runs Through It
Jul. 1st, 2006 @ 10:19 pm

About 15 miles upstream from my house the Mohawk River and the New York State Thruway pass through a natural cut in the Appalachian mountain chain, the only such break in the eastern United States until you reach Georgia and the end of the mountains. The Erie Canal transformed the country in the early 19th century, using this same route to open a water path to the West.

Locally these features are known as the Noses. Little Nose is on the left, Big Nose on the right (facing west, upstream). Ten thousand years ago, a mere blink of an eye in human time and almost too small to measure in geological time, while primitive men were already hunting and gathering in North America, a pre-Gore global warming caused the glaciers of the last great ice age to recede from this region. Not awfully far north the area that now composes the St. Lawrence River remained frozen. The Noses were still connected as part of a continuous ridge of the Appalachians and behind them, stretching back across all of central and western New York, lay the waters draining from the Great Lakes, seeking the path of least resistance to the sea.

A mighty river, known to geologists as the "Iro-Mohawk" roared through this valley and thundered over the ridge of the Noses forming a cascade several times higher and more powerful than Niagara Falls. Men could have been there to see it.

The heavy clay soil of our valley comes from the mud deposited by the old river. The lighter sands and silt eventually settled in the Pine Bush area between Schenectady and Albany.

We don't know when, exactly, the water forced open the ridge, but it surely must have created a tremendous flood. When the waters finally receded, helped along by the opening of the St. Lawrence which changed the direction of the Great Lakes outflow, various Indian tribes periodically settled both sides of the valley. Among the late-comers were the Mohawks, arriving a mere fifty years before the Dutch. They had villages on each of the Noses and a long cave ran down under the Mohawk River and connected the two. The opening on Big Nose collapsed in the mid-twentieth century, long after the Mohawks had left.

****

A few days ago we had one of those hundred year floods and much of the area of the Noses was under water. The Thruway was closed, the railroad shut down and the canal that uses the river may be incapacitated for months, stranding quite a few boats.

I don't think anyone was seriously hurt here in Montgomery County, but several hundred people were put up in Red Cross shelters and I'm sure hundreds more found their own temporary accommodations. My daughter Anna and I ran one of the shelters for part of the day Thursday. Notwithstanding all the training, something of this scale becomes a chaotic event, and we were pretty much left alone to make our own decisions.

But not a problem. People called to volunteer to board pets. The local hospital and some restaurants donated meals and supplies. After the first night a woman called and had us get clothing sizes from all our guests (we were in an elementary school) and made all the necessary connections with a local church to get ample quantities of appropriate stuff. She took up a collection at her office and bought fresh underwear and ran around on her lunch hour gathering everything together and personally delivering it with her family's help in huge bags.

Toiletries and towels and diapers and medical supplies all showed up. Anna arranged for a couple of people to get their prescriptions filled at a local pharmacy that didn't charge. A committee from the Chamber of Commerce came through and visited the four shelters to find out what their members could do and delivered truckloads of bottled water at the same time. Volunteer firemen from sixty miles away showed up to take the strain off their overworked brothers here.

As the waters returned to their banks, every available pump and firehose was emptying cellars. Neighbors from higher ground were all pitching in to start the cleanup and soften the blow.

****

The next day Hillary and Chuck and their entourages arrived with their photographers and reporters in tow to record their shock and dismay and sympathy and to promise somebody else's tax dollars to fix everything.

Thanks!

 Don't know what we could have done without you!

A Fudgenberry Sundae with carbonated water, please
Jul. 17th, 2006 @ 10:28 pm

I have been following the adventures of Nightfly as he and the Lady Bug wander around New Jersey seeking decent fast-food service and anything resembling ice cream.

Makes me more than happy that we have available but one hill away a genuine old-fashioned ice cream parlor parked in a residential neighborhood of the city comprised of mostly two-family houses. *Samuel Fariello Confectionary* it is now called, though when I was a kid it was just known as Sammy's or Fariello's, or Samiello's. The latter was Tim Blanchfield's contribution, I think. He used to pick up his papers there, along with a bunch of other guys from Market Hill, but at some point he and Sammy had a difference of opinion over the administration of the joint and Tim found himself banned for life.

It is a tiny place, long and narrow, with three booths, three or four small tables and half a dozen seats at the counter. In the olden days it was even tinier, because a good chunk of the floor space was taken up by a neighborhood branch of the post office, run by Sam and his brother Joe (who could have passed for any of those guys who filled the third slot in the Three Stooges after Curley and Shemp left us).

It was unbelievably crowded, especially when the paperboys were hanging out. They sold all kinds of odds and ends typical of a neighborhood all-purpose this and that store, but always, from the beginning, they had a reputation for being the home of the world's best hot fudge sundae, a little treasure well worth the lack of formal ambience.

The store disappeared for a while after the old timers retired, but eventually Sam's son brought it back to life, only too briefly as he died at a very young age. He did manage to sell the place and the recipes to a local couple who "restored" Sammy's to a glory it actually never had, and then about a year and a half ago it was sold to an old theater friend of ours, Gary Castler, who played Tommy Djilas to my Mayor Shinn in *The Music Man* about sixteen years ago ("You keep your premises off of my oldest girl!"). Amusingly, the young lady who played Gracie Shinn, my youngest girl, is a regular at Fariello's. She recently found herself elected to the school board. ("Will the members of the school board please stop bickering!")

Phosphates, egg creams, ice cream sodas, sundaes of all sorts, revolving stools with the chrome edge straight out of Norman Rockwell, old soda bottles and other relics, penny candy (well, that's what we used to call it), spectacular chocolates, bins of fresh nuts. It really doesn't get any better than this.

And the folks dropping in are neighbors and friends, or soon are.

Sometimes you just have to drift away from the mega-malls and the highway boxes and wander around the corner and inhale the smells of a thousand memories and walk back in time to when the most important decision in the world is whether to have nuts or no nuts, and your only challenge in life is trying to impress a pretty girl over a fountain glass of cherry Coke.

FOREBEARS

How Jamie Got His Name
Jun. 16th, 2005 @ 04:51 pm

[From the archives: a letter from a father to his son, c. 2002]

Dear Jamie,

You wonder how you got your name. (Actually, I think your exact words were, "How did I get such a stupid name as James Francis?"). The simple answer is I gave it to you. But then, you knew that. I guess you want to know why.

In 1848 Ireland was in the third year of the horrific potato famine. Potatoes were the principal crop or the poor of Ireland. When the blight came, millions of people died of starvation. The lucky ones were able to book passage to other lands.

These were not cruise ships. They were often called "coffin ships" because a large percentage of the passengers died before ever seeing the new land.

When he was barely older than you are now, James Going booked passage on one of those ships and came to America. All of his family was left behind. There were no handouts for immigrants. If they wanted to survive they had to work, and work hard. He managed to find work on a farm across the river in the Town of Florida. You can almost see that land from your window. Within a few years he was able to buy a small farm of his own, married and began raising a family. They were among the first parishioners of St. Mary's, back when it was only a small chapel on the south side of what would become Amsterdam but was then the canal village of Port Jackson.

Eventually he moved to another small farm on Van Dyke Avenue. If you walk straight up our street to where you can walk no more, that was his land. He was very mechanically inclined and went to work for the Shuler Spring factory where they made industrial springs for carriages. Within a short time he was running the factory and his sons, including James Going, Jr., came to work with him. He was 52 when he died in 1879.

His son James also worked at the Shuler Spring shop, and lost an eye in an industrial accident. He married and had two sons and two daughters. One of the daughters was Mark Lounello's grandmother, the other was Colleen Medwid's grandmother. His son James Edward was my grandfather.

James Edward Going was a fine horseman back when everyone had a horse. Because of his skill, during World War I (1917-1918), he was responsible for bringing horses from the South to New York City, where they were put on boats for France for use in the war. While he was in the army in New York, he met my grandmother who was a wonderful lady with an Irish lilt in her speech that she picked up from her mother and neighbors in Brooklyn.

They married, and first Aunt Marie was born, and then my father, Francis Going.

My grandfather was a very good man, everyone said, and he worked hard. The era of horses was over, so he bought a gasoline station in Tribes Hill which had some tourist cabins attached. (Motels hadn't been invented yet, but those little cabins were all people needed who were traveling overnight.)

By and by he developed an ice business (very few people had refrigerators) and the Going Ice Company was very big in Amsterdam. They cut the ice in winter and stored it covered with straw and sawdust in big barns and hoped it would last through the hot summer.

Aunt Marie and my father, Francis Going, went to school at St. Mary's. Back then it was located near where we park our car in the back of the church, and for a while they lived across the street in a building where the school district parking lot is now.

The business did well, and James Edward Going bought a house for his young family, one of the first houses on Wilkes Avenue up the hill from us.

Then he died. He was 41, ten years younger than I am now. My dad wasn't twelve years old yet.

There was no retirement account, no social security. My grandmother had to close the business, and they lost the house. She had to get a job working in a factory and they had to move to a dark, miserable four-family house on Williams Street, just about where you parked the car the other day in the Catholic Charities parking lot. (Years later the place burned down and a family with four kids were killed). They went from respectable middle class to poverty in just a couple of years. It was during the Great Depression and people were lucky if they had a job.

In that unhealthy environment my father became an unhealthy child, suffering from rheumatic fever and other diseases. The damage to his heart from those childhood illnesses later killed him.

But just because they were poor did not mean they gave up. My dad, Francis Going, studied hard in school and became salutatorian of his class in 1939 at St. Mary's.

There was no money for college, though, so he got factory jobs, and for fun he did some acting in radio plays in Schenectady. (Television had just been invented and was still extremely experimental).

When World War II came he could have gotten an exemption because he was the only one left to support his mother, but he joined the Navy. He was stationed several places in this country, including Newport, Rhode Island where Uncle Jay used to live. Later he was shipped to Scotland (aboard the Queen Mary, which WAS a luxury liner, but turned into a troop ship during the war.) He was the first one of the Goings to return to the Old World since 1848, though he never got to see Ireland. Right after D-Day he landed in France and eventually got to see Paris.

After the war in Europe ended, he was sent back to America and re-outfitted for the Pacific. They were going to assist in the invasion of Japan. He had been in the Navy three years when the war suddenly ended with the dropping of the atomic bomb.

The war changed everybody. The men came back from that war eager to make up for lost time and together turned the United States into the greatest economic, military and political power in the world over their lifetimes.

Because of his service to his country, Francis Going was able to finally go to college, six years out of high school. He spent four years at Siena College, and halfway through met my mother, your grandma. He wooed her, won her and finally married her just before his senior year.

He graduated in June of 1949 and then entered Albany Law School. Their first son was born at that same time, and they named him James Edward Going in honor of his grandfather. They called him Jamie, though later when he went to school, he decided to call himself Jay. He was always Jamie to Grandma.

I never talk much about Uncle Jay, but I have always been very proud of him. He was my big brother and always looked out for me. He wouldn't let the other kids pick on me or make fun of me. When we grew older, I always wanted to do what he did. He was very smart, and loved to read. When he found a book he liked, he would give it to me to read when he was done. We used to go down to the library together and spend the whole day just reading mysteries and science fiction.

He became the first valedictorian and first graduate of Bishop Scully High School. I wasn't a valedictorian, but he set a good example for me and I followed him to Albany State when it came my turn. We still had a draft in those days, and they instituted a lottery. Jay drew a low number, but he wouldn't have to go until he finished college. It was during the Vietnam War, and at a time when the colleges were being shut down by anti-war protests.

Uncle Jay was not someone who couldn't wait to go to war. He hated the idea same as most everyone else. But something inside him told him that he owed something to this country and at a time when soldiers were getting little or no respect, he dropped out of college early and volunteered to be drafted and went to Vietnam.

Meanwhile, Dad's health had its ups and downs. Scarlet fever in the Navy had weakened his heart further, and in 1955 with four kids he had his first heart surgery, to fix a valve that had become clogged with scar tissue. He insisted on checking out early so he could spend Christmas with us, then got so sick he very nearly died.

Five years later we moved to Amsterdam, his home town, to the house on

Trinity Place. He had his own law practice, and just as he was building it up, he got sick again, and had a second heart operation. He was out of commission for months, and we kids and our mom pitched in to keep his law business going.

After that, he got a job with the state and we finally had a steady income. He took a promotional exam, and failed it. Then he learned that half the people who took the test had four hours to take it (like him), while the others had eight hours. He sued on behalf of himself and all the others who failed, and the courts threw out the test results and ordered the civil service department to schedule a new test.

It was a great victory.

Then, on the Saturday before he was scheduled to take the new test, in 1968, he suffered a heart attack. He never got to take the test.

Six months later, his mother died. He got sicker and sicker. I remember sitting with him when he was coughing up blood and he kept apologizing to me. Over the next year he had a series of tests and finally another operation. This time they replaced the valve with a new artificial one. He was on the table seven hours. I sat with grandma in the lobby at Albany Medical Center, where Anna works, and remember how she jumped up when she saw the surgeon come out. He was alive. Barely.

He was in the hospital three months, home a month, and then back in for another month from hepatitis he contracted from a blood transfusion. (He had an extremely rare blood type and they had to take whatever blood was available.) They gave him five months to live. He lasted almost five years.

He never went back to work, and after his sick leave was used up, they terminated him, before he was eligible for a pension. We were back to poverty. But, at least we kids were older and we all worked our way through college.

He was in and out of the hospital. Finally, on December 3, 1974, the phone rang at six in the morning and it was all over. He was 52.

Uncle Sean was eight.

The life insurance policy he left got re-circulated over the years. It helped start a business for Uncle Jay, helped put Uncle Sean through college, and helped Mom and I buy this house we live in.

So I hope you understand why it is that on January 14, 1985 I could not think of a more honorable name to give you than James Francis Going. I hope you will always add to the honor of that name, as you always have.

Love,

Dad

A Doll's Boot
Sep. 29th, 2005 @ 08:35 pm

We had a built-in china closet in the house on Trinity Place where various and sundry items of trash and treasure were kept. The brother had taken it upon himself to rid the house of the former while I declared myself the preserver of the latter. Occasionally we had classification problems.

"What the heck is this?" he asked, holding up a tiny rubber doll's boot. I took it to Mom where she sat in the living room calmly dying.

She smiled. "When I was about five years old, my father used to take me along on the truck sometimes, delivering groceries. One day I found that little boot in somebody's house and the very nice lady told me I could keep it."

Keep it? Sixty-five years had passed. Mom had grown up, gone to college, left her home town, lived as a young professional woman in Schenectady, fallen in love, gotten married, moved to Troy, moved a couple more times, lived six years outside of Albany, moved to Amsterdam, raised a family, buried her husband and still had this little piece of footwear belonging to a doll she probably never saw in the first place.

But then, I suspect it wasn't the boot she was keeping. It was rather the memory of happy times spent with her father, a man still in his twenties that one night, the night he was riding in the rumble seat. He probably never even saw the uninsured motorist who plowed into him. No good night kisses or tucking her in snug as a bug in a rug, ever, ever again.

****

Guido Brunelli was the son of hard-working Italian immigrants who ran a grocery, a diner and a bakery and managed some real property investments. In his teens he became smitten with the girl down the street, wrote her a charming "Dear Miss Geromini" note in pencil, seeking permission to call on her. "I loved him so much!" Grandma Anita told me with tears in her eyes sixty years later when I found that note in a little box at her house. "Oh, how I loved him!"

He was a strikingly handsome young man, and the pictures we have of him exude a brassy confidence. It's not surprising that he considered moving his young family to Argentina to make his fortune. When a mobster wannabe came into the diner one day and offered to provide Guido with "protection" for a monthly fee, he reached under the counter, pulled out a gun and shoved it in the man's face.

"This is all the protection I need, and if anything happens to my store or my family I will personally use it on you."

The man never returned.

As sometimes happens, Anita became pregnant. Guido explained the situation to his father, Francesco Brunelli, who refused to allow them to marry until sometime after the birth of our mother, after which they had three more children. The neighborhood was Mom's home, but her bedroom remained at the Geromini house with her grandparents, even after her mother moved in with the Brunelli family down the street. Between births, Anita helped run the store, and there would always be a pot of sauce cooking in the back, and a wicker clothes basket that served as crib for the latest infant.

The Italians lived on the wrong side of the tracks, though they may never have noticed. The extended family of aunts and uncles overlapped generations, and there were dozens of shirttail relations and friends from the old village in Italy to keep them company.

They spoke only Italian at home. Mom never learned English until she entered school, but she had a keen mind and was an excellent student (as was her mother, who had completed the fifth and sixth grades in one year upon arriving in America, and who a long lifetime later could still recite the 48 states and their capitals in regional order, as well as "The Wreck of the Hesperus" in grandiloquent manner).

Guido was killed shortly after the birth of his first son and fourth child. It was during the last gasp of Prohibition and he was supplementing his income by running bootleg liquor to Omar Dupre's speakeasy. (Much later Omar's son married one of his daughters).

A few years later, Mom's grandmother Geromini died and her mother decided it was time she moved into "the new house" with the rest of the family. That lasted about two weeks and the stubborn young lady returned to her grandfather and an uncle and aunt and no one raised the subject again.

In her senior year of high school an intense academic rivalry developed between this child of an immigrant family and the son of an old-line New England WASP family. No Italian had ever been Valedictorian of Franklin High School. No one until Laurabelle Brunelli in 1943.

Imagine the pride they all felt, listening to her deliver her address on "Women in the Service". Years later, reflecting on having seen Carousel on stage in Boston, my grandmother wrote her that the graduation scene in the play reminded her of Mom's graduation. "That was the happiest day of my life," she said, "and you know I can count all my happy days on one hand and still have a couple of fingers left over."

Mom was entitled to a full college scholarship, but perhaps because of an oversight, or perhaps not, the paperwork never left Franklin High School. She nonetheless commuted by train for four years to Emmanuel College in Boston where she once again finished at the top of her class.

She took a job in nuclear research at General Electric in Schenectady and began a regular (often weekly) correspondence with her mother that lasted nearly forty years. She married Dad the following year and soon had four children, followed by the near death of her husband from heart surgery, then a second heart operation a few years later, then another child, then Dad's heart attack and third surgery, followed by a lingering five year death watch ending in 1974 when Dad was 52 and Mom 49.

By now her older children were leaving the roost. How she loved traveling to see them: Alabama and Florida and Newport and San Diego and San Francisco. Those were days of laughter and joy and the wonderful smells of home cooking and baking that followed her wherever she went. She was off visiting one of the sibs in July of 1986, about to come home in fact, when my uncle called me. I decided to wait before passing on the news.

I met her at the airport. "Your mother died this morning," I heard myself saying.

****

Nine years later and here she was dying herself, with as much dignity as she could muster, surrounded by her children and grandchildren, lovingly fingering a little rubber boot.

Someday, I suspect, my kids will be cleaning out my attic. They'll open up a plastic bag, reach in and grab a strange object and maybe hold that boot up to the light, taking turns touching it, rolling it in the palms of their hands, wrinkling their brows.

"What the heck is this?" one of them will ask.

"Boy, he never threw out anything."

Laura B. Going 5/22/25-11/07/1995
Nov. 7th, 2005 @ 09:52 am

Barely eight months after I had been triumphantly sworn in as Family Court Judge of Montgomery County, Mary called me. My mother was sick, she was on her way to the hospital for tests. They think it might be cancer.

For the moment, there was nothing I could do. I put down the phone, paced around my small office, wandered into the court room, sat down in the big judge chair, stared out the window.

I absentmindedly thumbed the court bible, the one we used for swearing in witnesses. I finally glanced down at it, a well-worn *Douay-Rheims* edition left behind by one of a long string of Catholic judges who had held my position.

My thumb was on the 4th Chapter of the book of Tobias (also called Tobit in other editions).

> *And he said to him: Hear, my son, the words of my mouth,*
> *and lay them as a foundation in thy heart.*
> *When God shall take my soul, thou shalt bury my body:*
> *and thou shalt honor thy mother all the days of her*
> *life,*
> *For thou must be mindful what and how great perils she*
> *suffered for thee in her womb.*
> *And when she also shall have ended the time of her life,*
> *bury her by me.*

The diagnosis was correct, the surgery fruitless; the stages of the disease advanced with numbing swiftness.

The siblings descended quickly on the old homestead, Dale for the duration, Jay and Sean on most weekends, Tim frequently, even bringing the California grandchildren. Mary and I and our kids were in town anyway. Sean was shy of thirty, the rest of us in our 40's, and we were totally helpless.

"What are we going to do? Who will take care of us?" asked Dale.

We looked at each other and the answer hit us simultaneously.

"Aunt Pia!" we both nearly shouted.

Aunt Pia is Mom's aunt on the Brunelli side, though being only seven years older, she was more like a big sister. Aunt Pia came all the way from Franklin,

MA and stayed with us for a month, until her own family reminded us that we were only borrowing her, we really couldn't keep her! By the time she left, we were only marking time as Mom could no longer communicate and had stopped eating and drinking and swallowing. We could only keep her moist and as comfortable as possible in the bed we had moved into the living room.

Her friends and family had all stopped by in those final three months. Among them was Maria (pronounced as rhyming with "aria"), a woman from Poland whom Mom had taught English a decade earlier.

As the end came nearer, we all stayed the night slumped in various locations around the living room, tuned in to her labored breathing. Father Gulley came to bring her the sacraments, and watched with us, reminding us of the most holy time we were in, approaching the moment when the portals of Heaven were opened in our presence, and the soul of the just passed seamlessly from this life to the next.

On November 7, election day, as it happens, we had just finished dinner when Dale called to us and we all gathered quickly around her, her five children and Mary and Dale's husband Philip. Our kids were playing upstairs.

Maria was there too. Earlier we had looked out the window and seen her parked across the street. She wanted to be near, but to leave Mom to us. Dale would have none of it, went out and told her she was family too.

I stood at Mom's feet as she took her final breath. Her eyes opened for the first time in days, and displayed a remarkable clarity. She looked right at me, and I smiled at her.

And that was all. We stood quietly for a while and Jay closed her eyes. Sean dropped to his knees, in solemn remembrance, as did the flight of angels that filled the room.

Moments later, I gathered the kids and explained what had happened. They ranged in age from 14 to 5. We all went down to spend some time with Mom until Mr. Riley the undertaker arrived.

Afterwards, when they had taken her away, five-year-old Louisa came downstairs again, looked around sadly and said to me, "Where's Gramma?" and I explained to her again, that Gramma had gone to heaven to be with God.

"Oh, I know that, Daddy. Where's her old body?"

The river of visitors at the funeral home never stopped. Our State Senator and Assemblyman, other political figures, relatives and friends, the immigrants she had taught to speak English, the generation of high school students she had educated, the mentally ill she had cared for.

An old friend approached me after saying his prayer for her.

"As you know, I've been to many, many wakes in my lifetime."

For sure.

"This is the first time I can honestly say that I have looked upon the body of a saint."

Remembrance
Nov. 8th, 2005 @ 12:19 pm

[Mom's funeral was a family affair, with children and spouses as pall-bearers, lectors and eulogists. Father James Gulley was the celebrant, assisted by old family friends Fr. Joe Cotugno and Fr. Joe Anselment. The readings included the one from the Book of Tobit which I had stumbled upon the day I learned of her cancer, and St. John's account of the Last Supper and the commandment of Jesus to "Love one another, as I have loved you." As is the custom, Father Gulley incensed the coffin at the Offertory. When he had finished, the incense rose and gathered and for a few moments formed a distinct halo over her mortal remains.]

Remarks of Dale Frances Going at the Funeral of Laura B. Going, 11/10/95

When I was 17, I gave Laura this e.e. cummings poem for mothers day. I remember feeling a kind of terror and urgency because I thought my mother had no idea how much love and awe I felt for her, and that once she read this poem, it would all be over, the cat would be out of the bag, I could never look her in the face again, it would change everything. I was an adolescent daughter, and I knew my mother was a saint. It was horrible.

When I came down for breakfast after slipping the poem under her door, all Mom said was, thanks for the poem. It was very nice but I don't think I understood it. It had never occurred to me that the poem wasn't clear as daylight. Well Mom, listen up. In heaven, everyone understands poetry.

> if there are any heavens
> my mother will
> (all by herself) have one
> it will be a heaven of lilies
> & lilacs
> of yellow & of blackred
> roses
> my father will be (deep
> like a rose
> tall like a rose)
> standing near my
> swaying over her
> (silent)
> with eyes which are really
> petals
> with a face really which
> is a flower with
> hands
> which whisper
> this is my beloved my
>
> suddenly in sunlight
> he will bow,
> & the whole garden will
> bow

REMARKS of Mary T. Going at Funeral of Laura B. Going 11/10/95

The first weekend we learned of Laura's illness we attended Mass together here at St. Mary's. Father Anthony Gulley's homily assured us that something good always comes when bad things happen to good people. I wondered what could possibly be good about Gramma having cancer.

For us, the past three short months has allowed the Going family to become reacquainted. We got to know each other again, we listened and supported each other. And during the last two weeks we even moved back in with her. Ma's house was alive with the grandchildren she loved so much, her family and friends and music and laughter; the way she always loved it.

Gramma often said, "Che sera sera." Her last words to me were, "Mary, day by day."

Recently Robert and I were inspired by Monsignor Glavin's prayer from his anniversary celebration:

> "God permits the sorrows and disappointments lest you become too well satisfied with this life and forget that you are on earth merely as a pilgrim on the way to your real home."

Laura has gone home to heaven leaving our hearts heavy,
    but filled with memories of her smile,
    her gifts of compassion, patience and wisdom,
    and her unconditional love.

REMARKS of Robert N. Going at Funeral of Laura B. Going 11/10/95

Our Irish grandmother, on her deathbed, summoned me to her side. "You know," she said, "when I first learned that your father wanted to marry your mother, I didn't like the idea at all because I knew she was (whisper) ITALIAN!

"But," she added, "once I got to know her, I realized she really is a wonderful woman."

That was her big secret, that Mom was a wonderful woman, a fact that was plainly evident to everyone who ever met her.

As long as we're giving away family secrets, here's another one. Most of you knew her as Laura, but her real name was Laurabelle Mae. She dropped the "belle" and the "Mae" as soon as she left home for college, but for some reason she shared the secret with our father, who ever afterwards would send her love letters addressed to "Miss Laura-belly Mae Brunelli". And he went on to share that secret with each of his children as soon as we were old enough to guffaw.

Many of you knew Mom as a teacher, not only as the Director of the Fulmont Adult Learning Center but also as an English and Math teacher at St. Mary's Institute, where she even taught a couple of her own children.

But we knew her as our First Teacher, and she taught us a great many things as we were growing up.

She taught us to laugh. She had a marvelous sense of humor and found amusement in the every-day trials of life. I think she would have really enjoyed watching her children, only a few hours after her death, composing a "TOP TEN LIST" of reasons Mom never threw anything out. (The number ONE reason: "Robert might want it.").

She taught us to love. Our house was always filled with love overflowing. If we truly wish to honor her, we can do no less than to take that love which she poured out on all of us and share it with each other, always.

She taught us to survive. She belonged to that wonderful generation of Americans who passed through the Great Depression and World War II and went on to build a better life for the rest of us. A child of immigrants, she spoke no English until she attended school at the age of 5 and went on to be Valedictorian of her High School class and finished on top of her class at Emmanuel College as well.

Dad's illnesses caused her married life to be a constant economic struggle. He nearly died in 1955 when she had four children six and under and was totally incapacitated for five years before his death in 1974 when Sean was only eight.

And in teaching us to survive, she also taught us to pray.

Some of my earliest memories are of Mom teaching me the basic prayers. Many evenings we knelt by her bed as a family reciting the rosary. She attended daily Mass whenever possible, even when we were on vacation. ESPECIALLY when we were on vacation.

She recited the rosary every day of her life, beginning each rosary, of course, with the Apostle's Creed, thereby confirming each day her belief in

> The Communion of Saints,
> The Forgiveness of Sins,
> The Resurrection of the Body,
>   And Life Everlasting.

And so, most gracious and loving Father, we are pleased to present to you this day your newest Saint.

A Saint of Love and Laughter,
Of Prayer and Survival.
Saint Laura-belly Mae Brunelli Going:
The patron saint
of Moms.

A Conditional Farewell
Nov. 16th, 2005 @ 09:20 am

Rheumatic fever as a child and scarlet fever in the Navy in Cherbourg weakened Dad's mitral valve, resulting in extremely serious and primitive heart surgery at the ripe old age of 33. There were four of us kidlings. Jay, the oldest, had just turned 6. Mom and Dad had just celebrated their seventh anniversary. He survived, but the health problems dominated the final 19 years of his life.

> [Autumn, 1955]
> Dear Laura
>
> Dr. John Carter of Albany Hospital says that "even a very good doctor" could not detect my 'murmur' with a stethoscope. He claims Beebe found it "because he is exceptional". If I should go out on this operation please keep the above in mind & if necessary contact Dr. Carter &/or Dr. Beebe to support claim against V.A.
>
> For legal advice I don't think you can do better than Jim Cahill and you can tell him I wanted it that way.
>
> Laura, darling, I can't tell you in the coldness of ink on paper what you've meant to me. I met you when I was undergoing pangs of uncertainty about so many things. Our courtship, and particularly our marriage made the semblance of a man of me. I was a difficult subject but all that is good in you somehow found its way into me to a lesser degree. I have no legacy to leave you & my darlings except my eternal love and, God willing, I shall be permitted to watch over you from eternity until the day we are reunited in God's Heaven.
>
> I leave with you my sincerest wish & hope that you shall marry again, knowing that you would do so wisely. It is not good for woman to be alone & my babies need a daddy.

Me too, my dearest and my sweet babes.

Frank

[Typical of Mom, she tore the above letter into six pieces. More typical, she saved it in the zippered compartment of an old pocketbook. Most typical, she kept the pocketbook, where Dale found this lost treasure. -RNG]

The Sandbox
Dec. 3rd, 2006 @ 01:46 am

My Grandfather Going met Grandma when she was a teenager during World War I, when he was a horseman bringing up the animals from South Carolina to ship them off to France from New York City. They married shortly after the War ended and settled down initially in her hometown of Brooklyn (which accounts for me rooting for the Dodgers over the Yankees in 1955 and 1956, when I was 4 and 5, respectively).

Aunt Marie, Dad's only sibling, was born in Brooklyn, but not much later they decided to move back to Amsterdam, his home town (there is a long family pattern of this, like there is some personal black hole that keeps sucking us back here even after we have seemingly escaped). The story is that he had passed most of the physical tests to join the Fire Department of New York, but asthma flared up and everyone thought it best for him to return to the healthy climate of upstate New York.

I don't know anything about Aunt Marie's birth, but Dad was born at home on April 30, 1922. We are a resourceful bunch, as can be seen by the fact that Grandfather Going delivered the baby. The Doctor arrived shortly thereafter, having been summoned from the pulpit while attending Sunday Mass at St. Mary's.

The tradition back then was to have the father present the child for baptism while the mother stayed home. Grandma had instructed him to have the child named James, the same as his father and grandfather and great-grandfather. When they came home from St. Mary's husband announced to wife that as far as he was concerned, there had been enough Jameses. "The boy's name is

Francis!" (after her brother, and father, and grandfather). The Christening gown has been used by every male member of the family since that day in 1922.

Jim Going moved his young family to nearby Tribes Hill in the mid-20's, where he ran an early service station (his horse-training skills being of lesser value then) and a motor camp consisting of a handful of one room cottages to provide minimal shelter for the traveling public. Later he started an ice company and moved back to Amsterdam where they lived relatively comfortably.

When Dad turned seven, he became an altar boy at St. Mary's. He had started school a year early at SMI simply by tagging along with his sister. (They lived across Maple Street from the school at that time, in a house later occupied by my classmate Frank Romeo).

Less than five years later, during a brutally cold (-28 F.) February in 1934, Jim Going developed a raging fever, demanding that Dad open the windows and shutters in their house on Wilkes Avenue. Grandpa Jim died shortly after, having just turned 41.

After that, it was just the three of them.

They lost the business, and the house, and Grandma had to go to work in the factories and later took an office job at the freight terminal. Dad peddled the *Evangelist*, the Diocesan newspaper, on a route he shared with his friend Tom Eagan, who would later become a Jesuit priest and the Director of the Shrine of the North American Martyrs across the river from Tribes Hill in Auriesville. When he was a little older, Dad delivered telegrams for Western Union on his bicycle.

He started his life-long relationship with the medical profession with a series of childhood diseases, including rheumatic fever, and an appendix removal.

From an autograph book he kept at the time, it appears he was a favorite among the nuns who were the nursing staff at St. Mary's Hospital.

From the stories he told later, we got the impression that he was quite the cut-up in school. Oh, the tales usually involved the antics of Ed Dirsie, or Bud Langley, or Packy McCabe, or Dick Turner. But I'm not stupid. He was into the mischief right up to his neck with the rest of them.

Aunt Marie dropped out of high school and went to work while Dad buried himself in his studies, earning the RPI Medal and finishing as Salutatorian of the Class of 1939 at St. Mary's Institute. He was also an accomplished orator and debater. He was already interested in politics and public affairs, an eager follower of radio firebrand Father Coughlin and an opponent of Lend-Lease.

College was out of the question, so he worked at the Freight Depot with Grandma and passed into honorable manhood. During Wold War II he served in the Navy, variously stationed in Cleveland, Newport, Norfolk and overseas in Scotland (where he fell in love) and Cherbourg, France (where he developed scarlet fever).

After the war he was finally able to fulfill his dream of college, Siena Class of '49.

Here's one of the first things he wrote for a class assignment:

English Comp
Francis Going

True Happiness

True happiness to me is the leading of a true Christian life in imitation of the Son of God. There is no greater satisfaction in the pursuance of the everyday tasks concerned with one's journey along the road to death than that which comes with the knowledge that one is doing unto others as he would have others do unto him. It gives one an inner glow, a sense of fulfillment, which can be obtained through no other medium. It is but a short time that we pass in this vale of tears and what happiness we have here is but a small amount in comparison with the boundless happiness which God has in store for those who keep His word. True happiness then may be expressed as the leading of our lives in such a way as to obtain the true achievement of seeing God face to face one day.

****

And then he met Mom.

It was love at first sight, love everlasting, love ever-perfect and a love that was stronger than death.

A whirlwind courtship, marriage, honeymoon in Nantucket, their first son (James) born a day shy of their first anniversary, followed by me less than two years later, then my sister Dale a year and a half later about the same time he was studying for the bar exam, then Tim the following year.

That was when we moved from Troy to suburban Albany into our own little house.

A year later Dad was near death from his disease-damaged heart. A team of brilliant young surgeons saved him, until the next time, and the time after that.

Dad had promised to build us a sandbox in the back yard in Westmere when we first moved in, but somehow he never got around to it. We didn't see him during that time when they were making the railroad tracks all over his torso, so we didn't quite understand that he would never be strong again. Listening now to the tape recorded message he made for us from his hospital bed after Christmas of 1955, I think I have a clearer picture.

The black hole sucked us back to Amsterdam in 1960 and by the following year he didn't have the stamina to walk the block and a half from the Post Office to his law office on Church Street. He had open heart surgery this time, and more railroad tracks and afterwards we all pitched in so he could keep his practice going from home while he recuperated. I helped with the filing.

We actually had a lot of fun in those years. We went camping and drove through Canada and drove up Whiteface Mountain, and we continued to spend a couple of weeks each July at the Brunelli camp in Jaffrey, NH. Dad helped Mom correct her high school English papers and we all very much enjoyed his company. He was witty and wise and awfully smart about many subjects, including politics, where, not unlike his second son, he was something of a contrarian.

He helped found the New York Conservative Party locally in 1962, then ran as a Republican for Alderman in a primary against a long-term incumbent in 1963 (he lost by seven votes). In 1964 the two of us were out trooping for Barry Goldwater.

The politics may not have panned out, but the apple of his eye and fourth son, Sean Thomas, came around in 1966, my brother the only child.

Then came the heart attack in 1968, the continuing deterioration of his mitral valve throughout 1969, the surgery again for seven hours in January of 1970 (by this time I was a freshman in college and fully understood the implications) and the nearly five years of being homebound when he wasn't hospitalized.

By then I was commuting to college and so got to spend more time with him than I ever had, and each moment was precious. Sometimes we'd stay up all night listening to the talk shows from New York City. He encouraged me to work on Jim Buckley's campaign for the Senate in 1970 and *mirabile dictu* (as Jim's brother might say), we finally won one.

I finished college and still didn't know what I wanted to do, so now we actually spent quite a few days as well as nights together.

We kids surprised our parents with a 25th Anniversary party in September of 1973, and a color tv. We cleaned him up and dressed him up and they looked pretty darn good for an old married couple.

By the following Spring he started improving, at long last. I took him to the putting green at the golf course, he attended all my plays, he'd go for walks in the sweet outdoors. He even occasionally climbed the stairs at home. I began to feel some hope. Though his vision was nearly gone (a consequence of the surgery) he even talked about maybe trying to go back to work.

But by the end of the summer he started to slide backwards again. The Nixon thing didn't help.

In and out of the hospital again. One day the visiting nurse couldn't find any blood pressure, so off to St Mary's we went and I stayed with him until he stabilized and I promised to be back the next day. He looked disappointed when I told him I had rehearsal for a benefit musical.

He died early the next morning, December 3, 1974 at the age of 52.

****

On Dad's 60th birthday, five months after Mary and Anna and I moved into our new house in Amsterdam (the black hole syndrome again), I painted a crude sign and drove it into the ground on the site in our back yard that would later include a swing set and sky fort that I built for our kids:

FRANCIS GOING MEMORIAL
SANDBOX
Dedicated April 30, 1982

Flag of My Country
Jun. 14th, 2006 @ 11:02 pm

Flag of My Country
A March, by William Going, c. 1911

Flag of my country,
A greeting 'ere I pass thee,
Child of a people who dared to be free;
Born with the birthright of Freedom eternal,
Sponsor of peace, love and true Liberty:

[Refrain]
Long may you wave,
Flag of the brave,
Wave over land and sea.
Long may you wave, flag of the brave!
Wave on eternally!

From thy white stars shown the first rays of freedom,
Thrilling, exalting the hearts of the brave.
All hearts turn to thee; oh, all voices hail thee!
Pride of the free man, the hope of the slave.

[refrain]

Long may thy folds bathe in God's holy sunshine,
Ever reflecting the joys of the free.
Long may the songs of thy children ascending
Blend with thy colors in sweet harmony!

[refrain]

****

Remarks of Robert N. Going, Corporation Counsel of the City of Amsterdam, to the students of William B. Tecler Elementary School, Flag Day, 2006:

Mayor Emanuele asked me to appear here today for him. He couldn't be here because he's teaching school in Fonda. I feel so bad for him. Imagine, such a beautiful day outside and he's stuck inside a school for the whole day. [laughs and groans].

You have many speakers on your program, so I thought I would tell a story about the flag that I'm positive no one else will tell. It's a story about a man from right here in Amsterdam, New York who wrote a song about the American Flag almost a hundred years ago. His name was William Going, and he was my great-great uncle.

Have you ever heard or sung the song, *You're a Grand Old Flag*?
[many nods and yeahs]

Well, he didn't write that one. That was written by George M. Cohan, the King of Broadway, but that was right around the same time that Will Going, the Prince of Glen Avenue was writing *Flag of My Country*. It tells the story of a man walking down the street who stops when he sees the American Flag. Here are some of the words:

> *Flag of my country,*
> *A greeting 'ere I pass thee,*
> *Child of a people who dared to be free;*

I love that phrase: *Child of a people who dared to be free.*

Dared to be free.

Boys and girls, ten generations ago when they first made the American Flag there wasn't a country anywhere in the world where ordinary people were allowed to think and speak and worship as they pleased and assemble and make their own laws and choose their own leaders except right here in the United States of America, when those people who gave us this flag dared to be free.

We honor the flag in many ways: we stand at attention, we uncover our heads and put our hands over our hearts as the flag passes by. We recite the Pledge of Allegiance, we sing the National Anthem.

But boys and girls, if you truly want to honor the American Flag, then

DARE TO BE FREE!

DARE TO BE FREE!

Grampa Des
Jun. 19th, 2006 @ 09:28 am

Today is Grampa Nichols' birthday. He would have been 110 today.

Now here was a character to end all characters. He wasn't our real grandfather, but he married our grandmother Going before any of us were born, then survived her by eight years, so we sort of inherited him, especially since he had managed to outlive all his close blood relatives, being the only one of the six siblings to marry.

He had some strong bloodlines. I have a family portrait of the Nichols crew from a summer outing in 1898. Des is a two year old. I was quite shocked to realize that I had personally met four of the adults in the picture, all in their mid to late twenties or thirties. One of them, Aunt Sarah, had come calling on Des in the mid 70's from her home in California. She brought along her daughter, grampa's cousin Lucille Bremer, a former Rockette and better known as an MGM starlet who appeared as Judy Garland's older sister in *Meet Me in St. Louis* and as Fred Astaire's co-star and dancing partner in *Yolanda and the Thief* and *Ziegfeld Follies*.

Des tried to get in the Coast Guard during World War I, but was declined and drafted into the army, where he was initially assigned to an artillery unit in Camp Jackson, S.C. From there he received his first public notice in a letter home from the troops to the Amsterdam *Semi-Weekly Democrat*:

> **"Red" Nichols is the battery joke. He keeps us all in an uproar with his jokes and tricks during our off time.**

He knew every old joke there ever was, and was something of a master of the sleight-of-hand, being able to pull a rubber ball or coin out of the darndest places. These skills served him well in his grampa era.

For some reason, he seemed to be the black sheep of his family. In a lot of the pictures he is off standing to the side. He was the only one of the family to leave the McCleary Avenue home, after the war, and would not return except as the upstairs tenant more than thirty years later.

When the war ended he returned to Amsterdam in uniform and took the Lyon Street trolley to the Rockton section of Amsterdam. A middle aged man got on at the next stop and sat next to him, staring ahead and not saying a word. It was only when they had reached their destination that Des turned to him and said, "What's the matter, Pop? Don't you recognize your own son?" He cried telling me the story more than half a century later.

Though he served only five months in the army and never left the states, Desmond F. Nichols became the greatest veteran the American Legion ever saw. Notwithstanding that there was an Irish post, he set his ethnicity aside and teamed up with the Post 701 Wyszomirski boys, rising through the ranks to become commander on multiple occasions. I gather that's where he met our widowed grandmother, and that watering hole was the prime site of their courtship for the next thirteen years. Dad remembered him hiding on their back porch one time (the reason was a bit obscure) and an old-timer related a hilarious tale of a couple of big guys picking him up and hanging him on a coat hook for several hours at a local tavern. The next night he walked by slowly, glanced in the window, and kept going.

During World War II he emceed the entertainment at the Post every weekend, adding to his repertoire. After marrying Gramma in 1949, the two of them bopped around the state and country hitting convention after convention. They particularly enjoyed the one welcoming General MacArthur back home. When they had that state funeral for him, beginning in New York City on a rainy day in 1964, I was staying with them for the day (home sick from school) and they seriously considered hopping in the car and driving the three and a half hours so they could see the cortege pass by. My illness sorta held them back, so we watched it on tv.

He never really recovered from Gramma's sudden death in 1968. A brother and sister followed quickly thereafter and his last much younger brother a couple of years later. His declining years were spent mostly in his underwear in front of the television. On July 4, 1976 he tripped and fell and lay on the floor until the paperboy found him the next day. While in the hospital he suddenly became young again, and thought he was back in the twenties and living in the Barnes Hotel.

He began drawing cartoons for the first time in years, and asked me to help him because some guy kept trying to sell him insurance.

And then, just when life was getting really interesting again, he died.

James Edward Going
Feb. 13th, 2008 @ 12:11 pm

The notice in the Recorder reported the events of February 13, 1934:

> **HEART ATTACK TAKES J.E. GOING**
> Amsterdam Business Man
> Taken by Death at
> His Home
>
> Amsterdam-- James E. Going died Tuesday morning at his home on Wilkes Avenue after a short illness. He suffered from a heart ailment but his death was unexpected. He was a lifelong resident of Amsterdam and a veteran of the World War, serving in the Medical Detachment at Spartansburg, S.C. being in the veterinary department.
>
> Born in Amsterdam, he attended the St. Mary's Institute. During the past eight years he has conducted a retail ice business. He was a member of St. Mary's Church, the Holy Name Society of that church and the John J. Wyszomirski Post 701 of the American Legion.

In 1918 he married Mary Goodison of Brooklyn, by whom he is survived together with a daughter, Marie, and a son, Francis; two sisters, Mrs. John Koch of this city and Mrs. Aaron Mondore of Albany, a brother, David, of Seattle, Wash., and his stepmother, Mrs. Sarah Going of this city.

Today, as I look into the happy, delighted, smiley, googling face of Laura Ann, I think about my own grandfather, whom I never met. Dad was eleven years old that winter, Aunt Marie only thirteen, and Gramma was six months shy of 34.

He was the first son and third child of James Going and Mary Agnes Maxwell when he came into the world in Amsterdam, NY on February 25, 1893. He took the names of his father (and paternal grandfather) and maternal grandfather (Edward Maxwell). His brother Dave was born a couple of years later and before he turned six his mother was dead.

Various relatives took care of the children. The girls, Rhea and Agnes, ended up staying with their maternal aunts, Catherine and Nora Maxwell, profoundly Irish immigrants from Manchester, England. (In her later years when Catherine was accused of being English she would say, "If you put bread in the oven it don't come out kittens!"). When their father remarried the widow Sarah Hussey, the boys went back to live with them.

Little Jim attended St. Mary's Institute through eighth grade.

Not much else is known of his childhood. His father died on May 28, 1916 (at 58).

When the World War came along he was considered a pretty competent horseman. He spent the war years transporting horses from South Carolina to Brooklyn, where they were shipped off to Europe. While in Brooklyn he met and fell in love with Mary Agnes Goodison.

He stayed in Brooklyn, married the Brooklyn Irish lass

before she turned 19, and applied for a position in the FDNY. He passed a battery of tests (only jumping off a building into a safety net remained), but flunked the physical due to recurring asthma. Aunt Marie (Mary Agnes) had come along on August 6, 1920. With the powers that be suggesting the fresh air of Upstate New York might be good for his health, he packed up his little family and moved back to Amsterdam, where he helped deliver my father, Francis, on April 30, 1922 (the doctor was called from the pulpit of St. Mary's Church and arrived at the house just a little behind Dad).

He bought and operated a gas station and tourist camp in Tribes Hill for a couple of years in the twenties, the type of tiny cottages as appear in *It Happened One Night.* The gas station still exists as a private residence and a number of the cottages remain scattered here and there in backyards in Tribes Hill serving as tool sheds. One dollar a night.

Later he started the Going Ice Company and delivered door to door in Amsterdam. I once had a client who, as a teenager, had worked for my grandfather. He told me that one of the customers was a house of ill repute on Division Street. My grandmother refused to allow my grandfather to step foot in the joint, so the kid had to make those deliveries. A dime's a dime.

The company did well. They moved out of rented quarters and into their own home on Wilkes Avenue. Then, in January of 1934 Gramma buried her father in Brooklyn. She returned home to find her husband gravely ill. That February was one of the coldest months in the twentieth century, but Jim, with his raging fever, screamed at Dad to open the windows. Twelve days shy of his 41st birthday, it was over.

Feb. 14, 1934

My dear May,

I was very deeply grieved to hear of the death of Jim, and we all sympathize with you in your grief.

You should be consoled in the thought that you did all you possibly could to relieve him in his suffering. Try to keep up for the children who I hope will always be a consolation to you.

I am sorry May that I could not go up and be with you in these trying times, but trust you will understand.

I will offer my Mass for Jim tomorrow that Our Dear Lord will be merciful to him and receive him so that Eternal Light will shine upon him.

Try to be composed, courageous and resolute through it all.

Knowing how you must feel I will be closing, trusting in Our Dear Lord to give you courage and hope I will be able to see you all soon with Love.

Your loving sister

Gertrude

Mrs. Aaron Mondore
266 Clinton Ave.
Albany, N.Y.
Feb. 22, 1934

My dear Sister and Children:

I trust you will forgive me for not writing sooner. Tonight, although it is now 12:25, I vowed I would not retire before I had written to you. Aaron went to work at 11:30; so far this week he has only had Relief jobs, or what they term "Relief engine", that is he remains at the Albany Station with an engine in case incoming trains have an engine which is out of order.

My heart is with you and wish I were near so that I could be with you and the children.

Anne had a gathering in her head, but, she is better now.

I forgot to get your 'phone number so please send it when you write. Our number is 4-2577. Do not hesitate to call, if you need me, and reverse the charge. Please let me know how you are and what plans, if any, you have made.

Did you have a heavy snow storm? I thought of you and wondered if you were isolated, as it drifted badly here.

I suppose Agnes and the girls have been to see you. We will be up soon as we can. In the meantime, take care of yourself and the dear children. Try to be reconciled and do not worry. I realize it is very hard.

Give Marie and Frankie a big hug and kiss for me. All four are sending love. May God bless and keep you, my dear ones.

Lovingly,   Rhea

A TREE GROWS IN BROOKLYN

The boast of heraldry, the pomp of power,
And all that beauty, all that wealth e'er gave,
Awaits alike th' inevitable hour:-
The paths of glory lead but to the grave.

-Thomas Gray, *Elegy Written in a Country Churchyard*

On a bright November Indian Summer day I undertook an oft-postponed pilgrimage, and set out to find the final resting place of my ancestors in Brooklyn. Finding Holy Cross Cemetery was not particularly easy, having on hand a city map with not quite all the streets on it, thereby providing me with about a square mile of "about there", and a subway map which doesn't necessarily correspond with true geography.

Nonetheless, after a couple of transfers I emerged into a neighborhood of Brooklyn once inhabited by Irish immigrants and now virtually exclusively a vibrant Caribbean community, whose unique ethnic food tastes no doubt were responsible for my most favorite business sign yet, the "Brooklyn Jerk Center."

A few blocks south, a few blocks east and I could see in the distance the open green space of my destination. Remarkably I had stumbled upon the main entrance to the cemetery, and even more remarkably upon the cemetery office where a very nice lady looked through the records to find my great-grandfather, Frank Goodison.

I knew something about him, that he was the son of a Civil War veteran Irish immigrant, that his mother had died when he was a small boy and that he remained with his father and new stepmother while his two sisters had been placed in an orphanage. He raised five children of his own. The youngest, my grandmother, was born in 1900. His trade was ornamental plastering, his skills employed all over New York City, including the old Wannamaker's building. I knew from photographs that, like many working men of his day, he looked far older than the 67 he reached on his ultimate birthday.

My grandmother left her young family in Amsterdam and attended her father on his death bed in January of 1934, writing this poignant letter home to her husband:

Dear Jim

Just a line, hoping you received the telegram.

Papa is just failing more all the time, is all I can say. Saturday he was very bad and the folks didn't think I would arrive in time, and did I rush over from the station. I am happy he knew me, and he had the idea I knew nothing of his being so sick, just thought I came on the excursion, but is now every once in a while asking if I got the train on time of course Gertie & Frankie & Lucy are continually making excuses, saying my ticket is good for a few days. Gertie is taking it so hard, my heart aches for her, & Lucy is all in, not having slept since Friday. Frank May & Frankie are attending to him, at different times.

Mrs. Leith and daughter were here last night & wonderful help.

Jim there is really no need of you coming down, as yet. I will let you know immediately if conditions change. The Doctor was here this A.M. and said he is filling up now, says it is only a matter of time. He was prayed for in church yesterday & people are continually calling up & calling at the house. He can not have any visitors at all now, people just sit in the dining room.

Poor Gertie, Jim, she said oh! May, how I try to keep up. I don't want him to know I cry. She tells him she has a very bad cold. She broke down today a couple of times. Frankie got through work at 3 o'clock, he is here now.

The weather is warm and so damp.

Tell Agnes I appreciate her taking care of the children. Hope they are O.K. also hope Agnes will be able to manage with the clothes for them. I know she will wash Marie's dress and Frankie's blouse. Tell them all to pray for papa please.

Jim I couldn't call you up. The talking annoys him and every once in a while he knows what you say, so I sent the telegram.

You will hear from me again. Let me hear from you and if you get a hold of a few dollars please send some to me. I will need it badly.

Lucy bought a new coat and said I could wear her other one.

Lots of love to all.

Good-night.

May

Barely a month after burying her father, my grandmother became a pre- social security widow at the age of 33.

Armed with a cemetery map, a section, a row number and a lot number I set out for a long walk, past magnificent monuments and mausoleums, tributes to the great and the mighty. The row and lot numbers are actually carved into the tombstones, so before long I was moving swiftly along our row until . . . nothing. I checked the numbers again and sure enough I was standing in the right place, but there where the tombstone should be was a blank space, an unmarked grave holding the remains of Frank Goodison and his wife Mary Philomena Hannon Goodison.

Well, not quite a blank space. Rising out of the lot was a tree, a magnificent tree, of a variety unknown to me, with a trunk a full eight feet around. I smiled, took a picture, and a leaf, and thought of the ironic fate of my great-grandmother, in the ground some eighty-four years.

She was born aboard ship, the daughter of Michael Hannon and Ellen Ford. Whether her parents were married is a matter of some conjecture, as records do not exist and the mother died in childbirth. Mary Philomena told her children that the ship was flying the Irish flag on the Irish Sea and that therefore she was as Irish as anyone from Cork or Tipperary. Even as a child I knew this yarn was a bit faulty because there WAS no Irish Flag back then.

Michael Hannon brought baby Mary to Brooklyn and placed her with her maternal grandmother Ford where she was raised as a sister to two of her cousins. Michael Hannon was never heard from again.

The rest of this story is based on family legend and has the added advantage that it just might be true. My grandmother believed it to be true, and believed it long before, as shall become obvious, it was particularly advantageous to do so.

Records show that there was a Michael Hannon, originally from Limerick, who settled in Massachusetts about twenty-five miles from Boston. My grandmother believed him to be the very same Michael Hannon who was her grandfather. The problem is that this Michael Hannon already had a family, a wife and several children. And while Mary Philomena Hannon was born May 2, 1865, this Michael had another daughter born October 31, 1865 named Mary Josephine Hannon.

So, it is possible that the two Marys were half-sisters, though I probably wouldn't credit the story at all were it not for the fact that Mary Josephine bore a striking resemblance to my grandmother.

When she grew up, Mary Josephine married a rising star in the Boston political firmament, John Francis Fitzgerald. When she finally left this world in 1964, just shy of her 99th birthday, she had lived long enough to see her husband elected Mayor of Boston, two of her grandsons become United States Senators, and a third nominated, and saw one of them inaugurated president of the United States.

Meanwhile, Mary Philomena grew up in poverty, had a child out of wedlock, married a common laborer, struggled through four more children, wept when her only son went off to war and died in a tenement of influenza in 1917.

But despite all her sorrows, she treasured her family and her God, possessed of the simple faith and virtues of the humble, which she passed on as her only legacy. She lies in that unmarked grave in Brooklyn, where a tree grows.

Let not Ambition mock their useful toil,
Their homely joys, and destiny obscure;
Nor Grandeur hear with a disdainful smile
The short and simple annals of the Poor.

The Other

Memories
Sep. 4th, 2006 @ 02:02 am

I did a little shopping in Office Max today and picked up a 250 gig portable usb hard drive for about 125 bucks with tax. That works out to about 50 cents a gigabyte in round numbers.

A far cry from the 32 meg internal drive I bought some years ago for about $300 and change. Let's see, rounding again that came to $10 a megabyte or $10,000 a gigabyte. That was probably mid to late 80's.

Of course, when I got my first job out of law school in 1980 I worked for a technologically advanced firm which purchased a TRS 80 Model II for the bookkeeper with dual 8 inch floppy drives, state of the art.

Our tech consultant told us that if we were interested, some after-market people were making available hard drives ("Winchesters") that could be rigged into the system.

They came in two sizes: 5 megs or 10 megs.

Five thousand dollars for the former, ten thousand for the latter, or a thousand dollars a megabyte.

Now they say you could daisy-chain up to 255 devices per computer, so, in theory at least, that could get you up to a gigabyte or two. That would make the cost, let's see, a thousand times a thousand equals ONE MILLION DOLLARS per gigabyte.

That would make the drive I bought today, not even taking into account the speed and power drain differentials, worth TWO HUNDRED FIFTY MILLION DOLLARS.

Of course, we have to adjust for inflation, so by applying the CPI change since 1980, that comes to a cool SIX HUNDRED FIFTEEN MILLION DOLLARS.

I'm glad I waited.

Young Republic
Feb. 21st, 2007 @ 08:06 pm

The realization that a grandson of President John Tyler (who was born while Washington still lived) is alive and living in the family homestead in Virginia prompted a discussion at *The Corner at National Review Online* which morphed into a degree of separation from John Quincy Adams game.

Here's mine:

In 1980 I met and shook hands with former Congressman HAMILTON FISH (I even have a couple of hand-typed letters from him). Hamilton was born on December 7, 1888, so he was a mere 91 when we chatted at the Republican National Convention in Detroit, Michigan. He had been an ally of Teddy Roosevelt and an enemy of Franklin Roosevelt.

His grandfather, also named HAMILTON FISH, had been Secretary of State in the Grant administration. Since he died in 1893, he most certainly would have met his young grandson. They all lived in the same neighborhood. (HIS father, by the way, had been a close friend of Alexander Hamilton).

In 1843 the elder Fish entered Congress as a Whig and served with

JOHN QUINCY ADAMS, who, on June 17, 1775 as an eight year old boy, stood on a hill behind the family home in Quincy, holding his mother Abigail's hand, and watched the smoke from the Battle of Bunker Hill in distant Boston.

How's that? It's 2007 and I'm only three degrees of separation from the American Revolution.

Young Republic II
Mar. 3rd, 2007 @ 06:37 pm

More fascinating leaps across history, this time with Fr. George Rutler, one of my favorite priests. If you're in the greater metropolitan NYC area, be sure to catch his Sunday Mass. I did. And will again.

The Corner on National Review Online:

Fr. Rutler on the Young Republic [Peter Robinson]

To the "Young Republic" postings of a week or so ago, Rev. George Rutler, the unofficial chaplain of this happy Corner, offers these addenda:

Item: When he was a boy, Fr. Rutler shook the hand of a man whose grandfather had shaken hands with Washington.

Item: Fr. Rutler once knew a man whose father had heard the Gettysburg address. A farmboy in Gettysburg, the man's father had helped erect the platform on which Lincoln and the other dignitaries were seated—and had then positioned himself underneath as they addressed the crowd. The man's father maintained for the rest of his life that Lincoln did not say "*of* the people, *by* the people, and *for* the people" but "of the *people*, by the *people*, and for the *people*."
03/02 12:45 PM

****

The Gettysburg story must be true, because my father the elocutionist insisted that Lincoln would have put the emphasis on "People". At least that's the way he taught the Gettysburg address to me when I was in fifth grade.

It was the custom to have a lad my age recite the address each Memorial Day at the services held at Green Hill Cemetery, up the hill in back of my City Hall office.

We worked on it for weeks. I would have to do it from memory, at the same time avoiding passing out and falling off the platform. My knees were shaking as I awaited my turn next to the young attorney who would be giving the main address, Vince Vicinanzo, for whom I would later work when I was a young attorney. He smiled and told me to relax, and I did.

Dad stood in front of me, beaming. He loved the cadence of Lincoln and I think saw himself as the Maestro conducting the Gettysburg Symphony. He waved his hands gently through the air as the speech built to a crescendo.

> That we here, highly resolve that these dead shall not have
> died in vain!
> That this nation, under God, shall have a NEW BIRTH OF
> FREEDOM!
> And that Government of the *People*,
> By the *People*,
> And for the *People*
> [And here the palm of his hand swept through the air with a final flourish]
> Shall not perish from the earth!

****

How I miss him.

COMMENTS
From: (Anonymous)
Date: March 4th, 2007 11:10 pm (local)

Your Honor-
That is a lovely story and beautifully told. Your father was a wise man. I understand that at a recent history committee meeting at the Union League Club across the street from me, the author of a book on the Address played a recording of it by an actor, and he got it right too.

I also knew a Mrs. Longmaid from Paterson NJ whose father knew Lincoln. He was born in Scotland and was going to set up a textile factory in Texas and went to Washington for advice and Lincoln packed him off to Paterson instead. I remember her saying, "Father always spoke very highly of Lincoln. "

[-Father Rutler]

Hill Hoods
Aug. 6th, 2007 @ 09:06 pm

I hope that my political antagonists don't read too much into this, but when I was a teenager I belonged to an organization known as the Hill Hoods.

Now, we weren't hoods in the traditional sense of juvenile delinquent hoodlums of that era, though some might have considered us a bit mischievous from time to time. Pretty much every kid who lived on Market Hill in Amsterdam was a "member", and most of our friends no matter where they lived. It didn't even matter if we went to Amsterdam High or St. Mary's/Bishop Scully. It didn't matter whether we hung out at Fariello's or Mac's or Vidulich's Bakery or just sat on Jack Fitzgibbon's porch making up awful puns and watching the trucks go down Glen Avenue.

It didn't matter if we were male or female. A good number fell in love for the first time and had first dates over nickel cokes without ever leaving the hill. Some even married ultimately.

The largest group of Hill Hoods were within a couple of years either way of my class of 1969, though with baby-booming our legacy passed on to the younger siblings for quite a while thereafter.

Back in 1981 Tim Kelly was getting married, so Tim Blanchfield organized the "First Annual Tim Kelly Stag Party and Hill Hood Reunion" and it was a smashing success, a lovely afternoon in Shuttleworth Park. So the following year we had the "Second Annual Tim Kelly Stag Party and Hill Hood Reunion". We did this off and on for a number of years, back when most of us were starting families and bringing the kids along.

After a while, though, it petered out. But the friendships didn't. Friendships of your youth seem to be the ones that last forever, the ones that seem most natural, the ones that don't require whole lots of conversations about what are you doing and how many kids and what are they doing. Mostly we can just pick up where we left off years or decades ago, and exchange a laugh again about some near-forgotten piece of foolishness.

After a long time, the 27th annual Tim Kelly Stag Party and Hill Hood Reunion took place this past Saturday. Most of our kids are grown now; some of the hoods have grandchildren. Something like a hundred people showed up, including some of the parents.

"I don't know, Bob. Do I qualify as a Hill Hood?" asked Mrs. LaBate.

Yeah, you do.

Her son Jim, originator of the LaBate Invitational (2-man basketball) Tournament (LIT), and author of two charming novellas about the old neighborhood, *Let's Go Gaels* and *Mickey Mantle Day in Amsterdam*, was there, and his sisters Marie and Kathy and their Dad.

Tim Kelly himself made a rare appearance. Tim Blanchfield, or course, and brother Dan. Lots of Rileys and Quandts and Hrycaj's. Sue was my Senior Ball date, a fact barely mentioned in one of her books (not available at Amazon) and not at all in mine (not available anywhere except this blog). There was a good turn-out from the McDermotts. They always lived on Division Street and not Market Hill. But they had relatives on the hill, so that qualified, I guess.

Though not formed as a political organization (not formed at all, really), the Hill Hoods did have one bright shining moment, the class elections of our sophomore year, 1966-67 at the brand new Bishop Scully High School. We ran Joe Cushing for president and Tim Kelly (of perennial stag party fame) for treasurer. Tim Blanchfield made signs saying "Free Shots from Dr. Kelly if Tim Wins" (Tim's dad was a prominent local physician).

Balloting took place during our lunch period, and on the honor system. At the time there were about 120 members of our class. Tony Centi, future restaurateur, shocked the principal, Father Oathout, by coming in first in the three way race for president with 250 votes, so much so that his votes were thrown out for this grave dishonor to the school, and Cushing, with 125 votes, was declared the winner. Kelly swept in on his coat tails.

Orest Babiak didn't show up at the reunion for some unknown reason. This six foot five concrete mountain, son of Ukranian immigrants, is one our more colorful members. He was my partner in the first LIT.

Besides having the memorable line, "FLIGHT 36 FOR GLOCCAMORA LEAVING IN FIVE MINUTES" in our eighth grade play, he is also known as a man of some deep mystery. About a year before the first Tim Kelly Stag Party, he tracked down Dan Blanchfield at his father's camp at the end of a dirt road in Galway toward the end of nowhere.

"Banchfield! I hear you're getting married!"

"That's right, Orest."

"Where?"

"New Jersey."

"I'll be there!"

No date, no time, no place, no invitation.

He showed up, of course.

I could have used his skills this Sunday when I found myself in New York City, on the day that my blogger friend The Nightfly was tying the knot somewhere in New Jersey, just a tunnel ride away. How neat that would have been.

Probably the highlight of the party was the surprise appearance of Virginia Raiano, co-proprietor with her husband of Mac's, the local confectionery, sundries and minor groceries store (they sold a lot of eggs around Halloween), the place where most of us gravitated. A good number of the girls worked there at one time or another.

The Welches were well-represented at the party, Barbara and my classmates Bernie and Gail and their spouses.

Once, over Christmas break in 1965, when we were 14, I met Gail at Mac's and bought her a nickel cherry coke and had one myself.

Funny the things you remember.

A Boy Named Hsu
Sep. 5th, 2007 @ 09:23 pm

(with apologies to Johnny Cash)

I was out in California just a while back,
Hopin' that a judge would cut me some slack--
Just a little fraud back in 1992.
Judge said,"Gonna sentence you another day.
"Now you make sure you don't run away!"
I told him, "Hell, you can trust a boy named Hsu."

Well we all thought that was some great joke
And everyone laughed (them legal folk)
And the next plane out I got on it and flew.
And I soon set up in old Hong Kong
Where every other feller's name is Huang
And no one's gonna notice another boy named Hsu.

And I coulda just looked around and stayed
And practiced at my garment trade
And maybe occasionally worked a scam or two.
But by and by I heard aroun'
That the Clintons moved to Washington town,
And I thought, "Easy pickins, for a boy named Hsu!"

It warn't no problem to get invited to tea,
I just practiced my diversity
With a wad of bills and an enigmatic smile.
So I said, "My name is Hsu;
"How do you do?"
And Hillary said,"Mr. Hsu, I like your style."

So I peddled some a this and I peddled some a that
And I was the world's best Democrat.
And my friends said,"We'd like to give a hundred thou' for
you."
So every cabbie and every maid
To all the Democrats they paid
And life looked awful swell for a boy named Hsu.

Well a guy can be smooth and a guy can be smarty
And own the Democratic Party,
But the long arm of the law can still come through.
And one day they came a'calling round
And I was California-bound
And bound with brand-new handcuffs just for Hsu.

The judge he set some mighty bail,
"Two million bucks or off to jail,
"And better not flee the country, 'cause if you do,
"This judge here will be awful sore!"
And I said, "Judge, just say no more.
"Everyone knows you can trust a boy named Hsu!"

Red Sox

The Division Series
Oct. 3rd, 2005 @ 01:01 pm

Our family has never been particularly lucky when it comes to lotteries and such. Oh, I've won my share of raffles, but nearly always during an election year when I feel a compulsion to give it back to whatever worthy cause sponsored my good fortune. Once I won a bottle of wine at a Holy Name Communion Breakfast and before I had even returned to my seat I had been talked into donating it for the St. Anthony Society Basket of Cheer. I didn't even know there was a St. Anthony Society. Frankly, I'm still not sure I wasn't conned.

Imagine then my delight a couple of weeks ago to learn that my beloved daughter Anna had won the lottery to purchase two tickets for the American League Division Series in Fenway Park!

Of course, the very next day the Sox had been knocked down to second place by the Yankees. At the same time, it looked like Cleveland was building a lock on the Wild Card. Now, we're optimistic fans this year, but there are still those 86 years of scars left over.

The family curse replaces the Bambino curse.

So then the day comes to buy the tickets and Anna's working so I had to go on line at precisely noon, at which time I was put into a "Virtual Waiting Room" for about 45 minutes. I had a meeting going on in my office so I kept one eye on the company and one eye on the computer. Suddenly I jumped up, grabbed the keyboard and started typing furiously.

First I had to pick the game, then the seats. Game One, of course. Sure thing if they make it into the playoffs. No seats except a couple of very expensive partial views. No standing room. OK, the heck with that. Game Two (or Game Four depending on who opens where in the best of five series). Standing room's ok. GREAT! TWO TICKETS RESERVED!!

You have three minutes and thirty seconds to complete the form and purchase your tickets.

OK, Anna laid it all out for me . . .the addresses, the password, the credit card numbers . . . Wait, they want her telephone number. What the heck is her telephone number? I grab the phonebook out of the drawer and feverishly look it up. Thank God they didn't change it when they moved last month. OK, all set.

Everything else goes in. ENTER!!!!

There is an error. You need to put spaces in the credit card number according to the following pattern xxxx xxxx xxxx xxxx. You have forty-five seconds to complete this form.

OK, Ok, I can do that.

SPACE SPACE SPACE . . .ENTER!!!!

There is an error. You need to enter the area code and the phone number as a single 10 digit number in the following format: xxxxxxxxxx. You have eleven seconds to complete this form.

Wait, the credit card number needs spaces, but the phone number needs no spaces. The pellet with the poison's in the vessel with the pestle but the chalice with the palace is the brew that is true. No, the pellet with the poison's in the flagon with the dragon and the vessel with the pestle is the brew that is true . . .

ENTER!! (Twelve seconds later, apparently).

We're sorry. We are no longer holding the tickets requested. Please try again.

AAAGGGGGHHHHH!!!!!! I screamed and the folks at my meeting were becoming a bit concerned and my secretary ran into the office.

Well, to ease the suspense, despite a couple of glitches I got the tickets second time around, and they arrived by priority mail and the Sox beat the Yankees two games out of three and ended up tied, but the Yanks were declared

Division Champs anyway and Cleveland lost a whole mess of games so the Red Sox open in Chicago tomorrow (Tuesday) and play again Wednesday then come home Friday and on Saturday, if neither team has swept the first three games, I'll be wandering around Fenway Park for nine or more innings because the Yankee-loving guy she married has no interest in the game so Anna's taking her Dad! Schilling will be on the mound and I'll have a big smile on my face, like I did last year when I was at Game 5 of the ALCS at Fenway sitting in the bleachers with my kid brother cheering our hearts out for 14 innings until Big Papi dropped that single in to end it and then we kept cheering for another half hour or more and rolled into the streets high-fiving everyone and singing about Tessie and come to think of it if I live to be a thousand I don't think there could possibly be another night like that.

But Saturday will be nice. If there is a Saturday.

[Editor's Note: There wasn't.]

I, Damon
Dec. 26th, 2005 @ 10:24 am

Is resistance futile?

Has the Yankee Borg assimilated Johnny Damon?

There can be no greater contrast in styles than the 2003-05 Red Sox and the 2003-05 Yankees. The former were composed of rugged individualists, each exploring the limits of his own identity and skills, joined in a raucous voluntary union with minimal direction; the latter equally talented individuals who completely surrendered their identities to become part of the Yankee collective, its perpetual mission to seek out All-Stars and assimilate them, governed by the ultimate Borg Queen George Steinbrenner.

There are many in Red Sox Nation who are showing signs of despair.

But wait . . . . Suppose that the transfer of Johnny Damon to the Yankees is NOT the most colossal management blunder of all time. For the sake of argument, let us suspend our belief in the utter stupidity and recklessness of the Front Office. Suppose, just suppose, that this is a move of pure genius.

I need hardly explain if you've gotten this far that in *Star Trek, The Next Generation* "The Borg" was a collectivist society wandering the universe and converting by conquest whole peoples. Individuality was crushed and each became a drone controlled completely by the collective.

Then along comes Hugh Borg, in the episode *I, Borg*, who, by accident, becomes separated from the collective and nurtured by the Enterprise crew. Eventually, he begins to think of himself as "I" and voluntarily returns to the Borg to change their ways. Once the Borg drones start thinking as individuals, their whole evil system breaks down and the universe is saved for another week or two.

So, WHAT IF the Red Sox deliberately sent Johnny Damon, the ultimate "I", the ultimate Individual, the ultimate IDIOT to infiltrate the Yankee Borg and ultimately weaken and destroy them? How long can the Evil Empire resist his infectious style? How long before Steinbrenner must suspend the entire team for growing chin hair?

Off season.

The time of dreams.

Promise Fulfilled
May. 23rd, 2006 @ 09:18 am

Well, as expected, Big Poppy had a grand old time with Anna and Bob and Bob's sidekick Jenna at Fenway Park last night. Just being with the kids is reward enough, but then Curt Schilling, he of the bloody sock, fulfilled the promise he made last week and pitched better.

It was, in fact, classic Schilling, totally dominant for the eight innings he stood on the mound, letting in only one run (I had my back turned at just that moment and missed Damon's hit, but I booed anyway), with five mostly scattered hits, a bunch of strikeouts, no walks (only Giambi came close to walking, to load the bases, in a classic showdown that Schilling won for the third out of a dangerous inning), a vicious splitter and judicious use of his new high and tight get-em-off-the-plate fast ball.

His strike to ball ratio was up over seventy per cent, and very, very few of the balls could be viewed as anything but deliberate.

Those of you who recall my story of how I helped Notre Dame beat LSU may appreciate (or not) the fact that I had the famed rosary with me, and numerous witnesses to my careful and sparing use of it with Ortiz and Ramirez. As soon as they each got their two RBI's (within the space of a couple of pitches) it went back in the pocket, though I nearly brought it out again with Foulke on the mound in the 9th. All praise to Our Lady of Victory!

****

Anna and I traveled by car and parked at the Riverside T station for the train to Fenway. Unfortunately we had to switch to a shuttle bus due to some track problem. Fortunately, the shuttle took us right past Emmanuel College, where I was able to tip my hat in memory of Mom's birthday in front of the school where she finished at the top of her class in 1947.

The afternoon was bright and sunny, so when we met up with Bob and Jenna we wandered the streets for a while, drinking in the atmosphere. Eventually, while waiting for Gate E to open, we bumped into Stewart O'Nan, author, with Stephen King, of *Faithful*, that just tremendous memoir of the 2004 championship season. We had seen him at the Hall of Fame in Cooperstown nearly exactly a year earlier. He was most gracious, bubbly even, as we swapped baseball stories of that and other years, including where we were when his hometown hero Bill Mazeroski hit that homer in Pittsburgh to defeat the Yanks in October of 1960.

I told him, sincerely, that I thought his part of the book was better written than King's and he laughed (he laughs most easily) and said that I shouldn't read too much into that, because he, Stewart, did all the editing.

When the gates opened, he hustled immediately to grab his traditional post at the point on the third base line, whipping out his glove and trying to snag every batting practice foul that came his way and calling out to all the players by name. He must have ten thousand scuffed balls in his collection by now, and still he stands there with the excitement of a Little Leaguer at his first Major League game.

God, I love baseball!

Confession
May. 29th, 2007 @ 10:36 am

I hope my political opponents never get ahold of this story, but the truth is that back in the 1956/57 school year I was thrown out of Mrs. Bealfeld's kindergarten class at Westmere Elementary School and forced to sit in the hall for about a million hours, all the while scrunching myself up in a tight ball to avoid being seen by Principal Cleary.

My transgression?

I had in my possession a plastic coin bearing the likeness of All-star third baseman Frank Malzone of the Boston Red Sox. While sitting in a circle on the floor with the teacher and my classmates, I absent-mindedly switched it from hand to hand. Mrs. B. told me to put it away.

A couple of minutes later I dropped it on the hard floor where it made a clunk.

Well, Mrs. Bealfeld noticed, and I was outta there in a flash, the first and only time anyone got tossed that entire school year.

I'll leave it to the opposition researchers to uncover the rest of my primary and secondary record.

****

Frank Malzone got a good chuckle out of that story last night when I met up with him at Fenway Park, as he autographed my ticket.

He told me I looked pretty good for a guy who was in kindergarten in his first full season with the Sox. He looked pretty darn good for 77 himself. A most pleasant fellow, and one of the heroes of my youth, notwithstanding his part in blemishing my Permanent Record Card.

-180-

ALCS Game One
Oct. 13th, 2007 @ 02:13 pm

Well, there we are, just under the middle of the Jumbotron featuring John Hancock in deepest center field. The color, the pageantry, the tradition, the crowd --- all fantastic from our cat-bird seats.

Little Bob and I sat right in front of a guy giving a non-stop commentary on the game, in case we missed anything, which was good, because to try to see the instant replay directly over our heads was kinda tough.

"The count's two and one, that's two balls and one strike. The last pitch was a 93 mile an hour fastball. There's two men on base, second and third, with one out. Now they're intentionally walking the batter so they can set up the double play."

Being kind by nature, you can ask anyone, I chose to assume he was describing the game to a blind friend rather than trying out for Joe Morgan's job, which, frankly, he could do better easily.

Turns out he had his son with him, maybe five or six years old. That was OK. I had my son with me, too.

So I told the kid how I was around his age the first time I came to Fenway Park. Ted Williams was playing left field.

****

I can't figure out why the Blessed Mother has such an interest in the Red Sox, like she did with Notre Dame a few years ago. I mean, Notre Dame you can pretty much understand without difficulty.

To explain, I have this rosary that used to belong to my father that still prays pretty well. I sometimes bring it out in certain athletic situations. In 2006 at Fenway, for example, it was responsible for 4 rbi's on two consecutive pitches, at which point I put it back in my pocket (I don't like to be piggish or push the envelope, though I later had to take it out again in the 9th when Keith Foulke got in trouble).

Last night the score was tied with the bases loaded in the third and Manny Ramirez at the plate. I figured this was as good a time as any for the Big Mom to do her stuff and figuring deep center field would work just as well as those seats behind the plate where that guy who looks like Redford sits, I took it out for a little while, and according to *Yahoo Sports* the following occurred:

> - M. Ramirez walked, J. Lugo scored, K. Youkilis to third, D. Ortiz to second
> - M. Lowell ground rule double to right, D. Ortiz and K. Youkilis scored, M. Ramirez to third
> - J. Varitek grounded out to third, M. Ramirez scored, M. Lowell to third, B. Kielty to second

That's enough. I put it back in my pocket. I hope nobody made fun of Coco Crisp when I left him standing there.

Well, the Sox did pretty well on their own after that and I only took it out again when Becket was having trouble getting a third strike for his fifth K, and he promptly got it, so that makes the Mother of God 4 for 4 with 4 RBI's, a walk, a double and a strike-out.

****

Before the game we hung out at the Sox bullpen and I tried my best to get the attention of Amsterdam native and Red Sox Bullpen Coach Gary Tuck, but the noise level was ridiculous and he never quite looked my way. He looks much better in red and white than he did in those stupid pinstripes.

Before even getting to the game I stopped in Mom's home town of Franklin, MA to pick up Bob Jr. who's working at Dean College for the week. We had time to grab a quick visit with my uncle and Godfather Bob Brunelli. The three Bobs talked baseball for about 45 minutes. His son (and my cousin), the fourth Robert, a life-long Red Sox fan, may be a little conflicted as he lives and works in Denver and has been to see the Rockies a few times (including the last game they lost) and it would be kind of hard NOT to root for that remarkable bunch who came out of nowhere to now take a 2-0 lead in the NLCS.

****

To throw out the first pitch they brought in that kid who pocketed the Ramirez pop fly last week, snatching it right from above the glove of the Angels' catcher, which ultimately led to the tying run. He received a most welcome reception. It will be interesting to watch over the next fifty years to see whether he'll ever be able to top this week in his life.

****

Whatever happens from hereon out, Bob and I witnessed one of the great teams of all time playing in beautiful and powerful sync last night, and it was a wondrous thing to behold.

Plus they had *Smithwick's* on tap.

Catholic

Were not our hearts burning within us . . .
Jun. 1st, 2005 @ 11:01 pm

Dueling bloggers over at the Dawn Patrol are busy debating the existence of God, a debate which includes the rages of a very bitter purported ex-priest. I will pray for him.

I'm a cradle Catholic. I missed out on the rush of being knocked off a horse and challenged directly by the Lord. I envy those who have had that experience, "the hour I first believed." My parents believed, and I believed them. And I've never doubted, which I suppose is a gift in itself.

Having a father who confirmed what my mother taught I'm sure made my faith stronger. When I was a boy I had a very naive faith. I remember talking to some younger kids through a fence in their back yard. They had never heard about God. I was surprised that their mother hadn't told them, and said so. They ran back into the house to check with her and came back.

"My mother doesn't believe in God."

Now I was truly puzzled.

"Is she a Communist?" I asked. They went back to check.

"No, she says she's not a Communist. Can we play the God game some more?"

So I told them about the Trinity (always a good place to start), about the Creation, and Adam and Eve, and Noah, and about Jesus of Nazareth, who was a prophet mighty in deed and word before God and all the people.

I had never seen those two kids before, and never saw them again.

Another time, when I was maybe eleven, Dad and I were riding in the car discussing the greatness of Douglas MacArthur.

"Dad, MacArthur is a great man [he was still alive at the time]. But why isn't he Catholic?" (I worried about his Episcopalian soul).

Dad struggled for a moment. "The Gift of Faith is a great mystery," he said. "I can't explain why God gives it so freely to some of us and not to others."

Mysterium fidei. Incredible as it sounds, I knew exactly what he meant.

There was hardly a thought Dad thunk that I didn't intuitively agree with. The oddball thing is that we were both by nature contrarians. We didn't much care for the existing political establishment. To be for Goldwater in New York, even upstate, in 1964 was not considered a great career move, for example.

I listen to my doctors, but take with a grain of salt the latest medical prevailing opinions, having seen them change so often in my lifetime. I didn't trust Walter Cronkite and have trusted even less the global warming "experts" who while I was in college were predicting the imminent arrival of a new ice age and that the world oil supply would be completely used up by 1983. Teachers, professors, even nuns gave pronouncements which I quickly ignored.

And yet, I believe. If anything my Faith has grown stronger and stronger. For me, it just all fits.

The events of recent months: the Schiavo case, the death of one pope and birth of a new papacy, the homilies of Benedict and the writings of John Paul, have filled me with a new fervor. I can't explain it, but I know it's there and very, very real. It brings me peace.

I shake my head, and all I can say is, "*Mysterium fidei*."

And I feel as one with my friends on the road to Emmaus, who recounted to the apostles what had taken place on the way, and how He was made known to them in the breaking of the bread.

My Spiritual Bouquet
Sep. 28th, 2005 @ 01:10 pm

I had the blessed fortune of attending a good Catholic parochial school in a working class multi-ethnic town before Vatican II. It was the era of the baby-boomers and the classes were huge, something like 43 in a room when I started in fourth grade in 1960.

I am reminded of that wonderful song in *The King and I*: "When I was a lad/World was better spot/What was so was so/What was not was not/Now I am a man/Things have changed a lot/Some things nearly so/Others nearly not."

No such problem as a young Catholic. The rules were all laid out neatly for us. We knew, for example, that our parents were pretty much destined for hell if they didn't vote for Jack Kennedy that year. (I was, even then, something of a contrarian. There were exactly six Nixon supporters out of the 43.)

On Friday, January 20, 1961, the father of one of our classmates delivered a table-top 19" black and white television up the three flights of stairs to our classroom so we could watch the historical moment of the inauguration of the first Catholic president.

"The President-elect began his day with a hearty breakfast of steak and eggs."

We all turned instinctively to Sister, who had gasped and was holding her hand over her mouth. She made a quick recovery.

"I'm sure he received a special dispensation, boys and girls. The Archbishop is empowered to waive the no meat on Friday rule for special occasions, and what could be more special than this?"

This nine-year-old contrarian chuckled to himself but otherwise kept his mouth shut.

****

We engaged, as a matter of habit, in what are now described as "the pious practices of the faithful", non-liturgical but spiritually enriching exercises. Like Bishop Sheen, we placed at the top of each paper the letters "J.M.J." with a cross beneath, a quiet invocation of the guidance of the Holy Family. Years later, in Sister Anna Roberta's Latin class we wrote instead "A.M.D.G." for *Ad Maiorum Dei Gloriam*, "To the greater glory of God". We learned and recited the *Angelus* prayers every day after lunch, sang the old hymns, took part in the May crownings of statues of the Virgin Mary.

It was a great honor to be an altar boy. We needed to be able to recite all the responses in Latin from memory. *Introibo ad altare Dei. Ad Deum qui laetificat iuventutem meum.* "I will go to the altar of God, the God who gives joy to my youth."

We'd be assigned a week at a time of daily masses. I always got the early one, seven a.m., which meant that I had to be out the door by 6:30 to walk the mile or so to the church with my cassock and surplice dragging over my back, in order to arrive in time to light the candles and otherwise prepare for the Mass. There used to be a short-cut through the City Hall grounds where I now work, dumping out on High Street. I remember one cold, pitch-dark winter morning when I was ten or eleven, taking that turn on High Street when a gray-haired, roughly-dressed woman emerged from the shadows.

"Boy!" she called.

I stopped. "Yes ma'am?"

She stumbled a bit.

"Boy. Say a prayer for me."

"Yes ma'am."

****

Saying prayers for people was something we did a lot. On All Souls' Day, we were told, if we made a visit to the Blessed Sacrament and said three Our Fathers and three Hail Marys and three Glory Be's we could release a soul from Purgatory to Heaven for all eternity. What an awesome thought!

After school the church was filled with young students dashing to the altar rail, saying nine quick prayers and dashing out the door and turning around and dashing back in for a new visit which would reset the clock to enable us to release yet another soul from the place of suffering. If we ran out of relatives and acquaintances, we could rescue souls at random, or by other identification, such as "the most neglected soul in purgatory." Any prayers wasted on those already in eternal bliss would be banked in the "Treasury of Merit" and of course all those souls freed by our good actions would spend the rest of forever praying for us before the Throne of God.

I wonder every once in a while if I was able to get through some of those rough times because some long-forgotten heavenly friend was putting in a good word for me with the Old Man.

****

On special occasions (other than inaugurations) we would make "Spiritual Bouquets" for our parents, usually with a hand-drawn picture of the Eucharist or the Sacred Heart of Jesus on the cover, wherein we would pledge to say so many rosaries, make so many Visits, offer up so many Masses, etc. so that God would pour forth spiritual blessings on them. And I'm pretty sure He did.

Mom kept them all. I've still got them. I was pretty generous. I think I may still owe a few of those rosaries.

"My Spiritual Bouquet," they all said.

Could there be a better gift?

How I Helped Notre Dame Beat LSU
Oct. 15th, 2005 @ 10:06 pm

Notre Dame's thrilling loss (if there is such a thing) to USC today brought me back to the day I helped the Fighting Irish beat LSU.

The year was 1998. LSU had a pretty darn good team, featuring a running back by the name of Kevin Faulk who went on to a substantial career with the New England Patriots. They did not seem to be intimidated playing to a packed house at Notre Dame with all the drama and spirit and history that goes with that legendary field. In fact, some of their fans even held a banner that read, "Faulk the Gipper".

I had driven the whole way from Amsterdam with my daughter Anna, hoping to interest her in that great educational institution that I had passed up so I could stay closer to home. Naturally, being the good parent that I am, I try my best to encourage my children to live as much of my fantasy life as is reasonably possible. My old high school chum, ND alumnus Pete Montenaro, had spotted me two tickets for the game and pointed the way to the nearest Motel 6 while Anna stayed in the dorm with his daughter Maria, the clone of her mother Mary Alice Mezzio Montenaro, also a high school chum.

Anna hung out with the students in the corner of the stadium closest to Touchdown Jesus, while I sat on the same side, but opposite end of the field with Maria's future father-in-law. Next to me on the other side sat a very pleasant deep-south LSU fan and behind me, of all things, a Southern Baptist Notre Dame fan.

The Irish have been playing valiantly throughout the game, but always a touchdown behind. Now we're midway through the fourth quarter and they're still down by a TD and LSU is marching down the field, deep into ND territory.

I can see that the team is up against it, things are wrong and the breaks are beating the boys.

I stand up.

"Gentlemen, I've had quite enough of this."

I reach into my pocket and pull out my rosary and hold it high toward the team.

"You know, that's really not fayah," says my friend from LSU.

I stand my ground. Next play the boys throw them for a ten yard loss.

"This is really not fayah."

Next play the quarterback rolls right and fires, right into the hands of a Notre Dame defender! I stand stoically, beads aloft, as he finds the sideline and dashes the full length of the field and in for a touchdown right in front of us.

Father-in-law and all ND fans surrounding us look at me with awe and suddenly we are in a group hug jumping up and down and screaming with joy.

Southern Baptist Notre Dame fan is in anguish as he cheers for the team while staring at my rosary.

"You know," he says finally, "it wasn't that graven image that caused the touchdown. It was MAH FAITH! It was MAH FAITH that I was sending down on the field! It may have bounced off your rosary, but it was MAH FAITH!"

"Monsignor O'Malley will be hearing confessions fifteen minutes after the game ends. I suggest you be there," says I.

With that, I drop the rosary back into my pocket.

They miss the extra point.

I'm sure my Southern Baptist pal could quote chapter and verse of that incident in the bible where the Israelites prevail in their battle so long as Moses (was it Moses?) has his arms outstretched, but retreat every time he puts them down.

And so it was that for the remainder of the game my heavy-laden arms outstretched with Our Lady of Victory's Holy Rosary led the Irish to triumph. It wasn't easy. They had to give up a safety in the waning seconds and in the process lost the quarterback for the remainder of the season.

But they won.

And when I told this story to the Admissions Office a couple of months later, it very nearly got Anna into Notre Dame, but not quite. It seems they had already filled their quota for beautiful, witty, charming, talented young women from Upstate New York whose parents help them win football games.

You may notice they haven't done very well since that decision.

Of course, Louisa will be starting to look at colleges next year.

****

Oh, by the way, for you Yankee fans who are wondering how they lost that 14 inning Game 5 of the 2004 ALCS:

It still works.

Sing an Old Song, Please!
Oct. 16th, 2005 @ 08:06 pm

The opening hymn at Mass today was that sing-songy *"Sing a New Song"*, which I guess was appropriate because the Responsorial Psalm was "Sing a new song unto the Lord," etc.

However.

Pardon me for being cranky, but I rather miss that blend of music, lyric and reverence that used to fill the Catholic churches on Sunday. A whole generation has grown up without being exposed to the great old hymns that somehow got discarded for no obvious reason.

Here are a few. Hum along if you remember:

O God of loveliness, 0 Lord of heaven above,
How worthy to possess my heart's devoted love.
So sweet thy countenance, so gracious to behold
That one, one only glance to me were bliss untold.

Thou art blest Three in One, yet undivided still,
Thou art the One alone, whose love my heart can fill.
The heavens and earth below were fashioned by thy Word,
How amiable art Thou, my ever dearest Lord.

And this one:

Jesus, my Lord, my God, my all,
How can I love Thee as I ought?
And how revere this wond'rous gift,
So far surpassing hope or thought.
Sweet Sacrament, we Thee adore.
O make us love Thee more and more!
O make us love Thee more and more!

Had I but Mary's sinless heart,
To love Thee with, my dearest King;
O with what bursts of fervent praise,
Thy goodness, Jesus, would I sing!
Sweet Sacrament, we Thee adore.
O make us love Thee more and more!
O make us love Thee more and more!

Or this one:

O lord, I am not worthy.
That thou shouldst come to me.
But speak the words of comfort.
My spirit, healed shall be.

And humbly I'll receive Thee,
The Bridegroom of my soul,
No more by sin to grieve Thee,
Or fly Thy sweet control.

O Sacrament most holy!
O Sacrament divine!
All praise and all thanksgiving
Be every moment Thine.

Or this one:

Soul of my Savior, sanctify my breast:
Body of Christ, be thou my saving guest;
Blood of my Savior, bathe me in thy tide.
Wash me with water flowing from Thy side.

Strength and protection may Thy passion be;
O blessed Jesus, hear and answer me;
Deep in thy wounds, Lord, hide and shelter me;
So shall I never, never part from thee?

Guard and defend me from the foe malign:
In death's dread moments make me only thine;
Call me and bid me come to thee on high.
Where I may praise thee with thy saints for aye.

COMMENTS
From: (Anonymous)
Date: December 6th, 2005 06:01 pm (local)

Every time I hear "Sing a New Song", I crack up my
daughters by making motions like I'm riding a carousel horse
(because that's what it reminds me of... calliope music).

-Tony
http://www.catholicpillowfight.com

Eucharistic Adoration

Oct. 20th, 2005 @ 07:59 am

For a while now we've had Eucharistic Adoration in our parish, one day a week for seven hours. During the last half-hour we are treated to a talk by a young and brilliant priest. Kinda like a blog with a microphone, but no comments section.

I confess I don't go as often as I should, and I'm not very good at it. There I am, face to face with the Lord and Saviour, the Answer to everything, the Way, The Life, The Truth, the easy yoke and light burden, and still my mind starts drifting.

I try to still the cacophony of exterior thought, and it is an interesting experience listening for the whisper in the corner of the cave. I try focusing by playing in my head some of those old hymns I posted a couple of days ago, first imagining my solitary shower-voice, which is good, and then expanding it (you can do anything with your imagination, according to Mr. Rogers) to full orchestra and chorus.

But then, because we are at St. Mary's, it is suddenly 1962 and the 11 o'clock high mass with the altar boy choir in the sanctuary on those rough little benches and Sister Anne Eugene and Sister Theresa Bernard sitting in the front row with those watchful stares that ensure that there is no flinching and the smell of the incense and the high school girls' choir in the loft with their mantillas neatly bobby-pinned and Miss Augusta Canale playing the organ and that petite woman with the booming voice occasionally warbling a response, or chanting the *Agnus Dei*.

> *Agnus dei qui tollis peccata mundi, miserere nobis.*
> *Agnus dei qui tollis peccata mundi, miserere nobis.*
> *Agnus dei qui tollis peccata mundi, dona nobis pacem.*

Now that's funny. Here I am drifting away from the object at hand and old Gussie Canale brings me right back where I belong.

I think I'll go back next week.

Eucharistic Adoration II
Nov. 5th, 2005 @ 09:50 pm

We've actually had Eucharistic Adoration once a week nearly continuously for several years now, though it has moved locations a couple of times, from the school chapel, to a neighboring village, and now on Wednesdays at St. Mary's Church, my home and ancestral parish. It's a fine devotion, and the organizers manage to find people to fill all the time slots from 1 to 8 p.m.

The last hour is the most popular, and that's when we go.
We have a young and enthusiastic and wise and insightful (as opposed to inciteful, which is what I originally wrote here until corrected by an actuary) priest, Father Brian List, SOLT, who has managed to hang around his hometown for the better part of the time since being ordained by John Paul the Great a couple of years ago. We were invited to the ordination. It was the same day as Bob's graduation from Dean College. I had this little interior monologue for a while:

"Hmm. Bob's graduation from a two-year school . . . the Pope. Audience with the greatest figure of the 20th century and probably a whole lot longer . . . standard commencement address. Papal blessing . . . 'Thanks, Pops'."

We went to the graduation.

Father Brian is well-versed in Canon Law, and he was so enthralled with the realization that All Souls' Day was one of three days a year when a priest is permitted to offer three masses, all with different readings, that he decided to improvise a little when it came time for the usual closing Benediction and homily. He decided to say two more Masses.

He had brought along one of his nephews to serve and of the 14 people who were present for Adoration, a full dozen remained for the Mass, which included one of his great extemporaneous homilies. One of the ladies did the readings. It was nice, and intimate. He said he would be doing another Mass right after that one and we were invited to stay, but there would be no preaching, he told us as he flashed that boyish grin.

Amazingly, only two people left and the rest of us decided to watch that extra hour with him and there we were plowing into yet another Mass. (For most of the folks in the group, this made their third Mass of the day.)

And after the Gospel, he got this apologetic look and pointed out that when the faithful are present, Canon law recommends at least a brief homily reflecting on the readings. So out of thin air he pulls yet another great homily, finding deep theological analogies and metaphors in *The Pirates of the Caribbean*.

We went away, finally, most refreshed.

****

I have been bringing along a pocket copy of the *Imitation of Christ* by Thomas a' Kempis, partly because my father had been fond of it and I had never gotten around to reading it, and partly because I remembered the story of the author being taught to me way back in the olden days.

Ordinarily, someone of the virtue and brilliance of this man would long since have been Saint Thomas a' Kempis, and certainly should have been on the fast track for Doctor of the Church, and after his death there was a great movement to have him canonized. No doubt there were shouts of "*Santo subito!*"

As part of the process they exhumed his body to determine, among other things, whether he might have exhibited the miracle of incorruptibility.

When they opened the coffin, however, Thomas was not as they had left him.

From the position of the body and the agonized look on his countenance and the scratch marks on the lid they learned that Thomas a' Kempis had been accidentally buried alive.

Because there was no way to determine whether such a situation may have caused him to despair and turn from God, the cause of his sainthood was abandoned forever.

Still a good read, though.

It is Good for Us to Be Here
Feb. 26th, 2006 @ 11:54 pm

After a week by ourselves with Louisa off in Ireland with Anna and Peter, Mary and I finished off with a lovely weekend in New York City, hosted affably and skillfully by our son Bob who even picked up the tab for dinner Saturday night at his favorite Japanese eatery in the Union Square area.

From his apartment in Jackson Heights I plotted out the options for Sunday Mass, based on a poll of friends more familiar with the local liturgical scene than I. We ended up at the Church of Our Saviour on Park Avenue at 38th Street. The Pastor is Father George Rutler, whom I have seen many times on EWTN. He is in the top tier of the finest homilists in the English-speaking world and today he didn't disappoint.

There is a side altar dedicated to St. Thomas More, one of my heroes and the patron saint of lawyers. I wanted to go over there and quietly sing the *Ballad of High Noon for All Seasons*, but alas, there wasn't enough time before Mass and the opportunity never presented itself again.

"This isn't gonna be all in Latin, is it?" Mary asked. She is that much younger than me that she has no recollection of the sublime beauty of the Tridentine Mass. "No, of course not," I replied without telling her that my second choice was the Tridentine Mass at St. Agnes which was even closer to Grand Central than this church, and at the same hour.

****

"Something old, something new." Father Rutler may have been in the midst of his brief history of Time, but he might just as well have been talking about the liturgy itself. For a *Novus Ordo* Mass, there was little evidence that the old order had passed much. Six candles, incense, sprinkling of the congregation with holy water, triple bell-ringing at the Consecration, and glorious Gregorian Chant sung by a magnificent choir whose voices filled the church. It seemed like dozens, but I think there were only about four of them, in wondrous harmonies, accompanied by a most-accomplished organist. First rate all the way.

When they did occasionally break into English, it was the good stuff, like *Holy God We Praise Thy Name*. (No *Gift of Finest Wheat* or that calliope number *Sing a New Song*). I never really understood why we abandoned *Gloria in Excelsis Deo* for the flat English translation. Hearing it again today, I would find it difficult to believe that anyone would not understand its meaning. And the *Sanctus!* To me, as an altar boy, that chant always sounded like the clink of censors and the tinkling of altar bells. It was in word and sound a brief glimpse of the Beatific Vision itself. It all came back to me today.

Fill the heavens with sweet accord
Holy! Holy! Holy Lord!

It really doesn't matter that they don't write hymns like that anymore. 'Cause we've still got 'em!

The first thing I noticed on entering the church was the long line at the confessional. This is something you don't see much anymore. The congregation was largely youthful, something we don't see at all at home, the demographics being what they are. It was most encouraging.

As I say, Father Rutler is an extraordinarily gifted preacher. My hearing has been steadily deteriorating in recent years, and it is harder and harder for me to place myself in an assembly where I can get much out of what's being said. I tried to capture each of the words today, and repeat them to myself as he went along. I felt, in the end, reassured, revitalized. Refreshed.

New York City is such a paradox. It is crawling with sin, sin of the worst kind, lost souls, drugs and alcoholism, diminishment and despair.

Yet in the midst of it all are these islands of hope and confidence, oases of grace and blessings in abundance. It is the surest sign that He wasn't kidding when He said, "I will be with you always."

High above the sanctuary of the church there is written this legend: "LORD, IT IS GOOD FOR US TO BE HERE."

Amen.

One of His Fans
Mar. 1st, 2006 @ 08:56 pm

In my last post I mentioned my wonderful trip to the Church of Our Saviour in New York (Park Avenue at 38th Street for those of you, including my children, who might be in the area). I was delighted to receive an e-note from Father George Rutler, the Pastor, who said, "You are most welcome anytime here, at what I like to think of as a village church in the midst of the big city."

I thought that was cute, but the more I reflected, the more I realized the truth in that short sentence. The church, though beautifully decorated, is on the small side and intimate. The congregation, though metropolitan, seemed friendly and there was an easy familiarity among many whom I suppose to be regulars. I certainly felt right at home. There was no sensation of being enveloped as sometimes happens in the great cathedrals. Sure, a village church. I've been to a few of those.

When the children were smaller we often took them camping in the summer in the southern Adirondacks. There were a couple of small village churches we attended and I always felt a sense of great faith abounding in the simple surroundings. We also got remarkably good preaching. It was especially remarkable because both churches were on the far fringes of their respective dioceses, Albany and Ogdensburg.

One of them we hit four summers in a row and I heard four of the ten best homilies I'd ever experienced from a simple unassuming priest of no obvious greatness. Yet, he somehow managed to startle with an old message newly told and I remember thinking that if I could only come there six more times he'd probably capture every spot in my top ten.

Most of what he said has faded away now with the passing years. If only I had blogged it. There is one story he told, however, that has stuck, and may be not a bad one for the beginning of Lent.

Back in the early days of the Civil Rights movement, an African-American preacher approached a famous white lawyer who had been sympathetic to the cause and asked him to take the lead publicly on some matter. Whatever it was, it created a great risk to the lawyer professionally. He was reluctant to get involved.

"I implore you, as a follower of Christ, to do the right and just thing!" begged the preacher.

"I'm a follower of Christ, too," said the lawyer, "but that doesn't mean I'm willing to be crucified!"

"If you're not willing to follow Him to Calvary," said the preacher quietly, "you're not one of His followers.

"You're just one of His fans."

Lent
Mar. 24th, 2006 @ 10:01 am

When we were kids, Mom made it a practice to take us to daily Mass during Lent. It wasn't easy. Mom was teaching at St. Mary's and the Mass schedules at St. Mary's Church were such that she couldn't quite get there and get ready for school too, so we would attend St. Michael's a block away up the hill which had a syncopated Mass at just the right time, which, however, because there were five of us, we were never on.

Day after day we would wander in at the Epistle, and the Cuban priest who was attending in the sanctuary while the pastor said Mass would glare at us fiercely. We often sat behind Gene and Nancy Catena and their large brood of mostly rambunctious young boys (and one poor girl). The boys were continually poking at each other and otherwise messing around and Nancy would firmly, but gently bring them back under control.

Gene later became Family Court Judge and served for the 21 years before me. One of the rambunctious lads is now the County Court Judge of Montgomery County, another is in the seminary, another a hospital administrator. None are in prison.

One day, probably by accident, we arrived on time. The Cuban priest saw us and flew into near-hysteria, naturally assuming that something must have happened to the pastor, who obviously must be very late for Mass.

After Mass we'd walk down the hill to school and open up our breakfast of buttered toast, neatly wrapped in wax paper.

****

Years later we were sitting near the front of St. Mary's Church and Mary and I were having a bit of a problem controlling our two boys who were, shall we say, behaving inappropriately for church and uncharitably toward each other.

I turned around and there sitting behind us were Gene and Nancy Catena.

Smiling.

Crossing the Tiber
Apr. 12th, 2006 @ 08:15 am

Call me an old softy, but I'm just a sucker for sentimental ritual moments like weddings and presidential inaugurations and a clergy choir singing *Thou Art a Priest Forever* at the funeral of their brother.

Nothing gets to me more, though, than the reception into the Church of a new member, whether it be infant baptism or adult conversion. In our parish the big night is at the Easter Vigil, and this week we'll have a few more coming over. Last year you practically needed a scorecard.

It is especially heartwarming when it is someone you know, and on several occasions I've had the opportunity to rejoice with the family afterward. There is a mystic bond among believing Catholics that is difficult to describe, but very, very real.

When I first discovered Dawn Eden and her *Dawn Patrol* blog a little over a year ago, I spent some time going through her archives and became fascinated by the development of her thought. She had previously converted from Judaism to Christianity and had continued to explore her faith in a deeper and deeper way. Like many of us, she became hooked on Chesterton and at one point, not all that long ago, really, had embarked on a Chesterton pilgrimage to England.

Looking back at those posts she sent of that trip, there is almost a sadness to them. But a divine sadness. The travel group, a friendly bunch I gather, was almost entirely Catholic and, in a nice way, they nibbled at her Faith around the edges, and tried to gently coax her into taking the Tiber plunge. She expressed some resentment at the time, but looking back you can sense the seeds having been sown.

By a year ago her daily pronouncements were such that I initially thought she already had crossed and I jumped around the archives looking for when that happened. But in fact there was no single point that I could find where she clearly started thinking of Catholics as US instead of THEM. There is no question in my mind, though, that she has been heart and soul a Catholic for some time now. And a darn good one.

On Holy Thursday Dawn will be formally brought into the Church and make her first sacramental confession and receive First Holy Communion. The process will be completed with her Confirmation at the Saturday Easter Vigil. I'm sure she will be surrounded by family and many, many friends.

Many hundreds more of her friends, most of whom she will never meet, will be praying and cheering and wiping a sentimental tear and joining with the choirs of angels welcoming Dawn Eden home.

God bless and keep her always.

Holy Week
Apr. 15th, 2006 @ 02:47 pm

The liturgies for Holy Week are truly beautiful and profound, particularly the mystic chords of the *Pange Lingua* and the veneration of the cross. A few years ago someone remembered that Msgr. Glavin had brought back tiny relics from the True Cross from his tour of duty at Vatican II and they've been mounted on larger wooden crosses that are brought out only on Good Friday, so at St. Mary's when we venerate we VENERATE.

Everything went pretty smoothly, except for the end of the Eucharistic Procession Thursday, when one of the altar boys bumped into an Easter lily and knocked it over starting a domino effect with the three other plants in line with it. No harm done.

I can't understand why more people don't go. The church should be packed instead of the 3/4 or so we usually get. More people clearly come on Ash Wednesday than Good Friday. Maybe we should be giving something away.

****

One year, when Jay was living in Newport, we attended Holy Thursday at a church which shall remain nameless. The service began with the washing of the feet by the pastor, which was ok. I had never seen that ritual before, and even though it took a while until all 24 feet were washed and dried and we couldn't see much, that didn't bother me.

Then, because it was the night of the Last Supper, the regulars were invited to bring their canned goods to the altar for distribution to the poor. This took a rather inordinate amount of time, I thought. I mean, I'm all for feeding the hungry and all that, but the sacrifice could have been made at the door on the way in and maybe the ushers could have rolled some Stop 'n' Shop carts up the aisle. That would have cut twenty minutes or so from a service that wasn't all that liturgical.

When the can-givers were safely back in their seats, the pastor got up and pledged another year of service to the parish, reading from a declaration that somewhat exceeded the length of Jefferson's, which he then signed with a flourish. He announced that the document would be framed and hung in the vestibule of the church. That's nice.

And then he invited each of the parishioners (each, not one per family) to come forward and sign the document at the altar as witnesses to his pledge to do good.

It was probably at about that point when my sainted mother began shifting in the pew and twitching her head and shooting me some glances.

One hour and fifteen minutes into the ceremony we began the Mass for Holy Thursday.

On Good Friday we switched and attended the service at Old St. Mary's in downtown Newport, the very church where Jackie and John Kennedy got married. It was lovely, and of moderate length.

****

Yesterday, during the mercy hour, EWTN broadcast Haydn's *"Last Words"* string quartet. I was in and out of the room, and struggled to remember what exactly were the seven last words of Jesus as he hung on the cross. As often happens when, for example, reciting Snow White's dwarfs, I kept getting to six and couldn't figure out which one was missing.

My daughter Anna was visiting with the grand-dog, so I poured out the problem to her. She says, "Tell me the ones you remember," and so I rattled off the six, "Father, forgive them,"This day you shall be with me," "Behold your mother," "I thirst", "Why have You forsaken me," "It is accomplished."

"What am I missing?"

"That's easy, Dad. It's 'PETER! I can see your house from here!' "

Now tell me, just *why* couldn't they have taken after their mother?

The Good Sisters
Apr. 22nd, 2006 @ 09:41 am

For well over a hundred years the Sisters of St. Joseph of Carondolet have served our parish. At one time they filled the halls of the old St. Mary's Institute and were responsible for much of my education.

I had a great-great aunt, Sister Mary Bartholomew, whom I never met, who entered the order in the latter quarter of the 19th century. She was sent from the emerging eastern mill-town metropolis of Amsterdam to the wild frontier fringes of Oklahoma, this before the "Land Rush", when it was still known as the Indian Territory. She worked in conditions of abject poverty, teaching Indian children in schools with dirt floors and little heat, for the greater glory of God. She served for over sixty years, including a stint running a college in Missouri. Not bad for the daughter of Irish immigrants, and one of them born a Protestant at that.

****

I was reading Frank McCourt's book Teacher Man last night and a segment reminded me of the drudgery of diagraming sentences. We had been doing this off and on for several years, I think, but it was our seventh grade English teacher, Sister Monica Agnes, who raised it to an art form. There was no part of speech too obscure, no subordinate phrase too remote, no participle too dangling that we couldn't find some space for it on the blackboard. Boy, did we think that was stupid. "When are we ever gonna diagram sentences in real life, S'ter?" we would ask, but to no avail, and so we kept plodding on and on until one day we realized we had somehow learned to write our own sentences. The understanding of how that happened came much, much later. Too late to say thank you, unless, of course, she happens to be reading this.

Sister Monica had a long hardwood pointer named Oscar which she claimed to retain primarily for disciplinary purposes, though none of us ever saw Oscar raised in anger.

I remember three specific things she taught us in that 1963-64 school year:

"Always use 'different from', never 'different than'."

"A lot is something you build a house on and dig with a shovel. Otherwise don't use it in your writing."

"I have a great deal of respect for Elvis Presley, boys and girls [I'll bet she almost said "a lot"], because he has staying power, but I guarantee you that a year from now no one will remember who *The Beatles* even were."

And then, of course, I will always remember her sitting quietly at her desk, as we were all sitting quietly, listening to the radio being pumped through the school's PA system, listening intently as the voice at the other end paused and said, "Ladies and gentlemen, the President of the United States is dead," and then the gasps and the tears and the playing of the national anthem and the dismissal and all of us wandering numbly into the bright sunshine of that beautiful November Friday, a day that we later, if we thought about it, would figure out had changed everything forever.

The Good Sisters II
Apr. 22nd, 2006 @ 10:58 pm

What's In a Name?

In the olden days, the Sisters of St. Joseph left their old lives behind completely, sealed by the adoption of a new name. Surnames were banished, which made them objects of great mystery to their students.

As shocked as we were to learn of a serious motor vehicle accident involving our junior high math teacher (and coordinator of altar boys and director of the altar boy choir), Sister Anne Eugene, imagine the guilty delight we felt to learn that her last name was Tranelli!

This led to a discussion that went on for months, carrying over into our eighth grade history class with Sister Samuel Joseph, she of the squinty eye and withering stare.

"I wonder what your real name is, Sister," said Barbara Curran. "It's probably something really ordinary like 'Jane Smith'."

Well, from my perspective it appeared that Sister Sammy Joe rose to her full six foot eight and emitted flashing daggers that enveloped poor six foot Barb and blew her up into a million pieces.

****

My love of history had gone back a ways, but Sammy Joe enriched it and cultivated it. Father Joe Cotugno told me then that when my formal education was completed, I'd probably be able to count the really great and influential teachers on one hand. Sister Samuel certainly gets her own finger (as does Sister Monica Agnes from my previous post).

American History came alive. She made us think and debate and work out solutions. As one of two Goldwater supporters in my class of 40 (the other one is now Family Court Judge in my old seat and a freakin' liberal), she called upon me to give a concession speech the morning after the election. Barry and I were magnanimous.

That year we were busy trying to preserve the union, with the class divided among pro and anti-slavery forces. We each made the points that would have been raised in the first half of the 19th century, a great Senate debate with Webster and Calhoun and others.

And when the arguments had been advanced sufficiently, J.D. Smeallie as Henry Clay would rise up and offer the Missouri Compromise and the Compromise of 1850, and that would settle things for that class. Then the first thing you know they sneak in the Kansas-Nebraska Act and the Supreme Court hands down *Dred Scott* and all hell breaks loose, only we didn't say hell.

Later we got into serious discussions about immigration, arguments that still seem fresh today. Some of our classmates were immigrants themselves. We all knew some war refugees and hardly anyone was more than two generations removed from another country, so the whole immigration thing wasn't totally theoretical.

****

Many, many years later, after Sister Anna Roberta's funeral at the mother house, Marie Guagliardo-Day called me over to join a conversation with a smartly dressed woman.

"Do you know who this is?" she asked.

I looked at the woman, and she looked at me and I smiled.

"Do that thing with your eyes," I said. And this woman whom I'd been looking down at suddenly rose to six foot eight, squinted her eyes and blew me into a million pieces.

"Sammy Joe!" I cried.

"Mary Jane Smith," she explained.

[CAVEAT: There is some dispute among my classmates as to whether the slavery debate took place in eighth grade or seventh grade, when we also had

-208-

an exceptional history teacher, also one of the Good Sisters. Throw in Richard Redznak in 6th grade and we had an astonishingly thorough background in history before ever entering high school. Even if I am wrong about some of the above, it doesn't affect my overall evaluation of Sammy Joe. And if anyone can remember the name of our 7th grade teacher, she will get due credit in the next addendum. Am I growing old?]

The Good Sisters III
Apr. 26th, 2006 @ 06:57 pm

What's In a Name? (cont.)

Our fifth grade teacher, Sister Florence Louis, volunteered how she chose her order name.

"My mother's name was Florence and my father's name was Louis."

I'll bet that was one of the easier ones.

****

Sister Patrick Francis, ninth grade homeroom and typing teacher (on manual typewriters, mostly, rarely electric and way before "keyboarding") told us that she had been instructed to select three possible names.

"And I wrote down 'Patrick Francis, Patrick Francis, Patrick Francis.'"

Patrick Francis Dunn was her blood cousin, but raised as her brother. After his christening he was known to the family as Parker. During World War I he volunteered to carry an important message across an open battlefield in France. He was shot several times, but kept going. The attention he drew somehow caused the recipient to understand the purpose of his journey and as a result, quite a few lives were saved, but not his.

He was, however, posthumously awarded the Congressional Medal of Honor and his name lived on in his sister, and in the bridge across the Hudson named after him in Albany. In the 1970's Sister Patrick was present when the new bridge replaced the old one. If recollection serves, she was well over a hundred when she went to her eternal reward.

****

Sister Patrick was wonderfully quotable. When making a point her index finger would seem to flap, especially when she was agitated.

"Turn around in your seat!' Flap. Flap. "Lee Oswald used to turn around in class!"

Flap. Flap. "Look at me when I'm talking to you!" Flap. "Stop staring at me!" (This she did on more than one occasion, most memorably when she had six foot four Orest Babiak standing in the corner.)

And during the 1966 World Series, "Who's got that transistor? Who's got that transistor??"

But more often than not her heart of gold would come out and she'd give us all candy for no particular reason.

When the nuns abandoned their old habits, Sister Patrick delightedly donned an otherwise modest suit of brightest green.

She was a good egg.

How Uncle Sy Got His Name
Mar. 24th, 2007 @ 02:22 pm

Uncle Sy was born at home on December 4, 1922. His birth certificate says December 5th, but that's the day they got around to registering it, I guess. Things were not quite so formal and legalistic back then.

There were ultimately 13 children born to Bronislaw and Anna Raczkowski Foltman and Sy was on the down side of the group, so potential names had already gotten scarce. So, it was potluck based on the feast day of the Saint of his baptismal day, December 31.

"So that's how I got named Sylvester and I've hated it all my life," he told me once.

Just out of curiosity, I pulled out my pre-Vatican II volume of feast days of the Church and thumbed through it.

"You know," I said, "You should consider yourself lucky. If you'd been baptized the next day your name would be Circumcision."

Origins
Dec. 29th, 2006 @ 08:04 am

The call of business brought me yesterday to the city of my birth, Troy, NY, for the third time in five weeks. The business was mercifully short, and we used my should-be-patented navigational method of follow-your-nose to wind our way back to the bridge over the Hudson.

I suddenly realized we had swung up to Fifth Avenue and when I spotted a church up ahead, I asked the driver, my former secretary, to pull over. For this was St. Peter's Church, the church of my baptism and our home parish until just before my third birthday.

Our other companion was her sister, also a former secretary of mine, and the three of us stepped smartly through the front door and back into the 1950's, for St. Peter's had hardly changed a whit from the days of my toddling.

Twenty-something companions were awed by the beauty of the architecture and decor.

"This is what churches used to look like," I told them.

It's the third oldest parish in the State of New York, following St. Patrick's in New York City and Old St. Mary's in Albany. A Catholic church has stood on that site since 1830. The present building dates from the 1850's, the interior decor from the late 19th-early 20th centuries. One of the early pastors was Rev. Clarence Walworth, whose name you might not know, but whose translation of a German hymn *Holy God We Praise Thy Name* should be on the lips of every English-speaking Catholic.

We wandered around, marveled at the marble high pulpit, the stations of the cross, the Christmas creche, the old confessionals. I realized I had missed the baptistry so I checked out the periphery until I found it in the back near the front door. (Churches are funny that way. You enter the front door to get to the back of the church, and the back door to enter the front).

It is astonishingly beautiful, dating, I later learned, from 1900, with an ornate baptismal font of marble, onyx and brass.

It was here that in July of 1951 I was given my name, and where, attended by my Aunt Marie Weise and Uncle Bob Brunelli, the stain of original sin was wiped away and I became, through the grace of Jesus Christ, a child of God and an heir of heaven.

****

I should mention that this church is the only place in the diocese of Albany where the traditional tridentine rite Latin Mass of the Catholic Church is regularly celebrated. The old altar is still in use.

Father Rutler, the Senator and Me
Aug. 5th, 2007 @ 08:34 pm

Sunday morning found me in midtown Manhattan in the greatest city in the world on as perfect a day weather-wise as I have seen since probably September 11, 2001. I parked the car on 37th Street with the initial intention of catching a bite before attending Father George Rutler's 11 a.m. Mass at Our Saviour, but the dearth of traffic on a summer Sunday in the big town had allowed me to cruise from Bob's place in East Elmhurst to midtown in twenty minutes, so I wandered in for the 9:30 instead.

I have previously written about this wonderful parish church four blocks from Grand Central Station and its exceptionally gifted pastor. His Masses exude sanctity in a way that's difficult to describe but wonderful to experience. *Christ in the City* would be a good thing to call it, and Father Rutler already has, on his EWTN series filmed there.

The homily was just magnificent, as always, Father commenting on the gospel of the day with references to Aristotle and Aquinas, and mixing in wonderful anecdotes and examples from the lives of St. John Vianney and a contemporary ordinary parish priest who could have been a baron and chose to serve God instead. Seemingly heading off in different directions, Father Rutler drew it all together and wrapped it in a bright ribbon for us and for God.

After Mass I introduced myself and he seemed delighted to meet me, a reception somewhat different from what I have received locally lately.

"That gentleman who was in front of you is former Senator Larry Pressler of South Dakota. You should go say hello to him."

Just like the Cure d'Ars! I thought. He sees my soul and recognizes me as a Conservative Republican Pro-life Catholic Red Sox fanatic!

Well, no, actually he reads *The Judge Report* once in a while.

And I really have no idea what baseball team South Dakotans traditionally root for. But otherwise, Senator Pressler has always been my kind of guy.

And he was most gracious. He had arrived alone a little early for the 11 and had no problem whatsoever spending time with a total stranger. He kept asking questions about Amsterdam. Ultimately the only things he could relate to were its distance from Albany and its connection to Kirk Douglas.

He's currently teaching at St. John's University in Queens, trying to teach our future leaders that it is indeed possible for a rich man to get into heaven, that free markets are not incompatible with virtue, and how both are important for the physical and spiritual well-being of the human race.

"What brought you to this church from upstate New York?" he asked me, and I tried feebly to explain as I did here how there's just something about Our Saviour that sets it apart.

"Maybe its just that there seems to be more faith in this little parish church than in all the great cathedrals," I said.

He nodded. He knew.

By this time Father Rutler was ready to begin the next Mass, and I stayed for the beginning, then wandered on my way, confidant that Senator Pressler would find much to chew on from the sermon he was about to hear.

Father Corapi, the Wife and Me
Aug. 12th, 2007 @ 12:34 pm

Week two of my impromptu EWTN Groupie Tour began Friday evening when Mary and I arrived at the Lowell (MA) Memorial Auditorium to take in a weekend of presentations by Father John Corapi, SOLT.

We are big fans of his, dating back to his series on the Catechism on EWTN which began playing in 1996 and has never been off the air. We also have a certain affinity for him. His conversion took place at the Shrine of the North American Martyrs in Auriesville, NY, only about six miles from our house, where he not only returned to the church after many wild years of decadent living, but decided to become a priest as well.

He hails from Hudson, New York, a city much like Amsterdam and about the same distance south of Albany as we are west. In the 1940's, 50's and 60's, St. Mary's of Hudson were the arch rivals of St. Mary's of Amsterdam in basketball. Rocky McCune remembers Father Corapi's father as being one of the star players of his era. What we didn't know is that Father Corapi had two aunts who lived in Amsterdam, one a Sister of St. Joseph who worked in the operating room of St. Mary's Hospital for about forty years and another who he mentioned in one of his addresses as the person who reconciled him to his father after a twenty year estrangement.

After the lectures he chatted with Mary and I far longer than he should have considering the long line behind us and autographed Mary's copy of the *Catechism of the Catholic Church.*

If Father Rutler, my host last weekend, represents the cerebral and the scholarly approach to passing on the teachings of the Church, with his perfect erudite references to Aristotle and Aquinas and his total immersion into sacred music and forms, Father Corapi presents more as a blue collar rock star, and so he was welcomed as he walked onto the stage on Friday night.

The warm-up act was a contemporary Christian music chorale and band. I confess it didn't do much for me, though later at benediction they handled *O Salutaris Hostia* and *Tantum Ergo Sacramentum* and *Holy God We Praise Thy Name* with exceptional skill.

But all those jumpy-clappy middle aged and later women scattered around the hall failed to enrich me, though I'm sure they felt quite spiritually involved themselves as they grabbed their tambourines and skipped up the center aisle in a sort of impromptu ecclesial Conga Line. But the Lord reaches everyone differently, and God bless them all.

****

Father Corapi is a mesmerizing speaker and every moment of his six-plus hours over two days was memorable. This new series, Easy Prayer for Hard Times was taped a few weeks ago and will be broadcast on EWTN sometime in the future. Particularly useful was the segment "Offer It Up", the substance of which most Catholics over the age of 50 should recognize immediately.

"Johnny, take the garbage out."

"But Grandma, it's snowing!"

"Offer it up."

He did his doctoral thesis on the theology of suffering, later published as a 333 page book. He gave a copy to his father.

"Dad, did you read the book?"

"Yes, I did."

"Did you like it?"

"Yes, I liked it a lot."

"Did you understand it?"

"Not much. Just the part where you said, 'Offer it up.'"

The simplicity of prayer. The simplicity of joining your sufferings to Christ.

A good message.

And one Father Corapi won't be giving before crowds of thousands any more. For after traveling millions of miles since his ministry began, more miles than Pope John Paul II flew in his entire pontificate, Father Corapi announced that we were witnessing his last public performance, at least until 2009. He is concentrating on books, television and his web site, where he will be giving weekly homilies soon.

Pray for him. Pray hard. He needs the strength of our prayers.

****

One more thing: I suspect I will never again be in a place with quite so many conservative Republican pro-life Catholic Red Sox fanatics as I was this weekend. Very nice.

Father Rutler, The Wife and Me
Mar. 17th, 2008 @ 11:30 pm

It doesn't get more solemn than the Solemn Palm Sunday Mass we attended yesterday in New York, from the grand opening procession, through the chanted Passion of Our Lord Jesus Christ According to Matthew, the incense, the Gregorian Chants by that spectacular choir and organist and the stunning silence of the recession.

Sanctus! Sanctus! Sanctus!

I said to Mary afterwards, "I love this church. It's the most peaceful church I have ever been in anywhere."

****

Father George Rutler is a most remarkable man. He mixes easily in the highest councils of the land. He thinks, and he writes wonderful books containing great thoughts. He conveys his message globally on EWTN. It is not unusual to spot famous people at his Masses. He is, among other things, the "unofficial chaplain of *The Corner at National Review Online*."

And he is the pastor of a church, just like hundreds and hundreds of other priests. He guides his parish flock. He pays attention to detail and is a respecter of the great traditions of the Catholic Faith. When he preaches the Gospel, you know he believes every word of it. When he consecrates the host, you know he knows that he is in the presence of Almighty God.

His parish church, the Church of Our Saviour on Park Avenue in New York City, four blocks south of Grand Central Station, exudes sanctity at any time of day. In slightly over an hour last Friday, Mary and I experienced quiet reflection, the Angelus, noon Mass with a fine little sermonette on the life of St. Patrick, Stations of the Cross and Exposition of the Blessed Sacrament. Father Rutler has his congregation well-trained. As he gently swung the thurible back and forth, the incense carrying his prayers to heaven, he alternated between English and Latin, with multiple voices echoing the responses in the appropriate tongue. (I did pretty good except for the middle of the second half of the *Pater Noster*, which I can never get right, though I present a strong finish.)

Afterwards he slipped gently out of the sanctuary, leaving the Blessed Sacrament exposed for worship, and quietly stepped into the confessional, where a long line soon formed.

For all his fame, he seems at heart a humble parish priest as we used to know them, bringing the mercy of God to his people one soul at a time. And that's what I really like about him.

****

And after the Solemn Mass on Palm Sunday he said to me, "Are you still judging? Justice Scalia had a bunch of us over Friday night for brandy and cigars. I had a great time! Didn't get home until after midnight!"

Frankly, I like that part of him too.

Merry Christmas

Dear Editor:

I must say, I just don't get it. Why do liberal intellectuals feel threatened by Christmas? Most of their core constituencies don't. Certainly African-Americans, Hispanics and blue collar labor unionists are among the most Christmas-loving people around.

Sure, I appreciate that some of the overly-educated consider the whole Christmas tale a myth, but so what? As myths go, it's a pretty good one. We're not talking about monsters and vengeance and people eating their children and stuff like that. We're talking about a story that has the Creator of the Universe looking down at this tiny spec of a planet that's filled with worthless and ungrateful people unworthy of His attention, let alone affection, and deciding to become one of us. Not as conqueror or king, but as a helpless infant in a smelly old stable relying on mere humans for his help and support. Then He grows up and teaches us how to act with charity toward one another and if that isn't enough offers Himself up as the supreme sacrifice for the sins of all mankind.

I happen to believe all that, but even if I didn't it would still seem pretty wonderful to me. And I think I would understand why commemorating the moment when the Word became Flesh would be pretty important to most people, and I would hope I would have the good sense to know that when folks said "Merry Christmas" they would be saying something to me that is at once both terribly friendly and awesomely profound.

Robert N. Going

Potpourri

Ted Olson
Sep. 14th, 2007 @ 07:50 am

I'm interrupting my mock campaign for Attorney General to express my outrage over the vicious partisan attacks being made on Ted Olson, former Solicitor General, who is on the president's short list for Attorney General. The senile moron who represents the majority of the Senate has in effect told the president not to bother to nominate Olson because he would see to it that he would never be confirmed.

Today's Wall Street Journal puts it better than I can. This is one of the finest and fairest legal minds in America, a man who would be an outstanding Supreme Court Justice, and a man whose dedication to public service has only brought him grief.

That the idiot leader of the Democrats in the senate would choose the week when we mark the anniversary of the murder of Mr. Olson's wife (she was aboard the plane that crashed into the Pentagon, though Mr. Reid may be one of those 35% of Democrats who don't believe that ever happened) to brandish his tarnished sword is enough to make a patriot's blood boil over.

Submit to the challenge, Mr. President. Hang in there, Mr. Olson.

Let the American people see.

It's Always Michael
Sep. 16th, 2007 @ 09:22 am

Way back in 1989 when I was running for re-election as City Court Judge, I went through the obligatory grilling by the editorial board of the Amsterdam Evening Recorder, as the paper was called then. It went well enough. They endorsed me.

Afterwards, the Executive Editor, Tony Benjamin (later fired for getting too close to the truth on an unrelated issue), pulled me aside and asked a strange question. There were rumors, he said, that one powerful person, acting behind the scenes, controlled everything that happened politically in Montgomery County. Did I know anything about that?

I looked at him like he was from Jupiter, muttered something incoherent, and went on my way.

When I hit the parking lot the light suddenly clicked and I doubled over in laughter. He was talking about my friend Michael Chiara!

Michael is an only child. Never married. He stayed at home and cared for his elderly parents until they passed away. The only companion he has is Miss Dog, whom he found half-starved wandering in the woods and fields behind his house, abandoned by her owners. She had pretty much gone wild and it took weeks of kindness before she would finally approach Michael and allow herself to be cared for.

Lacking other commitments, Mike has devoted his life to public service. He has been a lousily-paid employee of the City of Amsterdam for over thirty years. Name a committee or commission or agency, and he has been on it, and actively participated. Board of Trustees of the Community College, Private Industry Council, Chamber of Commerce, Charter Commissions, four times appointed (and three times fired) to the Amsterdam Industrial Development Agency. Took the Industrial Park out of bankruptcy and filled it, rescued the Mall, brought the Professional Wrestling Hall of Fame to Amsterdam, worked with developers on every kind of project imaginable, comes up with forty new ideas every day for making the city and county better.

When two guys from Europe came to town, it wasn't the Chamber of Commerce or the *Recorder*, or the guys with button-down collars and ties and new suits and fancy haircuts who volunteered to take them around and teach them everything they know about the history and culture of the city. It was Michael Chiara.

It's always Michael.

Earlier this week it was Michael who volunteered a morning of his vacation time to read the names of the September 11 dead on a local radio station.

-222-

Today, of course, the *Recorder* produces the biggest editorial I have ever seen devoted solely to mocking, berating, blasting and vilifying Michael Chiara. They call him a buffoon. They don't like the way he dresses. They criticize his haircut. They stick their noses so far into the air it must be hard for them to breathe.

It will be interesting to see how many civic leaders who for three decades have been running to Mike for confidential advice, political strategy, economic assistance , or just to cry on his shoulder, come to his defense. If the past predicts the future, I suspect that there will not be many.

When I think of words to describe him, buffoon is not on the list. Kindness and caring and character come immediately to mind.

I am proud, infinitely proud, to call him my friend.

Also way back in 1989, when Mary was pregnant with Louisa, we continued our family tradition that she would choose the name if it were a girl, and I would name the boys. When the outcome was still in doubt, she asked me what I had decided.

It was easy.

"His name will be Michael."

Mohawk Valley Autumn
Sep. 23rd, 2007 @ 10:22 pm

A lovely picture-perfect early autumn Sunday, so we hopped in the Caliber and took in some of the best of the Mohawk Valley, starting with the grand opening of the new Arkell Museum in Canajoharie, featuring a stunning art collection, including original works by Winslow Homer, Andrew Wyeth, Georgia O'Keefe, Thomas Hart Benton, etc.

In one gallery they have a full-size copy of Rembrandt's *Night Watch* covering one wall; in another fragile water colors and pastels in muted light; in another views of the Mohawk Valley. Pretty neat stuff for a village of 2,257 in a county of 49,708.

The Arkell family used to own the Beech-Nut Company, at one time an all-American operation, but now a subsidiary of some Austrian or Swiss outfit. They will be moving out of Canajoharie after a hundred and sixteen years or so. They had planned on leaving the state altogether, or threatened to, but the state government and county officials came up with millions in aid and tax breaks, so they'll be relocating nearer to Amsterdam. I need to talk to some of their people about water and sewer connections soon.

The grand opening included some Native American music and story tellers and lots of stuff for the kids and free apple cider and cookies. Great turnout.

Afterwards we wandered up to Wintergreen Park and walked the nature trail at the top of the Canajoharie Gorge to a lookout over the no-trespassing falls where some teenager or another breaks his neck every few years. A difficult spot for acrophobics like myself, but I like to challenge my fears every once in a while. Scientists figure the sedimentary rocks in the gorge were deposited upwards of a half a billion years ago.

And then another Mohawk Valley autumn tradition: Bellinger's Apple Orchard and we had Louisa's friend Earl Bellinger along for luck, even though he has no idea how, or if, he's related to them.

While others were picking apples and going on hay rides and wandering through corn mazes (should that be maize mazes?) I set my priorities right and waited in the long line for fresh cider donuts. It's not a big operation. You actually watch your own donuts being made, plopped one at a time into the hot oil and whisked along and flipped over before settling into the sugar and then hand packed in paper sacks. "Keep the top open and let the steam come out. Otherwise they'll get soggy."

I passed the open bags under the noses of everyone else waiting in line just to keep them encouraged.

The jug of cider washed them down real good later when we got home.

Big Pete
Oct. 8th, 2007 @ 09:30 pm

Aurora Montenaro's funeral today brought back memories, and visiting afterwards with her kids and grandkids and great-grandson and other assorted relatives and friends brought back many more, and I remembered a story I had started to write a long, long time ago and found it, happily transposed and saved through several generations of computers in still-readable format.

It is the story of the wake of Big Pete Montenaro back in the spring of 1995, I think. Mom seemed perfectly healthy at the time, though she died herself about six months later.

****

The line at the funeral parlor ran out the door, flowers everywhere. This was, after all, Big Pete's last farewell and everyone wanted to say goodbye to the gregarious, hardworking, hard-playing, sweet, loveable father of seven rough and tumble kids who were themselves now settling into ever-deepening middle-age.

Aurora and the kids and spouses lined up around the room. Family pictures, railroad memorabilia and Notre Dame paraphernalia were everywhere. We had something to say to them all, the usual mutterings, of course, but also a few lively exchanges, funny anecdotes, happy memories. For me, they were like an extended family, having grown up with the kids, worked for and with them selling snowcones through college, later their occasional legal counselor, always a friend.

Then there were Peter and Mary Alice, classmates and somewhat more than friends, subjects of numerous entries in my teen-age diary, high school sweethearts and parents of three. They had left town long ago, and though we saw each other occasionally, their kids had managed to suddenly grow up without my ever getting to know them. It happens fast, I've noticed.

Mary Alice had that soft, gentle glow as usual. She and Pete greeted Mom and Mary warmly and me not too badly either. By and by we made our way to the back of the room and took some seats and visited with some of the other mourners. Looking around I spotted three kids in the second row.

"Must be Pete's," I said to no one in particular. I decided to casually sidle up there, aiming to eventually engage them in conversation and tell them some rollicking good tales about what their parents did at their age. Eventually I took a chair in front of them and ignored them, noticeably.

The oldest, Maria, touched my sleeve. "You must be Bob Going," she said. "My father said you'd probably come over and try to tell us some stories."

I was shocked, I don't mind telling you, that Pete would ever suspect, let alone convey such a thing. So I pretty much saved the stories for another time, lest he should be proven right.

Maria had her mother's looks and charms and her father's spunk, not a bad combination, and *all that's best of dark and bright meet in her aspect and her eyes*, as could be said of her younger sister Gina as well.

The next day, after the funeral, I went up to the farm and spent some time with them.

"Maria wants to hear your stories," Pete informed me.

"Any restrictions?" I asked.

"None whatsoever."

Phew. Now there's a brave and trusting lad.

I decided to wait on it some more, and promised Maria a letter.

It was a good feeling hanging out with them. I felt like I had accomplished something, that my presence had helped lighten the load of their loss for at least a little while. I was rather proud of the way I had handled the whole day, and the maturity I had exhibited.

"So what did you do up there?" Mary asked later at dinner.

I smiled. "I did, I think, what I do best."

"You read their paper?" asked Bobby.
"You slept on their couch?" asked Anna.
"You sat on their toilet?" asked Jamie.

****

Dear Maria,

It was the best of times, it was the worst of times.

I take as my theme the words of Mr. Charles Dickens, for it was his A Tale of Two Cities *that our sophomore class was reading when the great race for the hand of Mary Alice Mezzio really began . . .*

And so I continued, ultimately telling my version of her parents' love story, including maximizing my part in bringing them together. I cast myself in the role of Sydney Carton, of course. Noble self-sacrifice and all that.

Anyway, I concluded the whole thing by asking her to read it aloud to her parents, and to watch for their reactions, especially to notice their middle-aged parent eyes suddenly looking young again.

I was delighted when she wrote back and informed me that all had gone according to plan, and that she had caught them each wiping a tear.

****

The careful reader will observe that in this unfinished excerpt I never really got around to talking about Big Pete Montenaro, the subject of the story and the object of the funeral. Before too many more decades pass, I hope to make up for that deficiency.

At Long Last Dawn
Nov. 10th, 2007 @ 07:51 pm

> *"I'm sorry, Adelaide. I can not get married tonight."*
> *"Why not?"*
> *"I have to go to a prayer meeting."*
> *"Nathan, that is the biggest lie you have ever told me!"*
> *"I swear to you, it's true!"*
>   - Guys and Dolls

This morning I drove up to East Syracuse to attend a breakfast meeting of about 85 Catholic women. Chaste Catholic women. Learning how to be chaster. Really.

Until the priest arrived, I was the only male. By and by a teenage bus boy popped his head in periodically, but that was it.

The occasion was an address by the remarkable Dawn Eden, with whom I have been exchanging emails and blog comments for the last two and a half years, mostly on her esteemed blog, *The Dawn Patrol*.

Shortly after I discovered her blog, I sent her an old piece I had written on Thomas More and the tough decisions judges sometimes face. Minutes later it was on *The Dawn Patrol* and in a brief exchange she encouraged me to start my own blog, and then when I hit a slow period she pushed me to start it up again and keep it going.

It was a crazy period in her life. She had just been fired by the New York Post on the eve of what is arguably her greatest front page headline, acknowledging the latest marriage of The Donald with LADY IS A TRUMP. She had put her first tentative toes on the bridge to Rome, having spent a few protestant years after a lifetime of living as an agnostic unchaste Reform Jew.

She landed on her feet, of course, took a job with the *Daily News*, wrote a book, *The Thrill of the Chaste*, now in its sixth printing, and has been on a whirlwind lecture tour on two continents for the last year, recently taking a position with the Cardinal Newman Society in Washington.

I had thought of driving to Worcester a couple of weeks ago to see her speak at the Bishop's request, but the City Hall boiler blew and we had an emergency meeting of the Common Council that same night. Over the years she has suggested getting together with Mary and me when we are in New York, but it never lined up. I've seen her on television, listened to her on the radio, seen her in numerous video clips and exchanged dozens of correspondences, but we had never met.

Until today.

****

"You know, you look like a judge! I didn't recognize you without your baseball cap."

Yeah, I guess I don't actually look like a judge in that picture, though I was. Now, almost seven years later, finally I look like a judge and I'm not.

****

The presentation was sensational and well-received by a mesmerized audience. I have seen the earlier clips from the tour, and it is amazing how much more polished she is now: relaxed and yet brimming with enthusiasm the whole time. She is in near constant motion and if I didn't know better I'd suggest a strong Italian streak in her gestures   [NOTE TO SAM ZURLO: THIS IS NOT MEANT TO BE STEREOTYPICAL OR DEROGATORY].

I'll have a second post on her speech after I have edited the video clips. That's how I got in. Dawn convinced them that I was her official videographer.

****

Near the end, she talked about her conversion to Catholicism and how difficult it had been and how she had been helped and aided by the encouragement of her friends at The Dawn Patrol.

"And one of those people is here today. His name is Robert N. Going, whom I met here today for the very first time, and I want to thank him."

Well. Wow.

If only the tiniest part of what she said is true, at long last I'll have something to say to The Lord if He should happen to bring up that other stuff.

****

"Hi, Daddy. What were you doing in Syracuse?"
"I went to a lecture, Anna."
"What was it about?"
"Chastity."
"Uh huh. Chastity."
"Chastity."

Archives
Nov. 11th, 2007 @ 07:44 am

Veterans Day Address
Bergen Park
Amsterdam, NY
November 11, 1989
City Court Judge Robert N. Going

How very profound are those moments of silence we observe leading up to the eleventh hour of the eleventh day of the eleventh month. How very different from those last moments of that same time in 1918 when every commander and every foot soldier on every side competed to fire the last shot of the Great War.
. . .

What are they all about, these veterans we honor today? The answer for them, and for us, can be found in the immortal words of that poem we just heard.

> *Take up our quarrel with the foe.*

Who is the foe? For the armed forces of the United States, the foe has always been the same: he is the enemy of human freedom, anywhere, any time. We have fought him at Lexington and Saratoga and Yorktown, the Barbary Coast, Fort McHenry and Gettysburg.

Our grandfathers met him at St. Mihiel and the Argonne Forest and our fathers at Saipan and Iwo Jima and Monte Cassino aand Normandy. Our uncles fought him to a bloody stalemate in Korea and our brothers faced him once again in Vietnam.

Throughout our history the United States has stood for one principle: Liberty. Oh, it has not always been possible or practical or prudent to send our troops in. Sometimes the struggle for liberty must go on without us. Sometimes we can only stand by with tears, as we did watching the brave freedom fighters of Hungary in 1956.

And this June in Tiananmen Square .

Sometimes, though, we stand by with cheers as we did in April when the Polish Parliament overthrew the communists, when the Baltic States declared their independence, when the velvet revolution swept through Czechoslovakia, and yesterday when the Berlin Wall came crashing to the ground.

For us, as Americans, we must honor our veterans in the only way we can: by proclaiming liberty throughout the land, and unto all the inhabitants thereof, and by standing with the friends of freedom in all places and at all times.

We cannot do otherwise.

> *To you from failing hands we throw*
> *The torch; be yours to hold it high.*
> *If ye break faith with us who die,*
> *We shall not sleep, Though poppies grow*
> *In Flanders Fields.*

Did Obama Go Too Far?
Feb. 1st, 2008 @ 10:14 am

In December of 1965, back when I was a high school freshman at SMI, I was invited to attend a Rotary Club luncheon as one of the three finalists from my school in the Four Way Test essay contest. Michele Bazan was the winner and got to read her essay (notwithstanding that 9th grade English teacher Mrs.

Going was one of the judges) and Gail Welch and I were along for the meal.

Mom gave me strict instructions on the finer social skills. Don't wolf down your food. Don't reach across in front of anybody. Please and thank you. All the basics. And by all means remember to hold the chairs for the two ladies.

It went well enough. After all, it was still 1965.

****

Seven plus years later I'm in college at SUNYA and there are no ladies, only womyn, but some of them are nice. Still, the tension level is a little high because Bobby Riggs is about to face Billie Jean King in a tennis match.

I'm walking out of a lecture hall with my friend the Manhattan dentist's daughter and I hold the door open for her, like Mom always said I should.

Ooops.

****

It's not like Barack Obama had the crazed womyn's vote lined up already, or anything, but I couldn't help wondering as he held the chair for Hillary at the last debate, *Is this guy out of his mind?*

Still, he managed to walk away without bruising.

And I'm sure Mom would have approved.

Torture
Feb. 23rd, 2008 @ 10:59 pm

So, I see where the Congress is talking again about banning "waterboarding" when interrogating terrorists who, by the way, happen to reject all norms of International Law and slit innocent people's throats on television, not to mention blowing up Downs Syndrome women and hailing them as Suicide Bombers.

Now, I don't know a whole lot about the process, but I gather it doesn't last long and provides no permanent physical injury and that our own special forces routinely experience it as part of their training. But hey, these same congressmen got all upset when somebody put panties on a terrorist's head.

Anyway, might I suggest a compromise: a perfectly legal and non-controversial method of interrogation which should get the job done in the same amount of time.

Give them all an MRI.

Sure, they know going in that it's only gonna take fifteen minutes and it's not really a sealed coffin.

Believe me, they'll talk.

So they tell me to lie down on this slab that's half the size of my posterior and tell me to lie still with my hands by my side and then the thing wooshes up and shoves me into this tube that's about the same size as me except for my hands which I have to squeeze in and the technician (whose tag reads "Fritz M" which I assume stands for Mengele) observes that if I tilt my head backward I can see the ceiling, which is just great because if I could tilt my head backward I wouldn't need the damn MRI.

Fifteen minutes.

Fifteen minutes.

Fifteen minutes.

They give you ear plugs, because the machine makes an awful lot of noise which bears an uncanny resemblance to techno music but I'm not into techno so I decide to play the score of *Oklahoma!* in my head, not the original cast album, but the motion picture soundtrack, and vinyl at that because I figure that with proper pacing fifteen minutes ought to be enough to cover the first side and I won't have to even flip it over to *People Will Say We're in Love* and the whole thing will be done.

Boom. (That's the kettle drum). And I start the *Overture* and I even go through it a couple of times because I keep thinking I left something out and then I'm riding through the corn fields singing about the morning and even the cattle which they cut that verse out of the movie but it's still on the album. I notice they did that a bit with the *Carousel* album, too. I wonder what ever happened to the Sinatra soundtrack of *Carousel*, 'cause he was in that playing Billy Bigelow and then he quit, but they must have recorded his songs, don't you think?

Then comes *The Surrey With the Fringe On Top*, which is an easy one because I sing that to Laura all the time, all the verses, and with that sealed coffin buzzing away I make sure that on the way home they slow it down to a real slow clip . . . clop. Then everything's going real smooth until I get to *Many a New Day* and I can't for the life of me remember what comes before I'll snap my fingers to show I don't care, so I try backing up to the beginning only it's the beginning I can't remember so I go back to *I'm Just a Girl Who Can't Say No*, which my sister Dale sang when they did *Oklahoma!* in High School right after I graduated, don't you know, when I was in my prime and woulda been perfect for the part, seeing as I knew all the verses to *The Surrey With the Fringe on Top*, except they probably woulda given me Judd Fry instead, *Poor Judd is Dead*. Wait, that's on the second side. So I finish my sister's song and wait for the sound of the click click between the tracks (you youngsters don't even know what I'm talking about, do you?) and I get to the beginning of *Many a New Day* and I STILL can't remember how it starts so I skip ahead to the part I know and many a new day will dawn, many a red sun will set, many a blue moon will shine before I dooooo and I repeat it a couple of times and the damn machine is still buzzin' and hummin' and quarkin' away. Side TWO!

And why DO they think up stories that link my name with yours and there I am listening to Shirley Jones singing away and all of a sudden I can't remember the second verse and say these guys are doing something to my head and it's not fifteen minutes it's two freaking hours and so I skip the verse I can't remember and give her her rose and her glove and don't dance all night with me and I'm thinking what happens if I get all the way to *The Farmer and the Cowman*, given my track record here I'm not sure I'm gonna be able to negotiate *All er Nothin* and I start to panic a little, but that's a long way off and it looks like I may be hearing *Poor Judd* after all, which is ok, because that's a funny one and Mom told me that when she saw *Oklahoma!* in Boston in 1945 with the original touring company, probably with John Raitt, that was the song everyone was humming as they came out of the theater and it's really a shame she didn't get to see it in New York, I mean there she was with tickets and all and nineteen years old bopping down to the Big Apple with a bunch of friends and that WOULD be the day Franklin D. Roosevelt decides to drop dead and they closed the theater out of respect, he being the president and all, and suddenly I'm wooshed out of the tube and ready to tell them EVERYTHING but the only thing Fritz has to say is do you wanna loosen up a bit before we start the next one?

RIP

Sunt Lacrimae Rerum
Apr. 2nd, 2005 @ 08:45 pm

Our church bell tolled 84 times. We draped the front door in purple and black. A framed action photo of the Holy Father was on display in the sanctuary, surrounded by the Easter flowers, propped between the new Paschal Candle and the baptismal font used only last week to welcome and sanctify the new members of our parish.

The mourning came twice: first yesterday, prematurely, when the false announcement came, then this afternoon when I was alone and Mary was teaching the new altar servers. An angel-weeping drizzle had been falling all day. I wiped some tears.

I turned on EWTN. That marvelous female voice with the British accent reading the text while appropriate photos and film from the life of John Paul the Great flashed on the screen:

> *Blessed are the poor in spirit, for theirs is the kingdom of heaven.*
> *Blessed are they who mourn, for they shall be comforted.*
> *Blessed are the meek, for they shall inherit the earth.*
> *Blessed are they who hunger and thirst for righteousness, for they shall be satisfied.*
> *Blessed are the merciful, for they shall be shown mercy.*
> *Blessed are the clean of heart, for they shall see God.*
> *Blessed are the peacemakers, for they shall be called sons of God.*
> *Blessed are they who are persecuted for the sake of righteousness, for theirs is the kingdom of heaven.*
> *Blessed are you when they insult you and persecute you and utter every kind of evil falsely against you because of me.*
> *Rejoice and be glad, for your reward will be great in heaven.*

Well, that did it for me. The pent-up emotion burst forth.

After communion I wandered into the family room (where families with rambunctious kids can watch Mass through a plate-glass window overlooking the sanctuary; it is usually occupied more by middle-aged to elderly people) and knelt with my old high school Polish-American buddy, Brother Alex. After Mass we reminisced briefly about our incredible and saintly Latin teacher, Sister Anna Roberta, CSJ, gone now to her eternal reward.

We looked out at the action photo of the young Pope, and the baptismal waters.

"What would Sister Anna say today?"

"I think," I said, "that she would first say, '*sunt lacrimae rerum*' ["there are tears for things", from the Aeneid].

I paused.

"And then she would say, '*Fiat*'."

Yes.

Fiat.

Fiat voluntas tua.

To SAR, With Love
Oct. 22nd, 2005 @ 09:31 am [written February,1994]

And Sister Anna Roberta said, "*Fiat Lux*", and there was light.

How extraordinary that a quarter of a century after my last Latin class with Sister Anna I reflect not on how excruciating the study of an ancient tongue could be, but on how exciting; not on how pointless, but on how many times a week I still point to things I learned from her; not on the deadness of the language, but on the magnificence of the life that one amazing teacher could breathe into it. (I also reflect that in writing this paragraph I make no effort to truly emulate the Ciceronian cadence which she cherished, which, after all, would require several more pages and somewhere around here would be the verb).

Sister Anna left us on February 15, 1994, for over sixty years a member of the Sisters of St. Joseph of Carondolet. Consider for a moment the depth of that commitment: an entire long life dedicated to service to others, to education, to enlightenment.

After her simple and moving funeral Mass at the Provincial House in Latham, NY, after the spontaneous bursting into song of her old friends and students as her earthly remains were carried away (the *Bishop Scully High School Alma Mater*, which she had written, and the somewhat strained strains of the *Gaudeamus*, which she had made her own), former students, former colleagues and friends mingled and shared their experiences.

"I had the ill fortune of replacing her in Saratoga in 1944," said one. "They told me they were sure I'd be all right, but there could never be another Sister Anna Roberta."

"I came after her in college. The professors told me that she was the finest student the college had ever produced."

Another former teacher of mine was there. She had been a student half a century earlier and said she had come because this was the greatest teacher she had ever known. All within earshot nodded in unison.

As Father Brad Milunski pointed out in his marvelous homily, words were her life and she could find endless wonder in a single phrase. I will do him one better. When I was a freshman she had one day in the front of her classroom a sign with the single word "meum" on it. The final "m" was lit up and blinking like on of those all-night eatery logos.

Of course, she waited till someone asked her what it meant. "The *'meum'* is the final word in the Consecration of the Eucharist in the Mass," she explained. "That last, glorious 'm' is the very moment when the Eucharistic bread is transformed into the Body of Jesus!"

She went on to further elaborate on how marvelous it was that the words of consecration should end in a liquid consonant, one whose sound itself trailed off almost infinitely.

You see, then, that not only a phrase could excite her, but that she could see volumes of theology in a single letter.

And oh, how she loved to sing. I would almost say we spent more time singing than we did learning our declensions, but for the fact that she had us singing AND learning our declensions simultaneously.

> -a is for the nom-in-A-tive
> -ae genitive and dative
> -am accusative, the ablative long -a,

et cetera for about another forty verses.

She translated quite a large volume of popular songs into Latin, and was a master of the parody form. On my way to her funeral, one suddenly popped into my head. (I say this with some hesitation, as Sister never much believed in things just "happening".) It was to the tune of that old World War I era waltz, *Till We Meet Again*:

> *Smile the while you count to thirty-one.*
> *Wonder which will be my setting sun?*
> *Which will be the day for me*
> *To begin Eternity?*
> *Every time a calendar I see,*
> *Wonder which will be the day for me?*
> *Every month I pass it by,*
> *Till the day I die.*

She considered the day of her death to be more important than her birthday, more important than ANY other day, the day she was to enter into her eternal reward.

If "m" was her favorite letter, Sister Anna's favorite word was "*fiat*" as in "*fiat lux*" ("let there be light"), but more importantly as in "*fiat voluntas tua*" ("Thy Will be done") and as in "Be it done unto me according to thy word". She firmly believed that if you cheerfully accept the pitfalls of living common to us all, the Almighty will personally reward you in this world as well as the next. Her entire life was a fiat and an inspiration.

Do not think that Sister Anna was some fuddy-duddy. On the contrary, she placed herself always on the cutting edge of technology and popular culture. One of my college professors, who viewed her with awe, told me that in the Classics community she was known as "Sister Anna Roberta Tape Recorder". What a shame that her teaching career ended at the dawn of the age of the Camcorder and the Personal Computer. What fun she would have had! Somewhere, probably in many somewheres, lie dusty overhead projector rolls; neatly grommetted black drapes; home-made Super-8 movies; slides of the class of '69 in The Legend of King Midas; endless audio tapes of generations of students featured in countless performances of song and silliness; *Veni-Vidi-Vici-VINGO* cards; boxes of unsold professionally produced *Alma Mater* records for a school that no longer exists.

Each school year concluded with the "Roman Banquet". Each year, in a long tradition, the banquet climaxed with a gift to Sister and an original song to her by the Senior Class. A year or two after my class the song was *To SAR, With Love*, which just about says it all. But since I'm writing this and since I wrote the song for Omicron Delta Class of 1969, I will quote from the latter instead. It is to the tune of *Try to Remember* and essentially in three verses attempts to cover four years of high school. Even though I was only 17 at the time and can probably be forgiven for excesses of youth, I will nonetheless skip over the parts about Caesar having a lot of Gaul and get down to the final verse:

> *Third year passed, though we*
> *Felt as it passed slowly*
> *We neared the end, and soon would part.*
> *And nearing the end, too, we'd all like to send you*
> *The deep'ning love that's in our heart,*
> *But most of all we know*
> *How much that we owe you*
> *And wish we could show you*
> *In some way not hollow.*
> *In life's last December, we'll fondly remember*
> *And follow.*

And so, dear Sister Anna Roberta, CSJ, you have graduated to glory, safe at last in heaven's freshman class, and we who are forever in your debt and left behind can only muster up a poor paraphrase of the Roman poet Catullus and ask:

That you accept these funeral offerings, wet with a disciple's tears,
And for all mortal time, Magistra, "*Ave Atque Vale*".

Hail and Farewell.

Cheer up! Life Isn't Everything
Jun. 9th, 2005 @ 09:09 pm

Long before Lucianne Goldberg founded Lucianne.com there was Trixie and Me.

Not that we ever met or anything.

Back in the bad old days, 1998, Lucianne was in the news for her role in advising Linda Tripp to tape her phone conversations with Monica Lewinsky about . . .well, you know. She also commented frequently as "Trixie" over at FreeRepublic.com and once, rather casually I thought, dropped her aol email address which I promptly plugged into my Instant Messenger buddy list.

Hey, part of me is political groupie. There's a semi-famous picture floating around of me at 9, squeezing into a shot with Richard Nixon. So, when Trixie signed on, I "IM"ed her a fan note and said there was no need to reply, but of course she did. (Even the famous appreciate compliments, I've noticed). Before long we were chatting away about Linda Tripp's legal problems. Even though I was a sitting judge and it was probably not proper for me to be handing out legal advice, I couldn't resist. (I don't think Linda ever took any of my free advice. If she had, she might have short-circuited the most agonizing ordeal of her life, but I guess I can understand that legal opinions given by some guy who broke into Lucianne's IM and claimed to be a judge might be taken with a grain of salt. It really was wonderful advice, however, and someday I may write a Law Review article on how Linda Tripp's lawyers missed the most obvious end-of-story-case-dismissed defense.)

Well, the months went by and the years went by and we kept chatting and emailing. Some of it was really hilarious stuff that neither one of us will ever be able to put in print. There were unforgettable times, too, like when we were both up early enraged over the Elian Gonzales raid, or the morning of September 11, 2001 when we kept the line open and learned simultaneously of the death of her friend Barbara Olson.

After she started *Lucianne.com* (I was a charter poster, SamuelSpade) she got into talk radio, and I would listen on the Internet at work, and when it was running fast enough to be nearly simultaneous I would sometimes be able to feed her jokes or other info which she would invariably use, except for the joke about Big Leroy which she hesitated about and then finally discretion prevailed (though she later emailed it to everyone she knew).

Her husband Sid joined the show from time to time and then all the time and they were just wonderful together. I knew he was some kind of big shot in the information industry. Obviously he was very comfortable having a wife with a strong identity and career of her own (though why she gave up being a book agent just before I finished my great American still unread novel I'll never know). I could just tell that they greatly enjoyed each other's company and I suspect there was a lot of laughter on the upper west side. She told me once how they would go out to dinner and if she was particularly enjoying her meal, he would sing to her a variation of Allan Sherman's parody of *Glow Worm*:

> *Grow, Mrs. Goldberg, bigger, bigger. . .*

The laughter ended last night with the death of Lucianne's beloved Sidney.

I learned about it this afternoon in a brief announcement at *National Review Online*, where their son Jonah is the editor.

I've never set eyes on Sid. Or Lucianne. Or Jonah, or Joshua. Yet I grieved for them as I would for one of my own. Realizing there would be hundreds of people doing the same, I nonetheless needed to send Lucianne a note of condolence, by email, of course. She always calls me "Bean", because I am her friend The Judge, just like Judge Roy Bean, the Law West of the Pecos.

Incredibly, with all she had to do, she answered almost immediately:

Thank you so much, Bean.

Sid has a phrase he loved: Cheer up, life isn't everything. Now he knows what he was talking about. I believe I will be with him again and I've promised him we'll get a dog.
We had a wonderful marriage and life and he left a huge part of himself here in his boys. I don't think any woman could ask for more.

Love to you,

Lucianne

I contemplated that phrase over and over. "Cheer up, life isn't everything."

Could there be a more joyous theology?

William Rehnquist, RIP
Sep. 4th, 2005 @ 01:01 am

Back in the old days when I was a real judge, and not just the titled-for-life kind, whenever a Justice of the Supreme Court died or retired, I would invariably get an excited call from Mary advising that I just went up a notch in seniority.

You'd have to climb mighty high to be able to jump into and fill Bill Rehnquist's robe. I met him once, back in the late 70's when he gave the Robert Jackson lecture at Albany Law School (Rehnquist had clerked for Jackson, an Associate Justice of the Supreme Court, Chief prosecutor at Nuremberg, and a graduate of Albany Law, just like me).

He seemed almost painfully shy, which surprised me. His talk was intelligent, coherent, precise. So were his judicial decisions.

More able people than I will write his epitaph. He earned his place in judicial heaven and made himself worthy of the real one with this dissent:

> The Court's opinion decides that a State may impose virtually
> no restriction on the performance of abortions during the first
> trimester of pregnancy. I have difficulty in concluding, as the
> Court does, that the right of ``privacy" is involved in this case.
> A transaction resulting in an operation such as this is not
> ``private" in the ordinary usage of that word. Nor is the
> ``privacy" that the Court finds here even a distant relative of
> the freedom from searches and seizures protected by the
> Fourth Amendment to the Constitution. ...The decision here to
> break pregnancy into three distinct terms and to outline the
> permissible restrictions the State may impose in each one, for
> example, partakes more of judicial legislation. ...Even today,
> when society's views on abortion are changing, the very
> existence of the debate is evidence that the ``right" to an
> abortion is not so universally accepted as the appellant would
> have us believe.

-Roe v. Wade, 1973

RIP Maynard G. Crebs
Sep. 7th, 2005 @ 02:00 am

It was this baby-boomer's favorite character of his favorite show of the era. I
don't know who that guy playing Gilligan was, but Bob Denver as Maynard
was pure genius at work.

Rest in peace, good buddy.

Simon Wiesenthal, RIP
Sep. 22nd, 2005 @ 12:23 am

The witnesses to the greatest horror of the twentieth century are fast disappearing, and the greatest of them all, Simon Wiesenthal, died this week at 96.

The lives of the last two popes were profoundly influenced by the Nazi terror, John Paul by the occupation of his native Poland and the witnessing of Kracow's own version of Kristallnacht and the sufferings of his Jewish friends, and Benedict by his forced military duty and his family's disgust and loathing of their regime. The result has been a body of theology and action to reassert the Jewish roots of Christianity and to attempt to heal the wounds and divisions brought about by centuries of perversions of Judeo-Christian ideals.

It should come as no surprise that as Europe has become decreasingly Christian it has become increasingly anti-semitic, not just in the subtle forms, but more and more overtly. Anti-semitism has become almost fashionable again, as it was in the days leading up to the Final Solution.

Dawn Eden presents an interesting perspective today from the point of view of a young Jewish woman about to become a Catholic. Let me throw in my two cents as a cradle Catholic.

Is it any wonder the Jews don't trust us? Anti-semitism, a defined sin, is lurking just beneath the surface in clubs and offices and bars and coffee shops all over the place. I have heard adults who are old enough to know better spout such nonsense as "Adolph Hitler wasn't all bad," (I'm serious) and how "the Jews" were responsible for much of the destruction of their own people.

One day at lunch, maybe fifteen years ago, some of the older guys were talking. There had been a television show about the death camps the night before.

"I am so sick and tired of hearing about the Holocaust!" pronounced one local businessman. "Is that all they have to talk about? That was fifty years ago! Why do they keep bringing it up over and over and over?"

And as the others started to nod in agreement I took advantage of the temporary silence to say, "Maybe because it happened."

A few of them, fortunately, looked ashamed.

I sat at a family function a couple of summers ago with my wife's sister's father-in-law. He told me what it was like to be a Jewish-American soldier in World War II, to be sent to Europe, to be among the first to liberate a death camp.

"It wasn't one of the big ones. You probably never heard of it. The things I saw you just couldn't believe."

He shook his head quietly.

"I'll never forget the smell."

Simon Wiesenthal forced us to remember when every fiber of our being and the inertia of many of our institutions conspired to make us want to forget.

We should honor him in the only way he would want us to.

We must remember.

Rosa Parks, RIP
Oct. 25th, 2005 @ 09:17 am

Somewhere back around the time I was about to enter kindergarten, *i.e.* 1956, Mom took us to a shoe store in downtown Albany. The sales clerk was a scrawny middle-aged woman with a tight bun and a weathered look. My memory is that she was wearing a gray dress, but maybe that's just because my memories of the 50's are mostly black and white.

An African-American youth, maybe twelve years old, examined shoes nearby. He picked one up, admired it, and turned to our sales clerk and said, "How much are these?"

The woman grew all flustered and said, "Oh, those aren't available to the public."

As I say, I was young, and had never recalled hearing "public" before. But I was a bright lad, and quickly examined the context. I learned a new word.

"Public" means "negroes".

****

Rosa Parks is dead at 92. Thank God and thank Rosa Parks that my children have no concept of the world she knew. It's hard to believe now that just a year before I got those new shoes THE LAW in Montgomery, Alabama said that if you were sitting on a bus and your skin was dark and a person with white skin wanted your seat, you MUST yield.

Rosa Parks did not yield.

She recognized what THE LAW did not, that she was a child of God, a human being, a PERSON with all the dignity that goes along with that.

She was one small woman, alone, who understood the true meaning of justice.

The movement she ignited with that single act of righteous defiance led nine years later to the Civil Rights Act of 1964, which spawned the Voting Rights Act of 1965. She helped liberate not only the black race in this country, but to a real extent the white race as well.

Remember Rosa Parks the next time you despair that one person can't do anything, or complain that you can't fight City Hall, or fail to act for fear of what others might think.

Enter into the Kingdom, Rosa Parks.

The public thanks you.

Your nation thanks you.

Eugene McCarthy, RIP
Dec. 10th, 2005 @ 11:19 pm

Former Minnesota Senator Eugene McCarthy has died at the age of 89. Back in 1968, when I was a junior in High School, he ran a quixotic campaign for president, challenging Lyndon Johnson in the early primaries. At a time when the really scummy look was becoming popular, "Keep Clean with Gene" was the slogan of his student volunteers.

He is often credited with having driven Johnson from the presidency. I don't believe he ever actually won a primary, but he beat the expectations game. He was on the ballot in New Hampshire and Johnson wasn't. Johnson's 55% of the vote came on write-ins. Still, McCarthy's 45% was astonishing. In April he finished strong in Wisconsin as well.

His success proved to be his undoing. Bobby Kennedy, suddenly realizing that Johnson was vulnerable, hastily announced his own candidacy, probably four years ahead of his previous game plan.

In an amazing week or so in April of 1968, Johnson got hammered in Wisconsin, Martin Luther King was assassinated (with the accompanying riots in numerous cities), Johnson announced the beginning of the Paris Peace Talks, and oh, by the way, I've decided not to seek or accept a renomination.

The whole game changed overnight. McCarthy now had to face not only another anti-war liberal in Kennedy, but also a traditional liberal and fellow Minnesotan, Vice President Hubert H. Humphrey. If enough wasn't already happening, Bobby Kennedy was shot and killed right after winning the California Primary in June.

While there was some talk of drafting 36 year old Ted Kennedy, who had given a stunning and emotional eulogy at his brother's funeral, McCarthy was really the only one left to carry the anti-war banner at the Chicago convention. The less-than-clean rioting demonstrators disrupted the affair and split the party wide open. The old pro-American wing never recovered. Their last gasp was Humphrey's nomination. The hate-America-first crowd took over for good in 1972, but their nominee was George McGovern, not McCarthy, for just as quickly as McCarthy rose, he faded away.

Eight years after his brief fame, as Spring ended in a year when Ronald Reagan still had a chance to dethrone President Ford at the Republican Convention, McCarthy gave the baccalaureate address the night before my brother Tim's graduation from RPI. At the reception afterwards, I noticed him just standing around, alone. I slipped my Reagan button into my pocket and went over to chat.

He was kind, gracious, witty, unassuming. I liked him.

Unlike many of the wackos who followed him, I think McCarthy was a sincere man, who opposed the Vietnam War for honorable reasons. There weren't too many guys like him, and way too many of the John Kerry types. It's sad that ultimately his legacy is wrapped up in his political progeny.

Rest in Peace, Senator. You never would have had my vote, but you earned my respect.

RIP Coretta Scott King
Jan. 31st, 2006 @ 07:53 am

Dignity. Courage. Class.

She taught us to love one another when she had no reason to.

Greatness in a small package.

Lyn Nofziger, RIP
Mar. 29th, 2006 @ 08:39 am

I'm most saddened at the passing of my fellow-blogger Lyn Nofziger.

Personally, I have never been a slave to fashion. Despite my profession, I don't think I even own a suit that fits me. I know I haven't worn one in a long time. When I was on the bench I rarely even brought a sportcoat to work. Usually had a sweater if it was chilly.

I never really understood the concept of a tie, but I wear them, because there are certain things you just have to do, but, unlike some judges, I never complained or felt insulted if a lawyer forgot to put his on.

Sure, he served his country and his president, Ronald Reagan, splendidly and deserves our thanks and blessings for that, but his lasting legacy is that Lyn Nofziger knew how to wear a tie. He liberated a whole generation of us, and for that there is no honor great enough, nor praise, nor glory.

Rest in Peace.

RIP Caspar Weinberger
Mar. 29th, 2006 @ 08:57 pm

The death of Lyn Nofziger, noted in my previous post, had me reflecting on the many truly extraordinary people Ronald Reagan kept in his circle. They were quite a bunch, not only talented, but articulate spokesmen of Reagan's core beliefs, who used their skills to implement those beliefs and in the process left this country and the world a much better place than they found it. I'm thinking of Nofziger, of course, and Ed Meese and George Schultz, William Bennett and Jack Kemp.

Maybe the greatest and most articulate of them all was Caspar Weinberger.

He was one of the Californians, instrumental in Reagan's early political career and a gifted advisor who first straightened out California's budget for Reagan and then went on to Washington to perform exceptionally in several offices in the Nixon Administration.

Reagan came to office determined to turn around our military from the doldrums and decay of the Carter years. He knew Weinberger was the guy who could do it. He became one of the longest-tenured Secretaries of Defense. He was self-assured, confident, determined. By the time he was done, the Cold War was over, and we won. Reagan set the policy; Weinberger believed in it and delivered.

In his calm, steady manner he made mincemeat of political opponents and media celebrities. He defended the cause as well as he defended the country. We should be eternally grateful for his life.

And what a happy place heaven is getting to be this week. I'll bet the members of the old gang are tipping a few and swapping yarns and hopefully still keeping a careful eye on the country they served so well.

Fiddlers
Mar. 31st, 2006 @ 06:06 pm

> *Before the fiddlers have fled,*
> *Before they ask us to pay the bill*
> *And while we still have a chance,*
> *Let's face the music and dance.*
> *-Irving Berlin*

Ed McBain's fifty-fifth, first posthumous, and perhaps final 87th Precinct novel, *Fiddlers,* may well be his best. The finest ensemble cast in the history of crime fiction takes one last bow, in style.

The plot begins with the shooting death of a blind violin player by what turns out to be a serial killer (I'm really not giving much away here), and Ed McBain's good alter-ego Steve Carella leads the gang in solving the crime, as he has for the past half-century. In the process we get a little bit into the head of the perp who is also, I suspect, an alter-ego of the dying author.

Wit, charm, emotion, pathos, courage, betrayal, romance, jealousy, revenge, terror: it's all here in grand doses.

The Berlin quote above is early-on attributed by one of the characters to Cole Porter, and I am sure that's not an author flub but an author joke, much as his later, "The French have a word for it: 'ambulance.'"

Many a fine evening I've spent in the last forty years with the Mystery Writers of America Grand Master. I tried to emulate his style, but I couldn't. No one could, though I have honored him in my own murder mystery, *The Evil Has Landed* (not available anywhere) by naming the mythical village of Fort McBain as the site of the principal murder.

Farewell, Ed McBain, or Evan Hunter, or whoever you really were.

> *There may be teardrops to shed,*
> *But while there's moonlight and music and*
> *Love and romance,*
> *Let's face the music and dance.*

Introibo Ad Altare Dei
Apr. 5th, 2006 @ 10:17 am

> *A teacher affects eternity; he can never tell where his influence stops.*
> *-Henry Brook Adams*

Newly-ordained Fr. Joe Cotugno joined the faculty of St. Mary's Institute in the fall of 1964 at the ripe old age of 25. He and Mom became fast friends instantly. At her funeral he told us about how she would cover for him when he would sneak out of school to appear in court with some troubled teen or another. That was Father Joe, always there when you needed him, always bending the rules a little, always knowing what was important.

He became a fixture in our living room. We had a pretty beat-up third-hand furniture set and one of the big stuffed chairs became "Father Joe's chair". His oversized body had destroyed the springs on his first plop.

His laughter was infectious, his joy boundless, his politics maddening. This was the autumn of the Goldwater campaign and Father Joe was a dyed-in-the-wool 1960's liberal. He and Dad would argue for hours on end, before, during and after dinner. When at last the hour grew late and the door finally closed, Dad turned to Mom.

"You now, I respect that man more and more every time I meet him."

****

He took a liking to me. I don't know whether he looked on me as a long-term project, or just another one of those early teens who needed a little guidance, or maybe he just enjoyed my company. I didn't shy from a good political debate myself, not even at thirteen.

The following year he became my freshman religion teacher, the first post-Vatican II. (Literally- the council had just ended.) He immersed us in scripture scholarship, and looking back I realize now that he was teaching

 first-year high school kids the stuff of later college work. I found it fascinating. One day he had Tim Blanchfield and me teaching a class on Hebrew cosmology. It was a noble experiment that failed miserably. Tim was one of his projects too. I believe it was he who gave Father Joe the nickname "Big Oscar".

****

At a CYO dance, you see boys and girls prance.
You wonder what they are doing.
It's that sort of thing where a priest starts to sing
With all of the spectators booing.

The music is slow, and then Father Joe
Begins with his mulish braying.
He may thrill the horde, but won't get far with the Lord
If that is his manner of praying.
-R. Poeta, 1965

****

"Mrs. G! You look like you're pregnant in that dress!"

Ooops.

"Robert, why didn't you tell me you mother was pregnant?"

"Sorry, Father Joe. I was the last to know."

It had been twelve years since her fourth child. Who would have thought? To make up for his *faux pas* he organized baby showers and little surprises for the next several months, and of course got the early-morning call from Dad.

"Father Cotugno is in bed. You must not disturb him!" cranked the Cuban priest.

Dad talked his way through to him anyway, and of course Father Joe did the Baptism, and had plenty of Uncle Nilo's meatballs afterwards.

****

He started youth groups, folk Masses, you name it. He spread himself pretty thin, but then, there was a lot of him to spread.

He talked me into joining the CYO at the parish where he served as assistant, St. Michael's. In a way, he was rather like Bing Crosby to Msgr. Beck's Barry Fitzgerald. Msgr. Beck liked him (it was really impossible not to), but couldn't figure him out, I don't think.

I sat with Msgr. at a CYO dinner one time.

"Tell me, Bob, do young people really need to have contemporary music to get them to come to church? Isn't the myssssstery and the magesssty enough?"

I laughed. "You're asking the wrong guy, Father! I don't get it myself, but at least the kids are coming to church." He nodded. With a very puzzled look.

In 1967 he took me with a bunch of other kids from the diocese and a whole mess of chaperones to the National CYO Convention in Miami Beach, which became one of the highlights of my life, for many reasons. He arranged for me to be a voting delegate, and I met some wonderful people from around the country, and got to see my music hero Allan Sherman, and Hubert Humphrey and Eunice Kennedy Shriver, long before my unfortunate incident with Maria.

I think that's when I began to emerge from my shell and developed some self-confidence. Life, despite its ups and downs, seems to have been a whole lot better after that.

Toward the end of that school year, Father Joe was transferred out of Amsterdam. The CYO gave him a farewell party. What I remember about it is that we were both exhausted. Bobby Kennedy had been shot the night before and we had both been up for 36 hours at that point. We said goodbye. It was hard.

But not as hard as this time.

****

He returned twice more to Amsterdam later in his priesthood, first as Chaplain at St. Mary's Hospital, and then as Pastor of St. Michael's when Msgr. retired. Later, three parishes merged and to make the transition complete the three pastors got bounced.

We kept in touch over the years, though not as much as we should have. He was there for the weddings, even flying to Martha's Vineyard on a private jet he commandeered for Dale's, but in later years it was mostly just bumping into him at funerals and such. Always the big hug and the mile-wide smile.

As I leaned over his hospital bed to kiss him goodbye, for the last time, he grabbed both of my hands in an iron grip.

"How are *you* doing?" he wanted to know, as he always did, even now.

I couldn't speak much, certainly not enough to find the words to thank him or tell him how I felt. But he knew.

He could barely move, and yet what little strength he had left, he was spending on me.

"How are *you* doing?"

Father Joe.

Thou art a priest forever.

Rev. Joseph P. Cotugno
Entered Holy Orders, 1964
Gone Unto the Altar of God
April 5, 2006

The Passion
Apr. 8th, 2006 @ 08:37 pm

Shortly before Palm Sunday, 1968, when I was 16, my mentor Father Joe Cotugno informed me that I would be taking part in the reading of the Passion. It was the first time for the "Performance Version" of the Passion, so I had little idea what he was talking about, but I did as I was told. We "volunteers" were dressed up in white albs and cinctures and foisted upon the startled congregation of St. Michael's Parish.

It was an awesome and moving experience for me, one I have engaged in nearly every year since at one place or another, and sometimes twice, as I have often done St. John's version on Good Friday as well. Usually I have been the Narrator, though for a few years Ray Jurus and I would fight over that part, the loser playing Jesus, who has some good lines, of course, and whatever woman they got to join us being stuck with the numerous "Voice" parts on our theory that it would not be proper for a male to play the girl at the gate asking Peter if he was one of the disciples. Somehow we always got away with that.

Ray eventually died, and since the role of Jesus in recent years has been read by the celebrant priest (as Father Joe himself did the first time, insisting there was no one more suited for the part), I've been pretty much exclusively the narrator.

The girl part thing has been quietly erased by the scriptwriters; her lines I noticed in this year's Markan version have been turned over to the "Crowd", *i.e.* the congregation, and I suddenly found myself this evening playing all the voices for the first time in many years, maybe twenty or thirty. It was a whole new experience.

And so I became the denying Peter, the treacherous Judas, the jealous High Priest, the cowardly Pilate: all those folks who remind us of our own human weaknesses, who can't find a way to do the right thing even when in the direct presence of the Creator of the Universe. That can be pretty humbling, if you think about it.

****

It rather gets you thinking about the virtues of suffering and self-sacrifice too. Earlier in the day Mary and I attended Father Joe's funeral Mass at our honeymoon parish, St. James in Albany.

Father Joe came down with diabetes while still in his thirties, with all the complications that go with it. His total kidney failure beginning twelve years ago made his ordinary ministry impossible, but it didn't keep him down. He worked his schedule around the permanent dialysis and filled in all over the place.

He brought his extraordinary brand of gregariousness among other places into the most opposite venue, the Capital District Psychiatric Center. Last Sunday, knowing he was about to die, he returned there in a wheel chair from St. Peter's Hospice and said Mass for his patients. He told them that he was there for selfish reasons, that from those shattered souls he drew strength, and that he came away from there with far more than he could ever give. He preached to them about suffering, and death, and of life everlasting.

The funeral was lovely and eclectic. We brought blind Rachelle Cotugno to sing for him, a promise she made at his bedside last Monday. Father Joe had given her her first job at St. Michael's where she formed a contemporary music group, and over the years she has held several positions as a music teacher, including now at St. Mary's. There seems to be so little disability in her disability, and that's partly because she drew plenty of strength and confidence from Father Joe over the years.

For a "modern" priest, his tastes were all over the lot. An Eastern Rite monastery sent a contingent of monks and nuns to perform several chants. Fulfilling his desire for the cutting-edge ritual of the bizarre, we had a sacred mother-earth type incense dance with a pot of smoke escorted up the aisle, all the time accompanied incongruously by the *a capella* monks. He would have loved it, and laughed heartily when telling about it afterwards.

The Bishop spoke for a while at the end, looking back nearly half a century to their first day together at Mater Christi seminary. Before that day was over, Father Joe was on a first-name basis with everyone in the place, including the professors.

"He was a man without guile. What you saw was what you got."

No Father Joe event would be complete without food, and so his sister-in-law's family organized a spread in the school gym afterwards worthy of Jiggers DiCaprio in his prime.

There were five items of remembrance on display. As Father Joe himself scrutinized every detail, I'm sure they were personally chosen. They included a baseball hat with his personal logo "Holy Man" with a cross beneath, an 8x10 framed photo of himself with his dog, a scrap book of cards received on his 40th anniversary as a priest, a photo album covering the last ten years or so.

And a poem by Dale Going.

RIP Clarabell the Clown
May. 17th, 2006 @ 01:30 pm

For us baby-boomers, a good friend and daily companion has passed away. There was a time, at least in this area, when the television day didn't start until late afternoon with Buffalo Bob and the Howdy Doody Show.

Seems to me that brother Jay had a Clarabell t-shirt with a built-in horn.

Buffalo Bob came to SUNY Albany when I was there. Quite the character.

I wonder if Princess Summerfallwinterspring is still with us?

[UPDATE: In viewing the comments at FreeRepublic on this story, it seems every male from that era is asking the same question!]

[UPDATE UPDATE: Here's a sure sign of age: the original princess, played by Judy Tyler, was killed in a car crash July 4, 1957 (the same fate as the original host of the Freddy Freihofer show for you capital district types). One of her final acting gigs was as co-star with Elvis in Jailhouse Rock. Later, Princess Summerfallwinterspring was reintroduced--- as a puppet! This probably explains a lot of baby boomer Stephen King's mindset.]

Marie Mercurio Hastings, RIP
Jun. 9th, 2006 @ 08:48 pm

Marie Hastings has died. That won't mean much to most of you, since she rarely traveled outside of Amsterdam, New York. She never had a driver's license and usually walked the three quarters of a mile to St. Mary's for the eight o'clock Mass every morning, often accompanied by her mother, who finally passed on to her reward three years ago after having lived in all of one and parts of two other centuries.

Marie was the same age as my father and shared the same circle of friends back in the thirties. Her life-long friend Dorothy Langley Sweeney, who choked back tears leading the rosary tonight, was my father's junior prom date and the sister of his best friend and later best man.

Marie married Ed Hastings the day I was born, June 30, 1951, and they had six kids together, two lovely daughters followed by four spirited boys. The second daughter, Karen, has been a good friend of my sister since high school, at least. Still, for the life of me I can't remember how Marie and Mom ended up being best, almost inseparable friends for the last twenty years of Mom's life.

I know the Hastings used to come over and play cards once in a while when Dad was still with us, and they were among a handful of couples outside the family invited to their twenty-fifth anniversary the year before Dad died. I suppose they had crossed paths at school functions. Must be all this developed while I was away at college.

Anyway, once Mom was free to get out after five years of around the clock taking care of Dad, she began to travel here and there and more often than not, Marie would go with her. It was always someplace where one of the sibs was living so the overhead was kept down. What they saved on accommodations they spent on garage sales. Of course, since Marie didn't drive and Mom didn't drive farther than church, they usually dragged somebody else along, too. They had oodles of fun.

And they started working together. When Mom became director of the Fulmont Learning Center, she brought Marie in as her assistant and together they learned to teach English as a Second Language without any competency in any other language whatsoever. Later, after the school closed, Marie hooked up with Montgomery Transitional Services caring for mentally ill adults and brought Mom in. This went on for years and years until the cancer hit Mom.

And then, in those last months, Marie was a regular visitor, sitting with Mom for hours, bringing her communion from church, praying the rosary with her.

****

The rosary is recited by the faithful every weekday morning after the 8 o'clock Mass. Until her illness, Marie had always taken an active role, generally leading a decade and devoting it to her special intention, "We pray for the salvation and sanctification of our children and grandchildren." It was her highest desire that they not be led astray from the Faith that she and her friends so carefully handed down.

Tonight a large crowd said the rosary together at Marie's wake. I brought my special one along.

I figured if it was powerful enough to help Notre Dame beat LSU and the Red Sox beat the Yankees, those super-prayers to the Blessed Mother would easily oil the hinges on heaven's gate to speed the entrance of a gentle saint.

The Godfather
Aug. 1st, 2006 @ 04:36 pm

We had taken the kids camping on the night of August 1-2, 1991. They were pretty small then: 10 ½, 8 ½, 6 ½, 1 ½. Moffit's Beach in Speculator, NY, about sixty miles north and way uphill from here on the Little Sacandaga Lake, pretty much the headwaters of the main branch of the Sacandaga River. It's a nice family-oriented state campground and a great place to escape the dog days of summer.

We had two cars with us, which turned out to be a good thing, because someone had left a door ajar and by the time we were ready to hop in the van on the morning of August 2nd for a trip to an old swimming hole on the east branch of the Sacandaga at Wells, the battery was stone dead.

After the usual amount of aggravation I managed to jump the battery and get it going again, but the clock had to be reset to make up for the lost hours. None of us had a watch, so I flipped on the radio to WGY in Schenectady, one of the few stations you can pick up in the daylight at such a remote spot. The local news had just started.

The flags in front of the Montgomery County Sheriff's Department in Fonda are flying at half staff today.

And here I held my breath.

Deputy Sheriff Gary Johnson was killed last night when his automobile . . .

Mary screamed.

I turned numb.

The kids couldn't figure out what was wrong.

"Bobby," I said, "your godfather is dead."

****

I had met Gary in passing outside of church one day, not long after we were married. He was from New Hampshire, but his wife was an old school chum of Mary, so the two of us just stood around awkwardly as the girls exchanged a couple of minutes of information for a half hour or so. It was always like that.

I got to know him, though, within my first couple of weeks as an assistant district attorney in 1981. At the time he was a full time patrolman for the Fort Plain Police Department and I was the brand new ADA assigned to the Town of Minden Justice Court. He was thorough, professional, creative, smart and just a great guy to be with. I began hanging out in the stationhouse after court and bounced around in the patrol car with him. He introduced me to most of the usual suspects in the village, which turned out to be pretty useful to me when I ended up investigating a murder up there one Palm Sunday morning, an event which after a little fictionalizing became the root of my novel.

We became fast friends, and a year and a half later when Bobby was born Mary and I asked Gary and Lori to be his godparents. Not long after that their first son was born, and then another and the families would get together a little bit now and again, though not as often as we would have liked. After I left the DA's office in 1983 the regular contact ceased, but irregularly we still kept up the friendship and Gary and I could talk shop and socialize every bit as well as our gabby spouses. He told me once how when he was a kid the fellow across the street had a visit from his uncle. Before even being introduced, Gary recognized the voice and that's how he ended up playing with Walter Brennan.

Eventually Gary became a full time Deputy with the Montgomery County Sheriff's Department and he was a whiz. One time he recovered some stolen property. Unfortunately, they had been unable to link the possession with the underlying burglary, a far more serious charge. Gary decided it would be a good idea to take one of the items, an 8mm movie camera, and have the film developed. As it happens these Darwinian wonders had taken turns filming each other burglarizing the house.

Then there were the goofballs who had a beer party in a mausoleum and started playing kickball with a human skull. Gary wrapped that one up in five minutes. He had seen the crew buying that brand of beer earlier in the evening. They all confessed.

So did the guys who broke into an abandoned hotel and stole some chairs. One of them even pointed out how he had deliberately broken one of the chair rungs because, "That way I figured no one would believe I would steal a broken chair." Unless Gary wanted to know.

****

It had been a routine domestic call. Gary was drifting back into patrol mode, just before midnight, heading down the Cooperstown Road, Route 80, on his way into Fort Plain. He entered a wide curve in the highway. Approaching from the other direction was a white van, driven by someone Gary knew. In fact, he had rescued this guy's sister from drowning a few years earlier.

The white van had a very defective steering mechanism, with several inches of play in the wheel. The driver overcompensated coming around the curve and slid into Gary's lane. In a split second Gary had to decide between a head-on crash or going off the road and down an embankment. He chose the latter, and a tree found him, and he died instantly.

The other driver paused for a moment and then moved on, circling around the area on back roads until he reached a point high on a hill overlooking the spot and sat there and watched while the rescue crews came, scurried frantically, and left.

****

It seemed like every cop in the state attended the funeral at St. Mary's. As parents of the godson, we rode fairly close to the front of the procession so that by the time we reached the grave site in Fort Johnson we could look back down the valley and see a mile of bumper to bumper police cars with their red and white lights flashing.

"It looks like a giant ruby and diamond necklace," Mary said.

They laid his coffin out and the bugler played taps and the pipes played Amazing Grace and the tears ran down my face and I never bothered to wipe them away.

Slipping the Surly Bonds of Earth
Sep. 1st, 2006 @ 12:45 pm

Rocco Petrone has died.

As director of the Apollo program that put America on the moon, that would be reason enough to note his passing. But here, in his home town where he grew up and went to school and earned admission to West Point, he is remembered especially, and fondly.

Some years ago we renamed the main intersection in town Petrone Square in his honor. It's two blocks down and one block over from Kirk Douglas Park.

The space program captured the imagination of kids my age and it was so neat to know that the man in charge went to school with our parents.

The last time I remember seeing him in the news was at the time of the Challenger explosion in 1986. He was working with the space shuttle builder Rockwell International by then. When it came time to decide to go or not go for launch, Petrone said don't go. They went.

It wasn't all just machines and computers. There was also this:

> He was watching launch operations center TV screens on January 27, 1967, when a fire in the Apollo 1 command module killed astronauts Gus Grissom, Ed White and Roger Chaffee during a launch pad countdown test.
> In an interview with The Associated Press 20 years later, he recalled feeling helpless.
> "When the cry came out, I looked at the screen," Petrone said. "I saw something going on, I saw a shake, I saw a flash inside the ship. It was just utter helplessness. Just nothing you could do. You could not get to them. The thing exploded in 19 seconds ... Those minutes were heart-rending."

Rest in peace, hometown hero of Amsterdam, NY USA.

Karen
Sep. 6th, 2006 @ 10:07 pm

"I have to stop at my parents' house. You don't mind, do you?"

Of course not.

Riding with Karen Partyka was always an adventure. I commuted with her my second year of Albany Law School while she was putting in her senior year away from Vermont Law School. Her father-in-law was a lawyer here in Amsterdam whom I knew noddingly (I had once impressed him greatly at the age of 12 or 13 by addressing him as "Judge", a title he had earned a couple of decades earlier via a short-term appointment). Karen I had met outside the book store at the law school her first day there, and before long I signed up with her one customer livery service.

With normal traffic, you could probably do the commute in 45 minutes. With Karen it was rarely less than two hours.

"I want to stop at Bonnie's house. You don't mind, do you?"

"I heard there's an old Dutch barn down one of these roads. I'd love to see it. You don't mind, do you?"

And the fact of the matter is, I didn't mind, because even though I had trouble keeping up with her thousand words a minute conversations, she was delightful company with an infectious laugh and non-stop enthusiasm about everything she experienced. She was probably the most ALIVE person I had ever met.

She and Rick had been married for a couple of years by then and had already seen most of the world together.

"You like this perfume? I got it in MOROCCO," which immediately conjured up images of her in Dorothy Lamour robe and veil, riding a camel into the nearest oasis and bargaining the salesman down to a dollar eighty-five American.

On one of the walls in their house they had a framed print-ad for a hotel in

Athens, featuring Rick and Karen poolside with the Parthenon as a back-drop. Once they sat around debating whether one of their daughters might have been conceived in Peru. In France they found themselves on first name bases with most of the local vintners.

* * * * * * * * * * * * *

Before long the three of us were young lawyers in Amsterdam and Mary and I started having kids and then they had their two girls, so the families would get together, mostly at their camp. Almost every 4th of July found us spending a day of barbecue and beach and boating and margaritas, followed by bonfires and fireworks. And not just fireworks, but FIREWORKS, grand displays courtesy of the good vendors of North Carolina and the very good Partykas.

Looking back, I'd say that if I were to pick the twenty very best days I've spent over the last thirty years, Karen was in one way or another involved in at least fifteen of them.

I remember once sitting behind her parents at a Community Concert featuring a dance company from Harlem, clearly not her father's cup of tea as he sat squirming deeper and deeper into his seat.

At intermission Karen came running down to him, just bubbling right over.

"Oh, Dad! Aren't those guys SEXY?!?!?"

I think she was quite oblivious to his agony.

* * * * * * * * * * * * *

I talked to another formerly young lawyer today.

"I was just sitting around one day and all of a sudden I hear this noise and I look up and it's three females riding in a car with the radio jacked up singing away at the top of their lungs to songs from the sixties. It was Karen and Olivia and Cassandra."

Karen never really got past that 18th birthday she reached in 1969, and

-268-

eventually the girls caught up with her.

Rick and Karen came to Anna's wedding, of course, but were a little late because of Cassandra's fencing tournament.

And they threw such a nice party at the lake when Cassandra graduated from high school last year. Things being how they are, I think that may have been the last time I saw her, though we spoke by phone a few times in between.

Just as they lived for each other, they lived for their kids and I never saw parents who enjoyed their children more. The girls are both in college now: fine, lovely, warm and funny young ladies.

****

I didn't even know she'd been sick.

The cancer got her Monday, I heard about it Tuesday and I've been numb and worthless ever since. God, she's my age. How can this be?

Rick is being strong, as he always has been.

Time will temper the agony of the moment. Life will go on, as it must.

But, oh, there's a mighty rip in the fabric of the universe tonight.

****

Back when I had some troubles of my own, ever so much easier than these, Rick came into my office at Family Court, closed the door and sat down.

"You know," this deeply private man said, "they say that if you're lucky you can count your true friends on one hand. I just want you to know that I consider you in that category."

If it's any solace to you now, my friend, ditto.

Milton Friedman, RIP
Nov. 16th, 2006 @ 08:27 pm

In the near giddy days after the fall of the Soviet Union, the Mayor of St. Petersburg commented that they had gone past communism and socialism to Reaganism.

He might well have said "Friedmanism", for Milton Friedman, more than any man in the twentieth century, was responsible for the economic theory of freedom that became known as Thatcherism and Reaganomics, but which was basically nothing more than trusting that the best good came from free people freely choosing.

"You can't repeal the business cycle," I used to hear all the time. Friedman did, and his followers have brought us a quarter of a century of economic prosperity and the spread of political and economic freedom at an unprecedented rate. His theories are responsible for the global boom that has raised the standards of living for people everywhere.

Winner of the Nobel Prize for Economics, he has also earned a coveted niche in the *Judge Report Hall of Fame*.

And if all that wasn't enough, Milton Friedman was also one of the kindest, wittiest and most gracious men to walk the earth in his long lifetime, which began five years before the Russian Revolution and ended yesterday at the age of 94.

May we never forget the good he has done, and may God bless and keep him always.

Gerald R. Ford, RIP
Dec. 27th, 2006 @ 06:57 pm

De mortuis nil nisi bonum dicendum est.

Art Buchwald, RIP
Jan. 18th, 2007 @ 10:02 pm

The great American humorist Art Buchwald has joined the ever-growing list of famous dead people I have met. He gave a lecture at SUNY Albany while I was there, took numerous questions from the audience and afterwards just hung out with us in one of the lounge areas of the Campus Center for a couple of hours. Easy going, gentle-hearted, and just a naturally funny guy.

NBC, I think, hired him to do color commentary for the 1968 conventions. The Republican convention, which would nominate Nixon, was not yet a sure thing, so he did a piece comparing how uncommitted delegates were treated compared to the pledged delegates. The uncommitted had fruit baskets, wine, Godiva chocolates etc. waiting in their rooms. The pledged delegates found a note on their pillows reminding them of check-out time.

Well, now it's check-out time here on earth. I trust his new room will be to his satisfaction.

And the next roll of thunder you hear will most assuredly be the chuckling Almighty.

Boris Yeltsin, RIP
Apr. 23rd, 2007 @ 09:10 pm

Great moments in world history: Yeltsin on the tank.

I often wondered what would happen if the dictators gave orders and no one obeyed. Boris Yeltsin proved what one man can do.

Joseph Michael Purtell, RIP
Mar. 21st, 2007 @ 07:19 am

Some years ago, soon after the bishop closed St. Joseph's church and merged the congregation with St. Michael's and Our Lady of Mount Carmel under a single new pastor, groups of disgruntled parishioners from St Joe's and St. Mike's began quietly showing up at St. Mary's on a regular basis.

"You know," I said to stalwart fellow Irish-Catholic Joe Purtell, "we need to let these people know they're welcome here and that our church is their church. I've got a great idea."

"What's that?" the perennial basket-passer asked.

"We'll rename St. Mary's after you. We'll call it 'St. Joseph Michael Purtell.'"

****

Even then, Joe would have been the first to tell you that he'd be an unlikely candidate for *santo subito*. He was born into the rough and tumble world of old-style democratic politics in Troy, NY. His father died when he was eight years old, at which time his mother placed him at the head of the table, informing him that he was now the man in the family. They scraped their way through the Great Depression. He saw death enough for a hundred lifetimes at Anzio.

A butcher by trade, he supplemented his income at the A&P with purloined cuts of meat to feed his rapidly-growing family and would then run to confession. Somehow they survived, because Joe was nothing if not a survivor.

The family peaked at seven kids. For a while. That's when Theresa had her last pregnancy. Twins.

****

In the late 60's a "Christian Family Movement" began here in Amsterdam, and groups of Catholic adults would meet in each other's homes to discuss how they could utilize the message of Christ to strengthen their families and

-272-

communities. At one of these gatherings Joe Purtell heard the call from God to run for Alderman of the Eighth Ward.

The ward included a pretty solidly Republican "Mustang District" where many of the residents were Scots-Irish Ulster Protestants of the deeply entrenched variety. The Irish-Catholic *Erin go Bragh* Democrat candidate did not receive the warmest of receptions, but he earned their respect with his tenacity. He confronted their prejudices with an in-your-face attitude and found himself elected, and re-elected and re-elected and re-elected. Then they threw him out for good.

My local political career began as a Young Republican thorn in Joe Purtell's side. The administration he served reeked of corruption in the old-fashioned political way. Joe later admitted to systematic kick-backs from contractors (5% was the going rate). If a cable television company wanted a franchise, it seemed to him only natural that the regulators should have free service including the fledgling Home Box Office.

Joe was not happy when Dave Pietrusza and I exposed this.

"Listen, you Young Turks! Someday you guys are gonna be in charge and when you are, some kid who's in diapers now will come here and bust your balls just like you're busting mine, and you won't like it any more than I do!"

But I liked Joe Purtell.

And, eventually, he liked me. After his forced retirement from politics, we began having lunch together regularly as part of a larger group, and by the time I ran for Family Court Judge, far from seeking revenge, he threw a couple of fund raisers for me, calling in chips from long-distant vendors for whom he could not possibly deliver any more favors. But they remembered him.

Fact is, Joe may have been a rogue, but self-interest was the farthest thing from his mind. He took care of his family, he took care of his friends. He took care of strangers and he took care of anyone who came to him. He got people jobs and he put food on their tables.

I can't recall a single time when anyone who fled to his protection, implored his help or sought his intercession was left unaided.

And if that's not enough to be a saint, well, I don't know what is.

God grant him rest, and blessings to his family.

COMMENTS
From: (Anonymous)
Date: March 29th, 2007 09:09 am (local)
One of nine

Thank you for remembering a man, of great courage and as you said, tenacity. I knew Joe, probably better than most... Not a saint by any-means, but anyone with nine children should be at least beatified.

He would have been proud to have seen the response at his wake and funeral. It was a overwhelming and powerful statement to him.

Thank you again for the kind words... his legacy remains, hopefully with another generation of Mustangs.

From: (Anonymous)
Date: March 29th, 2007 12:37 pm (local)
Re: One of nine

I want to thank Robert Going for his kind words regarding my Dad (obviously this is not an anonymous reply, although try and figure out which one of nine children wrote this). I would like to add a few more bits of information about Joe's life. When he was growing up in Troy's 5th Ward, it was controlled by a Ward Boss. This was a robust Irishman (according to Joe). When my grandfather died in 1929, leaving my grandmother with three small children and three older step-children, life was difficult. The Ward Boss made sure that all the families received the help they needed. My Dad's family was one of them. My Dad was grateful to that man. My grandmother was a Registered Nurse. She worked for one of the hospitals in Troy. Nights. In the morning, neighbors and the poor in South Troy would be sitting on the 'back stoop' with broken arms, or needing stitches, or a wife about to deliver. My grandmother took care of these people and they reciprocated with food or favors. In this way my father became a person who believed in helping others. He also realized that a position of influence was the most likely way to accomplish this. During my life with him and during his employment with the A&P, he fed us and the homeless with meat and bread that was to be thrown out because it was past its selling date. The homeless men and women who lived down by the RR tracks would wait outside the A&P near the loading dock. Dad would send out a package of meat and old bread for them to split. As I grew older the A&P insisted that everything be thrown out, absolutely. So he would triple wrap the food and put it in the dumpster and later that evening the homeless people would come to get it. My father took in youngsters in the area of the Walnut Street store and brought them home to our house in order to give them a place to play. These were poor boys without fathers.

I was unaware of any 'kickbacks' Dad was receiving through his political connections. It is hard to tell exactly what period of time in our lives in which this was happening because we never had a new car or even two used cars or new clothes, gifts, furniture or vacations until my Mom started her own business. I didn't realize he was 'driven out' City politics. I thought my Dad just lost the 4th term election. As I said in his eulogy, "My father was an honest man, sometimes to a fault, he was a man of valor. If you were his friend, he would defend you, verbally, emotionally and sometimes physically. He was a man of his time." I'll miss him.

From: rgoing
Date: March 29th, 2007 02:03 pm (local)

Re: One of nine

I greatly regret not having been able to attend the funeral, which was at the same time our 84 year old uncle who lives with us was having surgery in Schenectady.

As for the "kickbacks", sometimes Joe had a tendency to romanticize these things and I would be greatly surprised to learn that he ever kept any of it if there was in fact any to be had. At one time he was one of 7 out of eight Democrats on the council, with a democrat mayor and really wide-open money flow with all of the urban renewal and other money pouring in to the city. In fact, once Ray Hall got elected as a maverick Democrat, he and your father joined forces and occasionally allied with the then 2 Republicans to create their own little reform group and a real balance of power. As legend has it, that was the end of the graft era. As I say, I don't know how much of that is true.

He was a grand and good man and I loved him as I loved my own father. You were truly blessed to have him.

RIP Tom Poston
May. 2nd, 2007 @ 12:15 am

You youngsters probably remember Tom Poston as the perennial sidekick of Bob Newhart in his various shows ("Climb upon my knee, sonny boy . . .). Maybe if you're a little older you know him as a favorite panelist on the old game shows, where he now joins Kitty Carlisle. (Which raises an interesting philosophical question: Would To Tell the Truth be allowed in heaven?)

Me, I think of him as the star of *ZOTZ!*

Now this is probably one of the worst movies ever made, though having seen it contemporaneously with *The Three Stooges in Orbit* I didn't think so at the time. As I haven't seen it since it first played at the Mohawk Theater lo these many years ago, I'm a little hazy on the plot. As I recall, Tom gets ahold of this magic coin. If he says "Zotz!" while holding it, people start moving in slow motion. If he points his finger at someone, I guess they get zapped, and if he points his finger and says "ZOTZ!" simultaneously, why, he can kill people. Didn't your mother always tell you not to point your finger, someone might get hurt?

The first zillion kids got plastic ZOTZ coins to take home with us.

Wish I still had mine.

Heh heh.

Anyway, Tom seemed like a real warm human being and he certainly delighted me through most of my lifetime. God rest him.

The Right Stuff
May. 3rd, 2007 @ 03:51 pm

His dad flew bi-planes in World War I and on the county fair barn-storming circuit thereafter. His mom was a wing-walker at those early flight exhibitions. Wally Schirra was born with the Right Stuff already in his genes.

He slipped the surly bonds of earth, put out his hand and touched the face of God earlier today at the age of 84. For boys my age there were no bigger heroes than the seven Mercury astronauts, and time has not diminished their glory.

Schirra, and only Schirra, flew in Mercury, Gemini and Apollo capsules. (Grissom would have, had he not been burned to death on the launch pad. Shepard was grounded during Gemini).

And Wally Schirra remains the only astronaut to date to have smuggled a corned beef sandwich into space.

God speed, and rest in peace.

REQUIEM II
May. 20th, 2007 @ 08:26 am

The faces of the Amsterdam war dead haunt me. So many look so familiar, yet I didn't know a one. Some intrigue me, like this guy, Fenton Brown:

S/Sgt. Fenton E. Brown
Oct. 5, 1944
France

He looks so mild-mannered, so young, almost as though his uniform is too big for him. I was thinking that if they had made a war-buddy comedy about him they would have cast Wally Cox.

Fenton Brown served in the 36th Division. In late August of 1944 their job was to trap and destroy the German Army retreating from the south of France after our landings on the soft underbelly of Europe. Our artillery set up a sixteen mile gauntlet that the Germans had to run.

But the infantry always has to finish them off.

Here are some excerpts from the division history, edited by John Hyman:

But while the artillery brought the German's rear areas crashing down around his ears, the outnumbered infantry slugged it out with his tanks and foot troops. There is no animal more deadly than man, and a trapped man is the most dangerous of all. The infantry was mere yards away from the wounded, cornered beast that had been an overwhelming juggernaut. The men with the M1's and BAR's and thin-hulled bazookas had to stop him.

They stopped him.

. . . Men like Sgt. Fenton Brown, Amsterdam, N.Y., stopped

him. When Germans attacked his rearguard positions, Sergeant Brown machine gunned and killed over a score of the enemy before they withdrew. Two tried to infiltrate and get at his rear. He picked up a rifle and shot them both.

Fenton Brown never saw a victory parade.

I wonder if there is anyone alive today who mourns him, who remembers.

Sister Mary Perpetua, RIP
Jun. 24th, 2007 @ 11:50 pm

Word comes of the death of Sister Mary Perpetua Gibson, CSJ, just after her 90th birthday and in her eighth decade as a Sister of Saint Joseph of Carondolet.

Her family moved to Amsterdam in time for her to attend high school at St. Mary's Institute, and later she returned to teach grammar school there.

Doing a little backwards calculating, she must have been 43 when she governed the combined 5/6 grade across the hall from my 4th grade class on the top floor of the old SMI on Forbes Street back in 1960.

Although she never taught our class, she was a frequent visitor. Back in those days when a nun walked into the room all 43 of us would leap to our feet and say, "Good morning, Sister. God bless you!" and Sister Mary Perpetua would say, "Thank you and God bless you, boys and girls. You may be seated."

One time our regular teacher stepped out for a few moments and left us on our honor to sit quietly until her return. The honor soon became a dull roar, but not as much of a roar as we got from Sister Mary Perpetua who stormed into our classroom and demanded to know who had been talking.

Approximately half of my classmates turned and pointed accusing fingers at their neighbors.

Sister was stunned.

God is not fond of tattlers, it seems. Might have had something to do with the

Commie tactics behind the Iron Curtain where kids were taught to rat out their parents.

"This is terrible! I want to know right now which of you just tattled on your friends!"

Whereupon nearly the entire other half of the class turned and pointed out the offending tattlers.

****

God's honest truth: this time I was innocent on all counts.

And greatly amused.

Barbara
Jul. 30th, 2007 @ 11:32 pm

It's always tough to write about the death of a friend or a family member. In the case of Barbara Reidy, one was the same as the other. If you were her friend, you were her family.

I first met Barbara thirty-two years ago when Bob ran for Mayor of Amsterdam. She had a stubborn mixture of Polish and Lithuanian blood that served her well in handling a stubborn mixture of Polish and Irish in her husband and maintaining control of a household that included four strong-willed (and lovely) daughters and numerous pets.

Notwithstanding that Bob and I began working together, first when I became attorney for the Department of Social Services while he was Commissioner, and later when, as Family Court Judge I occasionally needed to remind him of my contempt powers when some underling stepped over the bounds, and still later, now, in City Hall where he is our Employee Relations Director, the Reidys continuously included us in all their major family functions and not a few minor ones.

What fun Barb had at all four of their weddings. How she adored her grandchildren. How she enjoyed a quiet evening at home, when Mary and I would drop by while we were out walking and she'd beg me to play the piano for her, which I did, badly.

One of the last things she said to me was to come over again and play for her. But a week later the symptoms of an unknown brain tumor kicked in, and she spent Mother's Day in the hospital. And her anniversary. And her birthday.

"I'm scared," she told me the night before her surgery was scheduled. She hung on for two months more and finally passed over Sunday at 67.

She didn't need to be scared. The love of family and friends poured over her, and rightly so, because she was a good woman, strong in all the right ways, proud in all the right ways, loyal as any wife or mother or friend could be.

Her sufferings in this life by themselves should earn her a straight ticket to paradise. Her virtue insured it.

Gabe
Sep. 30th, 2007 @ 10:31 pm

I didn't know Gabe Vertucci very well, but I liked him and he earned a special place in my heart when he allowed us to place one of my campaign signs on his front lawn when I ran for Family Court Judge, the very one I needed to win the battle of Market Street. I knew him as a contractor and local businessman. When I was a kid we used to walk out to his place in Fort Johnson and climb over the government surplus tank he had overlooking Route 5 and the Mohawk River.

I knew he was from the World War II generation, but never gave it much thought. Lots of guys from here were in the war, and very few ever talked about it. They just went on with their lives.

Recently, however, there was an article in the paper about his brother and how the two of them ended up on Iwo Jima but never saw each other. Back home their family saw a newsreel after the battle, and there was Gabe's brother wandering through the temporary graveyard, looking for Gabe's name.

As could be expected. There were over two hundred guys in Gabe's unit on Iwo Jima. Three survived.

Here's some of the story I never heard him tell, from his obituary in today's paper:

> Gabe served as a corporal in the 3rd Platoon, E Company, 2nd Battalion 25th Marines, 4th Division during World War II. He fought in Tinian, Saipan and Iwo Jima. On Saipan, Gabe was shot in the head. The bullet exited the back of his helmet, allowing Gabe to kill the Japanese soldier. In a counterattack, Gabe was hit with a piece of hand grenade in the arm, receiving his first purple heart. As the fighting grew more intense, a Japanese soldier shot him in the pocket, the bullet was deflected by an ammo clip, but slashed through his hip. He was then awarded his second purple heart. On Iwo Jima, four hours before the battle was over, Gabe, one of only three men left in his company, was shot in the eyes . The bullet ricocheted under his helmet causing a serious head injury. Medics operated in a tent under a lantern. He received his third purple heart for valor.

I've previously posted my tribute to the Amsterdam war dead. There were plenty of guys who survived who were heroes too. Too many to name, though I think of Malcolm Tomlinson and his four D-day invasions (North Africa, Sicily, Italy and Normandy); Mario Villa on the beach at Anzio (along with Joe Purtell, an adopted Amsterdamian); Steve Rutkowski, who lost a brother and a leg in the war, but danced a polka at my wedding nonetheless; Michael Chiara, Sr. and Richard Dantini, both left for dead but who managed to come home.

They're dropping away rapidly now. Too late to thank most of them.

Not too late to remember.

Rest in peace, Gabe Vertucci. *Semper fidelis.*

Aurora
Oct. 8th, 2007 @ 12:16 am

I'm not sure when I first met Aurora Montenaro. I think it was in eighth or ninth grade when her son Pete was recuperating from a knee injury in St. Mary's hospital and a bunch of us went down there to create havoc with him.

Peter often proved a challenge to the educational establishment. Our Bishop Scully High School Principal Father Anselment has said, "Peter and I occasionally had differences of opinion on the administration of the school."

Oddly enough Sister Maria Christina discovered a similar pattern in her English class. Once she attempted to settle some disruption issues by spacing Pete and Mark Olbrych and myself as far apart as was physically possible.

She failed miserably. I leave it to my biographers to dig up the details.

(Peter, naturally. went on to become a school psychologist).

Pete and I had more than a few things in common, and one of them included his future wife, Mary Alice Mezzio. All three of us had mothers giving birth while we were in high school, all in their forties. Sean and Stephen came within days of each other in May and Aurora brought forth Anthony the same October.

After high school I went to work for the Montenaros as Snow Cone Bob, and worked alongside Snow Cone Pete, Snow Cone Frank (Romeo) and Snow Cone Mr. Harrington the Mailman.

And I got to know Aurora.

Taken as a group the Montenaros were the hardest-working family I have ever met. They would have made great pioneers. None of them worked harder, and with more cheer, than Aurora.

She was simply a wonderful woman. Selfless, caring, devout, long-suffering (she had five rambunctious boys before producing Marilyn, who frankly could hold her own with her brothers as far as I could tell), and in endless motion, whether working in the big kitchen making sandwiches for the food truck, or

-283-

mixing the snow cone syrup, or cashing us in at the end of the day, or teaching Marilyn to use an iron, or just trying to figure out where everyone was.

Once, early in my second season, I had a difference of opinion about the administration of the snow cone business when Jimmy Dick, who couldn't drive, got to milk the city swimming pool traffic by himself instead of sharing it with the rest of us. I tendered my resignation.

Aurora came to me with tears in her eyes and begged me to stay.

Aw, shucks. I stayed. And my commission on those fifteen cent snow cones paid my way through college.

I always felt right at home at the Big M farm. Aurora made everyone feel that way.

Years and years later I performed weddings for a couple of the kids. After the last one Aurora came up to me and said, "Bob, what do we owe you?"

"Are you kidding?" I said. "You're family!"

And then the tears came again.

As they did for me this week when I picked up the paper and learned that she had died.

There's probably no grief worse than losing a mother, but losing your friend's mother can come pretty close, especially when it's someone who did so much for so many for so long, who loved so well, and who left the world so very much better than she found it.

Margaret Louison
Oct. 21st, 2007 @ 11:16 am

If I were forced to choose a favorite family member there would be many candidates, for I have been blessed with wonderful, wise and amusing relatives on both sides, near and distant. But there's no doubt my Dad's cousin Margaret Louison would be a finalist.

She left us the other day at 92, her last years spent in unfortunate befuddlement, though with occasional glimpses of her old self, such as when she was at the Park Hill Adult Home and began going from room to room to cheer up the other residents, thinking she was back in her old uniformed days as a nurse at St. Mary's Hospital where her infectious smile brought many a patient back to recovery.

Cheerfulness was her cardinal virtue, and she exercised it better than anyone I have ever known. That impish grin would light up a room. She had no fewer sorrows in her life than anyone else, losing three children along the way, including my friend Robert who starred in the national touring company of *No, No Nanette* back in the 70's, and her husband Arne immediately after he retired. But she bore her sorrows like the saint that she was, is, and set a standard for the rest of us who think life is tough.

She took the command, "Be fruitful and multiply" quite seriously, and though she didn't quite fill the earth, she still managed to populate a good part of Amsterdam, particularly her old neighborhood, high up on our hill, where Ruth Street ought to be renamed Louison/Luffman Estates.

We would run into her sometimes when we were out walking, and once she took me down Wilkes Avenue to show me my grandfather's home, where my father lived as a child. "This was Uncle Jamie's house," she noted proudly, speaking of her mother's little brother who died suddenly in 1934 at the age of 41. (Aunt Agnes, with seven children and a husband at home, didn't hesitate to take in her widowed sister-in-law and her two kids until they could get back on their feet.)

Margaret's gentle spirit has been passed down through all of her children and grandchildren and hopefully will continue spreading ever outwards as the fruits of her life refresh and invigorate generations to come.

For now, she is at soft, tender and well-deserved rest.

Gentle Giant
Nov. 22nd, 2007 @ 11:34 pm

> *To try, when your arms are too weary,*
> *To reach the unreachable star!*

The call came early this morning from Mike Chiara, while I busied myself at the stove melting down celery and onions and Jimmy Dean Maple Sausage for the stuffing.

"Jimmy Marks died."

****

He was at the house with Paula. She asked him to call me to make sure I knew before it hit the news.

Death is always an intrusion, but worse on holidays. My kids didn't know him. Mary only met him a couple of times. I kept my grief to myself, and the day went on. A happy day with family and the joy of a new life, making her first appearance at Grandma and Grampa's house. Not the appropriate time to beg the Lord to welcome into the kingdom His good and faithful servant James Marks. But I remembered him in my own helpless way.

Tomorrow the papers will doubtless speak of his public life: City Historian, former Secretary of Urban Renewal, member of the Amsterdam Industrial Development Agency, only two months into his first full term as Montgomery County Republican Chairman, having taken over last Spring when the former chairman stepped down.

He didn't attend his own election, still in the hospital with near-catastrophic fluid retention, bad heart and kidneys shutting down.

But he rallied and made it home. Even from his hospital bed he had barked orders for the fall campaign and pulled out all the stops. His new regimen required frequent dialysis; he had started to stop by City Hall again on his way home from treatment.

Only a week ago I sat next to him at a spaghetti dinner he threw for the Republican Committeemen, a post-election social gathering designed to regroup and fight the good fight. He was brimming with optimism, planning for the future, announcing time tables, promoting unity, inspiring the troops.

And filling up with fluid again.

****

Jim had a tremendous understanding of local history and its lessons. We called him "The Professor" and Mike and I loved having him as a talk show guest. He was our first choice for mayor last Spring, but even then it was becoming obvious that the rigor of a campaign would be too much for him.

For the last four years he was among a handful of people who got together on an almost daily basis to discuss city policies and ideas, and he had a million of them. He was not afraid to take an unpopular position if he thought it was the right one, and he suffered a great deal of public abuse as a result. Maybe the most honest man who ever walked the face of the earth, the demagogues accused him (and others) of every nefarious intention imaginable.

Even as he lay near death in St. Peter's Hospital, Alderman William D. Wills attempted to block his re-appointment as City Historian and demanded an ethics investigation.

It was disgusting.

But I will remember Jim Marks as I knew him: a sweet and gentle man whose personal kindness knew no limits, whose humor brightened every moment of every day, a friend with whom you could be totally candid, and most of all as someone who loved his hometown more than it deserved and far more than that love will ever be appreciated.

RIP Henry Hyde
Nov. 29th, 2007 @ 09:29 am

In an age of wishy-washy wind-checkers, Congressman Henry Hyde stood out by taking stands on issues as bold and as bright as the colors of the flag he loved and served so well.

In the beginning he had many bipartisan allies in his Right to Life cause. Over the years, many of them, for the sake of political expediency, drifted away. The sad case of Jesse Jackson comes immediately to mind.

But Hyde stood his ground. He knew what he believed in, and he fought for his beliefs. He managed to keep the Hyde Amendment, which prohibits federal funding of abortions, virtually intact for decades, despite the shifting sands of politics and public opinion.

According to *National Review*, the National Right to Life Committee conservatively estimates that the Hyde Amendment prevented over a million abortions in the last thirty years. That's a million people walking around today who owe their lives to the tenacity of this one man.

I think it is fair to say that he has justified his life here, and will be welcomed heartily in the next.

RIP Johnny Podres
Jan. 14th, 2008 @ 04:19 pm

Johnny Podres died yesterday in Glens Falls. Somewhere in my attic is a tape recording of his greatest moment of glory, the day he delivered the one and only World Series championship to the Brooklyn Dodgers, shutting out the Yankees 2-0 in game seven back in 1955. At 8 ½ McCleary Avenue in Amsterdam, my Brooklyn born and raised grandmother shook the rafters while her second husband, Grampa Des Nichols, recorded it all for posterity, meaning me, who, even as a four year old living in suburban Albany, fully understood the significance of the occasion. I vividly recall the downcast faces of the other kids in the neighborhood the next day. Heh heh.

As a skinny high school kid playing in deepest upstate New York he was spotted by Amsterdam's Alex Isabel, legendary Athletic Director of my alma mater, St. Mary's Institute, who scratched a little bonus cash scouting for the Dodgers. On his recommendation they signed the lad, and the rest is baseball legend.

He was a parishioner of my high school principal and hiking pal, Father Joe Anselment, but unfortunately our paths never crossed. Still, it's nice to know that somebody I know knew the guy who stunned the invincible Yankee machine of the 50's. That glory has lasted more than half a century and is probably still good for a long time to come.

Dick
Jan. 28th, 2008 @ 04:59 pm

Back when Dick Healy was a cub reporter for the old Schenectady Union Star, he used to hang out at the Maxwell House Diner on Chuctanunda Street with older guys like my Dad and Phil Spencer and Mike Riccio. Politics was generally the subject, state, national and local. Pretty much the same conversations were still going on a decade later when I took my father's place after the table moved around the corner to the Topaz.

I didn't meet Dick until 1975 when he popped out of nowhere as the campaign manager for Bob Reidy, young upstart candidate for mayor, though not as young and upstart as me.

I joined the team, another of those quixotic adventures. Dick and I ended up running for the Board of Supervisors as well that year, me against a very popular second cousin of mine, and Dick against a former mayor who held the ward seat once belonging to Dick's father-in-law Mike Sagarese. None of the three of us was elected that year, but we had fun. Dick went on to win the next time around and served several terms on the Board of Supervisors, including as Chairman. He was one of those guys who insisted on doing things the right way, rather unusual for Montgomery County, and he made a few enemies as a result.

-289-

Along the way Bob Reidy became Commissioner of Social Services, beginning a long and distinguished career, and I was rescued from the oblivion of my own ill-fated run for mayor by being appointed Social Services Attorney, the beginning of my come-back.

After he stepped down from the Board, Dick became Deputy County Administrator and Clerk of the Board. He had a talent for getting things done, despite political opposition. He suffered much frustration, but he always hung in there. He may not always have been right, but he fought for what he believed in. Such a man is, unfortunately, quite rare.

****

June 6, 1994, the fiftieth anniversary of D-Day, and the night of my greatest political moment.

My fellow City Court Judge had announced his candidacy for Family Court ahead of me, and I was gamely fighting my way back into the race when the incumbent judge suddenly switched gears and announced he was running for a third term after all. He was my friend and mentor and a really good judge and I was caught betwixt and between. If I dropped out in his favor, the other guy would stay in the race and might just beat him, leaving me out in the cold. If we all stayed in, he and I might split a similar constituency and allow the other guy in with less than 40% of the vote.

I had two speeches in my pocket going into the meeting of the Montgomery County Republican Committee: one staying in and one pulling out.

"What are you going to do?" asked a committeeman lawyer friend.

"I'm going to make a speech, and when I'm done, the judge is going to decide not to seek reelection after all."

He laughed.

I gave my speech.

The judge decided not to seek reelection.

-290-

****

I couldn't sleep with all the excitement. I woke Mary up about 2:30 a.m. and told her about Col. Chamberlain on Little Round Top at Gettysburg, as related in *The Killer Angels.* (That's just what I do).

"They run out of ammunition, and here come the Confederates up the hill again. He knows if he retreats, the Union left will be turned, the army routed, and the war lost. Without hesitating he gives the order, 'Fix bayonets! Charge!!' Afterwards, when it's all over, he leads his men up Big Round Top and as he's trudging along with his game leg, he thinks to himself, 'Savor this moment, Lawrence my boy, for this is as good as a man ever gets to feel.'

"And that's how I feel right now, here."

Mary was asleep.

****

The next morning I got the call.

"Dick Healy had a massive heart attack last night. He's not going to make it."

At the request of Louise, I quickly prepared a will and power of attorney and drove them down to St. Peter's Hospital in Albany. They were already making the funeral arrangements, but Dick managed a smile for me and made his X in the appropriate locations. I said my last goodbye.

Next day a kid in New England crashed his motorcycle. His heart was a perfect match for Dick. They rushed him to Boston. Two months later I chatted with him in his living room.

He was quite surprised to find his office in Fonda had been turned into a storage room. Who knew?

He went back to work and eventually retired in the ordinary course of business.

****

There was one more last hurrah as he ran for his old seat on the Board a couple of years ago. Then, last year, he and Reidy dusted off the old game plan and considered re-issuing the Reidy for Mayor bumper stickers. But it was not to be in either case.

It appears that the drugs that kept him alive all these years may have caused the damage to his organs that brought his noble life to an end on Saturday. His warmth, his wisdom, his humor, his courage and determination and his honor all live on. He was one heck of a guy, and my friend.

Dick II
Jan. 29th, 2008 @ 10:51 pm

Looking over the remembrance card at Dick Healy's wake tonight reminded me of a time when I was placed in rare company when I was able to give the correct response to a Dick Healy puzzler.

"I was born the day World War II started," he would tell people, many of whom immediately assumed he meant December 7, 1941, but of course, that was the day the Japs bombed Pearl Harbor, whereas the war itself had been going on for some time.

The really clever would respond "September 1, 1939," the day Hitler invaded Poland.

Knowing Dick, however, and his love of precision in such matters, and the fact that he wouldn't even be wording it that way if there wasn't a little trick to it, I promptly responded, "Ah, September 3, 1939, the day the British Parliament declared war on Germany."

His eyes twinkled, as they often did.

"Very good, counselor."

Dick loved old movies and old radio shows and old tv shows. He had miles and miles of audio and video tapes, more than he would ever be able to listen to or watch. He opened a very early video store on Main Street, Reel Images, which he later changed to Real Imagery after somebody in another state threatened to sue over the name. I had lifetime membership number 2 (a cousin of his wife got number 1) and was a faithful customer. I also helped out a bit by making minor repairs to the cassettes as the need arose.

The store has been closed for years and years, but Dick's Goddaughter, Alison Reidy-Bialobok, remembered with a beautiful floral arrangement in the form of a movie reel. Nice touch.

I usually don't rate wakes, but this one had a certain special air to it with a nice mixture of family and friends. For the most part, the phonies stayed away.

Dick would have liked that.

WFB
Feb. 27th, 2008 @ 02:34 pm

William F. Buckley, Jr. is dead.

He never held elected office, yet few people have had greater influence over the course of human events than he has over the last fifty years through the sheer power of his intellect, wit and drive. We already knew who he was at my house even before he founded *National Review* in 1955. By the early 60's my dad was a subscriber and I devoured each issue, building up a store of arguments to buck me up any time some junior high smart-ass liberal wanted to debate social security or the Tennessee Valley Authority.

Long before *Firing Line* I would tune into distant WNBC radio in New York to listen to Buckley extemporize all night long on any and all issues. He was in his intellectual and physical prime when he ran for Mayor of New York City in 1965 and I followed that race with a passion that only a 14 year old political junkie could have. He finished third, but then, so did Teddy Roosevelt when he ran for the office.

By the time I entered college I was a full steam ahead member of Young Americans for Freedom, founded at the Buckley estate in Sharon, Connecticut in the early 60's, and chairman of our local College Republicans and Youth for Buckley (brother James, that is) and got to see the whole clan when Jim was elected US Senator in 1970. I finally met Bill when he gave a series of four lectures at Russell Sage College around 1973 and he graciously hung around to engage anyone who cared to chat. And I like to chat.

We kept up a correspondence for a while, nothing earth shaking or worth reprinting, but the fact that he would bother to even answer every letter from every young hero-worshiper I found pretty amazing. He even invited me to lunch, but our schedules never meshed.

Two years ago, early the next morning after his big 80th birthday bash, he emailed me to thank me for what I had written about him on this blog, at a time when I'm sure he had about ten thousand thank you notes to write to people far more important than this lone blogger. It's hard not to like a guy like that.

Buckley made the conservative movement respectable and he kept it respectable, no small achievement.

It's hard to imagine Reagan without Buckley playing John the Baptist. As well as being ideological allies, they became fast friends, and even when they disagreed, they did so in good humor. When Bill was supporting the Panama Canal Treaty and Reagan leading the fight against it, the Reagans invited the Buckleys over for dinner. As Buckley drove up the long driveway he found neatly spaced, like Burma Shave signs:

> *We bought it.*
> *We paid for it.*
> *It's ours.*
> *We're gonna keep it!*

His writings, his voice, his television shows, his spirit we will always have with us, but as he observed when his sister Aloise died, things are just not going to be as much fun anymore.

Rest in peace, and welcome into the Kingdom.

****

From: (Anonymous)
Date: November 18th, 2005 7:55 am (local)

Delighted by your blog! You didn't say whether you were still reading us! I hope so. WFB

Rosebud

The Impossible Dream
May. 8th, 2006 @ 01:32 pm

(slowly)
There's no business like show business,
Like no business I know.
All made up and soon you'll be appearing---
Every bit of nervousness is gone---
(pick up tempo)
And the sound that's music to your hearing:
To hear them cheering when you come on!

Annie Get Your Gun happened this weekend, which is why I've mostly been away from my keyboard. It went well, quite well as local theater goes. You want Broadway, go to Broadway. If you like families having fun singing and dancing their hearts out and ad-libbing through crises as well as some wonderful magic moments, come see the Galway Players. They've been around for thirty-nine years now and next year the director and accompanist will be doing their last show, they say.

The cast call came two hours before show time Sunday, and as I had a bit of time to kill, I sat on the edge of the stage (didn't Judy do that in *A Star is Born*?) and played *Name That Tune* with Melissa, the choral director, and Tilda, our veteran piano player. What I would do is sing the lesser-known introduction to a famous song and they would have to come up with the rest.

After a while, Tilda says to Melissa, "You know, this is all he ever wanted to do, his entire life. He doesn't really like what he's doing. All he wanted was to get up on the stage and play all the big parts from all the big musicals and that would have made him happy."

She turned to me with her big smile. "Am I right, or am I wrong?"

More right than you know, Tilda. Except on a certain level I didn't want to *play* Billy Bigelow, or Frank Butler, or Curly, or Harold Hill, or Sid, or Higgins or Don Quixote de la Mancha. I wanted to *be* those guys.

I wanted life to be a musical.

I wanted to fall in love on a park bench near a carousel when you can't hear a sound, not the turn of a leaf, or the fall of a wave hitting the sand. I wanted her to wonder how she'd feel, living on a hillside, looking on an ocean beautiful and still. I wanted to be younger than springtime, to see that old devil moon in her eyes, to be able to shout out, "Who cares what happens now? Just keep your hand in mine. Your hand feels so grand in mine! Let people say we're in love!!!"

And of course there would be children, and when the children were asleep we'd sit and dream, just an ordinary couple.

And I knew there would be struggles, and I'd fight the unbeatable foe, bear the unbearable sorrow, run where the brave dare not go. And maybe there'd come a point when we'd have to give up everything except ourselves and our kids and climb over those mountains, yet never walk alone.

And when the end came, I liked to think I would be surrounded by my loved ones, while in the background someone is singing:

> *This is a man who thinks with his heart,*
> *His heart is not always wise.*
> *This is a man who stumbles and falls,*
> *But this is a man who tries.*
> *This is a man you'll forgive and forgive,*
> *And help protect, as long as you live...*
>
> *He will not always say*
> *What you would have him say,*
> *But now and then he'll say*
> *Something Wonderful.*
>
> *The thoughtless things he'll do*
> *Will hurt and worry you*
> *Then all at once he'll do*
> *Something Wonderful*

He has a thousand dreams
That won't come true,
You know that he believes in them
And that's enough for you.
You'll always go along,
Defend him when he's wrong
And tell him, when he's strong
He is Wonderful.
He'll always need your love
And so he'll get your love-
A man who needs your love
Can be Wonderful.

That would be nice.

And maybe to top it off I would get up for the curtain call to thunderous applause and hear the chorus and the audience sing together:

And the world will be better for this,
That one man, scorned and covered with scars,
Still strove with his last ounce of courage
To reach the unreachable stars!

And then we'd do the whole thing over the next night and the night after that and the night after that for all eternity.

****

I always think there's a band, kid.

For more thoughts, opinions, projections and fantasies of Robert N. Going (and free at that) be sure to check in regularly at *The Judge Report,* http://rgoing.livejournal.com.

Comments, criticisms, corrections and hopefully praise my be directed to rgoing@yahoo.com.

And if you're in the mood for a humdinger of a murder mystery, feel free to purchase *The Evil Has Landed*, almost certainly available from wherever you got this book.

www.ingramcontent.com/pod-product-compliance
Lightning Source LLC
Chambersburg PA
CBHW061336280526
45784CB00001B/39